LESSONS FOR
MULTIPLYING AND DIVIDING FRACTIONS

GRADES 5-6

THE TEACHING ARITHMETIC SERIES

Lessons for First Grade
Lessons for Introducing Place Value, Grade 2
Lessons for Addition and Subtraction, Grades 2–3
Lessons for Introducing Multiplication, Grade 3
Lessons for Introducing Division, Grades 3–4
Lessons for Extending Multiplication, Grades 4–5
Lessons for Extending Division, Grades 4–5
Lessons for Introducing Fractions, Grades 4–5
Lessons for Extending Fractions, Grade 5
Lessons for Multiplying and Dividing Fractions, Grades 5–6
Lessons for Decimals and Percents, Grades 5–6

Teaching
ARITHMETIC

LESSONS FOR
MULTIPLYING AND DIVIDING FRACTIONS

▲▲▲▲▲

GRADES 5-6

MARILYN BURNS

MATH SOLUTIONS PUBLICATIONS
SAUSALITO, CA

Math Solutions Publications
A division of
Marilyn Burns Education Associates
150 Gate 5 Road, Suite 101
Sausalito, CA 94965
www.mathsolutions.com

Library of Congress Cataloging-in-Publication Data

Burns, Marilyn, 1941–
    Lessons for multiplying and dividing fractions: grades 5–6 / Marilyn Burns
        p. cm.
Includes index.
    ISBN 0-941355-64-0 (alk. paper)
1.   Fractions—Study and teaching (Elementary) 2.   Multiplication. 3.   Division.   I. Title
    QA117.B88 2003
    372.7'2—dc21

                                            2003013246

Editor: Toby Gordon
Production: Melissa L. Inglis
Cover & interior design: Leslie Bauman
Composition: TechBooks

Printed in the United States of America on acid-free paper
07 06 05 04 03   ML   1 2 3 4 5

A Message from Marilyn Burns

We at Marilyn Burns Education Associates believe that teaching mathematics well calls for increasing our understanding of the math we teach, seeking greater insight into how children learn mathematics, and refining lessons to best promote children's learning. All of our Math Solutions Professional Development publications and inservice courses have been designed to help teachers achieve these goals.

Our publications include a wide range of choices, from books in our new Teaching Arithmetic and Lessons for Algebraic Thinking series to resources that link math and literacy; from books to help teachers understand mathematics more deeply to children's books that help students develop an appreciation for math while learning basic concepts.

Our inservice programs offer five-day courses, one-day workshops, and series of school-year sessions throughout the country, working in partnership with school districts to help implement and sustain long-term improvement in mathematics instruction in all classrooms.

To find a complete listing of our publications and workshops, please visit our Web site at *www.mathsolutions.com.* Or contact us by calling (800) 868-9092 or sending an e-mail to *info@mathsolutions.com.*

We're eager for your feedback and interested in learning about your particular needs. We look forward to hearing from you.

SOLUTIONS®
Publications
A DIVISION OF MARILYN BURNS EDUCATION ASSOCIATES

CONTENTS

INTRODUCTION   ix

MULTIPLYING FRACTIONS

ONE   Whole Number Multiplication: The Building Block   1
TWO   Introducing Multiplication of Fractions   11
THREE   Making Estimates   23
FOUR   Drawing Rectangles   33
FIVE   Multiplying Mixed Numbers   46
SIX   The Multiplying Game   57

DIVIDING FRACTIONS

SEVEN   Whole Number Division: The Building Block   67
EIGHT   Introducing Division of Fractions   75
NINE   Division Patterns   84
TEN   The Quotient Stays the Same   97
ELEVEN   Division with Remainders   111
TWELVE   Tool Kit for Dividing Fractions   123

ASSESSMENTS   139

Halfway Between   141
Multiplying with Rectangles   143
Multiplying with and without Rectangles, Version 1   145
Multiplying with and without Rectangles, Version 2   147
Explain Your Reasoning   149

Problems with $\frac{3}{4}$ and $\frac{1}{4}$ ... 151
Five Problems ... 153
An Experiment with Mice ... 155
Two Ways ... 157

BLACKLINE MASTERS ... 159

The Multiplying Game Record Sheet ... 161
The Multiplying Game ... 162
The Quotient Stays the Same ... 163
Multiplying with Rectangles ... 164
1-Inch Squares ... 165
Explain Your Reasoning ... 166
Problems with $\frac{3}{4}$ and $\frac{1}{4}$ ... 167
An Experiment with Mice ... 168
Two Ways ... 169

INDEX ... 171

INTRODUCTION

How to teach students to multiply and divide fractions so that they develop both understanding and skills has perplexed me for quite some time. (I've been teaching for forty years, which is what I mean by "quite some time.") Over the years, teachers have told me that it's actually easier to teach students how to multiply and divide fractions than it is to teach them how to add and subtract fractions because the standard algorithms for multiplication and division are fairly straightforward. To multiply, you simply multiply across the numerators and then across the denominators, and that's that. To divide, the only extra step is to remember which fraction to invert first before you multiply across the numerators and denominators. Of course there are a few extra steps if the problems involve mixed numbers or whole numbers—students first have to change these to fractions before applying the rules. But the rules are doable, both for teachers to teach and for students to master.

I've long been bothered, however, about teaching these rules. While I know that learning the algorithms allows students to do the computations, I also know that merely teaching the rules for algorithms does not contribute to students' understanding of why we follow these procedures. Even more distressing is that teaching algorithms as rules that we should memorize and follow runs the risk of giving students the message that they are not expected to make sense of these operations. Worse yet, students may think that rules in general don't really make any sense but merely are there to be learned and practiced. They may learn "this is the way we do it," but they may not learn "this is why we do it."

My goal for instruction is to help students bring meaning to all of the procedures that they learn. I believe that students should consistently receive the message from their math instruction that learning mathematics calls for making sense of mathematical ideas and skills. The process of making sense becomes even more important when students face more advanced mathematics courses where they encounter increasingly abstract ideas and complex procedures. Yes, teaching the rules for multiplying and dividing fractions may be fairly easy, but I believe that we truly serve students mathematically when we emphasize understanding.

I also want students to understand that a standard algorithm, such as for multiplying or dividing fractions, is just one of many strategies that are useful for computing. I want to avoid teaching that supports the idea "yours is not to question why, just invert and multiply." Rather, I want to help students develop a tool kit of strategies that they can use, alone or together, to solve problems that call for multiplying and dividing fractions.

When teaching the lessons in this book, I held off introducing any standard procedures, curious about what students would do when asked to think about a problem that was new to them. How would they make sense of a problem like $\frac{1}{2} \times \frac{1}{3}$? Or $1\frac{1}{4} \times \frac{2}{3}$? Or $\frac{3}{4} \div \frac{1}{8}$? Time and again, I was astounded by their ingenuity and perserverence when faced with the challenge of making sense of a problem.

For example, to solve the problem $2\frac{3}{4} \div \frac{1}{2}$, Eddie doubled the dividend and divisor, changing the problem to $4\frac{6}{4} \div 1$. (In a previous lesson, Kayla had noticed that doubling the two numbers in a division problem didn't change the answer.) Eddie knew that any number divided by one was equal to itself, so he knew the answer to $4\frac{6}{4} \div 1$ was $4\frac{6}{4}$, which he then rewrote as $5\frac{1}{2}$.

To solve the same problem, Annie wrote: $\frac{1}{2}$ goes into 1 two times, so it goes into 2 four times. $\frac{1}{2}$ goes into $\frac{2}{4}$ one time, but I still need to put $\frac{1}{2}$ into $\frac{1}{4}$. $\frac{1}{2}$ of $\frac{1}{2}$ is $\frac{1}{4}$, which goes into $\frac{1}{4}$ one time, but that's half of $\frac{1}{2}$ so it goes into $\frac{1}{4}$ $\frac{1}{2}$ times. $4 + 1 + \frac{1}{2} = 5\frac{1}{2}$.

Craig changed the dividend and divisor into fractions with the same denominator—$\frac{11}{4} \div \frac{2}{4}$. He then wrote: Now I had to figure how many $\frac{2}{4}$s were in $\frac{11}{4}$. If I had five $\frac{2}{4}$s that would be $\frac{10}{4}$, but there's one more fourth to make $\frac{11}{4}$, and $\frac{1}{4}$ is $\frac{1}{2}$ of another $\frac{2}{4}$. So it's $5\frac{1}{2}$.

What did I do to elicit this variety of reasoning from the students? In general, I first of all told them that learning to solve problems was the purpose of learning mathematics and that their job was to seek to make sense of problem situations that were new to them. Next I helped them see connections among mathematical ideas, helping them draw on their previous learning when faced with something new. Finally, I encouraged the students to take risks, even if they made mistakes, assuring them that errors are most often opportunities for new learning. These general ideas were the backbone for how I structured lessons, and I outline in each of the chapters in the book the specific pedagogical steps I took to help the students bring meaning to multiplying and dividing fractions.

Just as I know that trying out new ideas can be uncomfortable for students, I also know that teaching lessons in new ways can feel uncomfortable for us as teachers. Even so, I push myself to take pedagogical chances when I think they can result in furthering students' mathematical progress. The rewards can be incredible, and I encourage you to try.

I did not originally set out to write this Teaching Arithmetic book. I intended to follow *Lessons for Introducing Fractions, Grades 4–5* (Math Solutions Publications 2001) with *Lessons for Extending Fractions, Grade 5* (Math Solutions Publications 2003) and include in those two books all that I felt was important to teaching fractions. Working on the second book, however, made me realize that multiplying and dividing fractions demanded more attention and in-depth treatment than I had anticipated. Therefore, I have devoted a book entirely to these two operations and am pleased to introduce this third Teaching Arithmetic book about fractions.

I was determined to figure out ways to help students understand what I myself was never taught about multiplying and dividing fractions when I was in elementary school. I wanted to answer several questions: Why do we say that *of* means "times" when we think about multiplying fractions? How can we help students understand why we invert and then multiply in order to divide fractions? What are effective ways to teach these topics so that students do only what makes sense to them? What do students first need to understand about fractions in order to make sense of multiplying and dividing them?

What's in This Book?

Whenever I teach something new, I try to build on the students' base of understanding so that they can connect new ideas to what they already know. To put this idea into practice for teaching multiplying fractions, I first thought about what students knew about multiplying *whole numbers*. As you'll see in the first chapter of the book, I discussed with the class the following list of six statements about multiplication of whole numbers.

1. Multiplication is the same as repeated addition.
2. *Times* means "groups of."
3. A multiplication problem can be shown as a rectangle.
4. You can reverse the order of the factors and the product stays the same.
5. You can break numbers apart to make multiplying easier.
6. When you multiply two numbers, the product is larger than the factors.

We discussed these statements, one by one, and I asked students for examples to illustrate each of them. The students agreed with all of the statements but the first and last ones. They edited the first one so that it read:

1. Multiplication is the same as repeated addition when you add the same number again and again.

They edited Statement 6 so that it now read:

6. When you multiply two numbers, the product is larger than the factors *unless one of the factors is zero or one.*

Then, in Chapter 2, I asked the students if they thought that the six statements were also true for multiplying fractions. Julio's hand shot up. "I don't think that we know how to multiply fractions yet," he said in his typical matter-of-fact tone. Others in the class seemed relieved to hear his comment. I responded to Julio's comment by telling the students that I thought that they could figure out how to solve problems that involved multiplying fractions. I wrote a problem on the board—$6 \times \frac{1}{2}$. I asked them to read the first statement on the list and talk with their neighbors about how multiplication is related to repeated addition and see if this idea could help them solve the problem. Animated conversation broke out. I had purposely chosen a problem that involved multiplying a whole number by a fraction because it's possible to figure out the answer by repeated addition—$\frac{1}{2} + \frac{1}{2} + \frac{1}{2} + \frac{1}{2} + \frac{1}{2} + \frac{1}{2} = 3$. The students easily came to this conclusion and agreed—that the first statement could also work for fractions, at least for the problem $6 \times \frac{1}{2}$. I then continued down the list of statements, using the same problem to analyze each of them. By the end of this lesson, we had established that the statements about multiplication, once we again edited Statement 6, all held true when fractions were involved. Statement 6 now read:

6. When you multiply two numbers, the product is larger than the factors unless one of the factors is zero or one *or a fraction smaller than one.*

In Chapter 2, I also addressed why it makes sense to use *of* to mean "times" when we multiply fractions, and you can read about how I did this in both the "Teaching Notes" and "The Lesson" sections.

My goal in these first two chapters wasn't to develop the computational fluency that the standard algorithm provides. Rather, I wanted students to begin to think about strategies that would help them multiply fractions by reasoning in various ways. At the end of the lesson in Chapter 2, you'll read that Celia noticed that you could get the answer to a multiplication problem by multiplying across the numerators and denominators. It's typical for at least one student to make this discovery when I'm teaching about multiplication of fractions. I responded as I typically do when a student reports the discovery, by acknowledging that Celia's idea worked for all the problems we had solved so far. Then I asked, "Do you think that would work for every problem?" Celia wasn't sure!

In Chapters 3, 4, 5, and 6, you'll read about how the strategy that Celia suggested, the standard algorithm, becomes available to students along with the other strategies they learn. The lessons in these chapters focus on having students make estimates, represent problems as rectangles, figure out the area of rectangles when the lengths of the sides involve fractions and mixed numbers, and practice a variety of strategies for multiplying fractions. From these lessons, the students develop a tool kit of strategies that can be used alone or in combination with each other, depending on the particular multiplication problem to be solved.

Chapters 7 through 12 focus on dividing fractions, and I began this instruction the same way I began instruction for multiplying fractions, by presenting a list of statements relating to dividing whole numbers. I told the students that all but the last statement was true and asked them to think of whole number examples to illustrate each of the ideas:

1. You can solve a division problem by subtracting.
2. To divide two numbers, $a \div b$, you can think, "How many bs are in a?"
3. You can check a division problem by multiplying.
4. The division sign ($\div$) means "into groups of."

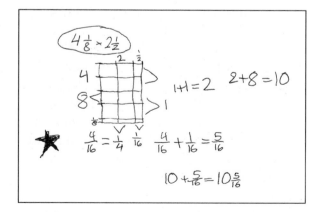

▲▲▲▲▲▲Figure 1   *To solve $4\frac{1}{8} \times 2\frac{1}{2}$, Maggie drew a rectangle with dimensions of $4\frac{1}{8}$ and $2\frac{1}{2}$ and figured out its area.*

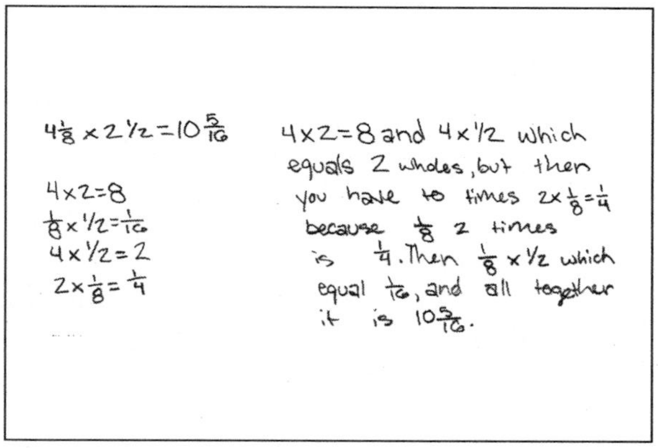

▲▲▲▲▲▲Figure 2   *Gloria figured four partial products and then combined them to get the correct answer of $10\frac{5}{16}$.*

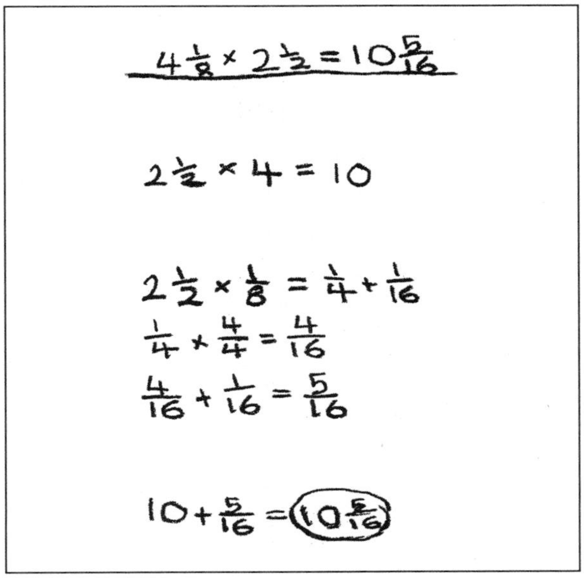

$$4\tfrac{1}{8} \times 2\tfrac{1}{2} = 10\tfrac{5}{16}$$

$$2\tfrac{1}{2} \times 4 = 10$$

$$2\tfrac{1}{2} \times \tfrac{1}{8} = \tfrac{1}{4} + \tfrac{1}{16}$$

$$\tfrac{1}{4} \times \tfrac{4}{4} = \tfrac{4}{16}$$

$$\tfrac{4}{16} + \tfrac{1}{16} = \tfrac{5}{16}$$

$$10 + \tfrac{5}{16} = \boxed{10\tfrac{5}{16}}$$

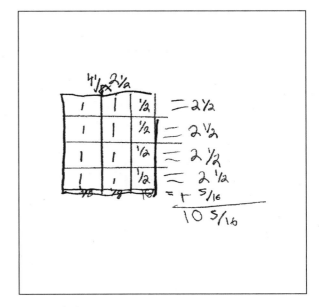

▲▲▲▲▲▲Figure 3 *Kayla broke the problem into two partial products—$2\tfrac{1}{2} \times 4$ and $2\tfrac{1}{2} \times \tfrac{1}{8}$. To figure the second partial product, she figured that $2 \times \tfrac{1}{8}$ was $\tfrac{1}{4}$ and $\tfrac{1}{2} \times \tfrac{1}{8}$ was $\tfrac{1}{16}$.*

▲▲▲▲▲▲Figure 4 *Julio also drew a rectangle and figured the area of each row of squares, getting the correct answer by adding $2\tfrac{1}{2} + 2\tfrac{1}{2} + 2\tfrac{1}{2} + 2\tfrac{1}{2} + 2\tfrac{1}{2} + \tfrac{5}{16}$.*

5. The quotient tells "how many groups" there are.
6. You can break the dividend apart to make dividing easier.
7. Remainders can be represented as whole numbers or fractions.
8. If you divide a number by itself, the answer is one.
9. If you divide a number by one, the answer is the number itself.
10. You can reverse the order of the dividend and the divisor, and the quotient stays the same.

(**Note:** None of the statements addresses the sharing, or partitioning, model of division. See the "Questions and Discussion" section at the end of Chapter 7 for information about this. Also, in Statement 2, I didn't include that b could not be zero. We had discussed earlier in the year why it's not possible to divide by zero, and I didn't repeat that discussion at this time. See the "Teaching Notes" in Chapter 7 for an explanation.)

In Chapter 8, I asked the students to use the ideas in the statements above to figure out answers to problems that involve dividing fractions. For this first experience with dividing fractions, I purposely chose problems with divisors that were smaller than the dividends and for which the answers were always a whole number, for example, $3 \div \tfrac{1}{2}$, $\tfrac{3}{4} \div \tfrac{1}{8}$, $4\tfrac{1}{2} \div \tfrac{1}{4}$, and $3 \div \tfrac{3}{4}$. For each of these, the students should be able to figure out how many of the divisor fit into the dividend, either by reasoning numerically, making drawings, or both. In later lessons, I introduce problems for which the divisor is larger than the dividend, for example, $\tfrac{1}{2} \div \tfrac{3}{4}$. (Students learn to reason that all of $\tfrac{3}{4}$ can't fit into $\tfrac{1}{2}$, but $\tfrac{2}{3}$ of the $\tfrac{3}{4}$ can, so the answer is $\tfrac{2}{3}$.) I also introduce problems for which the divisor is smaller than the dividend, but there is a remainder to deal with, for example, $3\tfrac{1}{4} \div \tfrac{3}{4}$. (For this problem, students learn to reason that there are 4 $\tfrac{3}{4}$s in 3 with $\tfrac{1}{4}$ remaining. The answer, however, is $3\tfrac{1}{3}$ because the remainder of $\tfrac{1}{4}$ is $\tfrac{1}{3}$ of the divisor, $\frac{3}{4}$. See Figures 5 through 8.) You'll see other samples of students' solutions throughout the book.

In Chapters 9 and 10, I have students investigate patterns in sequences of problems to help them think about how multiplication and division of fractions relate, relying when appropriate on examining the patterns with whole numbers first. From these explorations, students learn how to change a division problem to a multiplication problem with the same answer using the dividend in the division problem as one of the factors in the multiplication problem. For example, to change the problem $8 \div 2 = 4$ to a multiplication problem with the same answer and using 8 for a factor produces the problem $8 \times \frac{1}{2} = 4$. After doing this for many problems, students see the reason for and benefit of inverting the divisor (or flipping, as they described it) and then

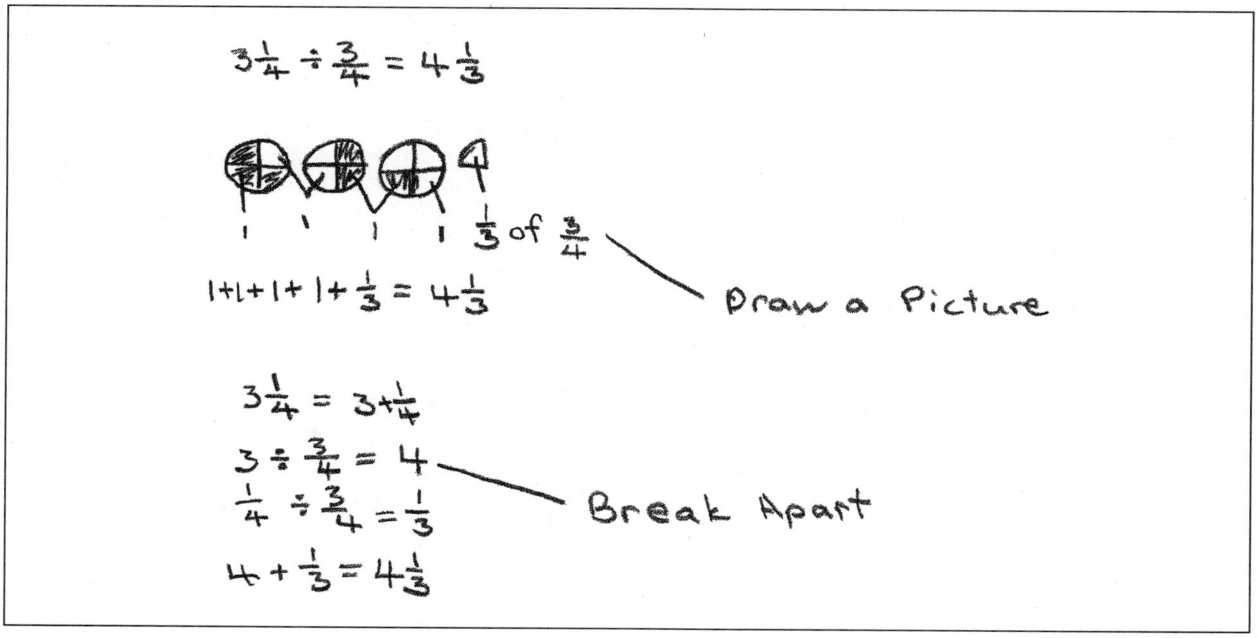

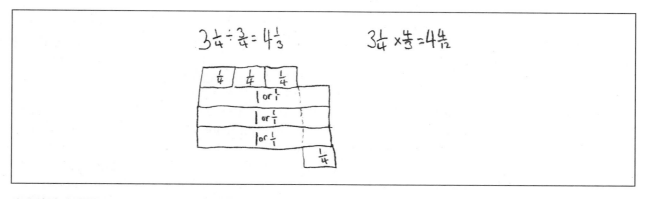

▲▲▲▲▲▲Figure 5 *Kayla used two strategies from the tool kit to solve $3\frac{1}{4} \div \frac{3}{4}$—draw a picture and break apart.*

▲▲▲▲▲▲Figure 6 *Kara made a drawing to divide $3\frac{1}{4}$ by $\frac{3}{4}$ and then also used the invert-and-multiply method.*

multiplying as one strategy for dividing fractions. This is just one of the strategies in the tool kit that gets developed in Chapter 12.

Also, students add another strategy to their tool kit when they investigate the pattern that if you double the dividend and the divisor in a problem, the quotient remains the same. For example, $6 \div 2 = 3$ and $12 \div 4 = 3$. Doubling the 6 and the 2 doesn't change the answer. It may be easier to understand this relationship if you think of the division problems as fractions—$6 \div 2 = \frac{6}{2}$ and $12 \div 4 = \frac{12}{4}$. Doubling the dividend and divisor is particularly helpful when dividing by $\frac{1}{2}$ since doubling $\frac{1}{2}$ results in a divisor of 1, which is easy for students to do. For example, $\frac{2}{3} \div \frac{1}{2}$ can be rewritten as $\frac{4}{3} \div 1$, and since anything divided by 1 is equal to itself, the answer to $\frac{4}{3} \div 1$ is $\frac{4}{3}$, or $1\frac{1}{3}$. And this is also the answer to $\frac{2}{3} \div \frac{1}{2}$!

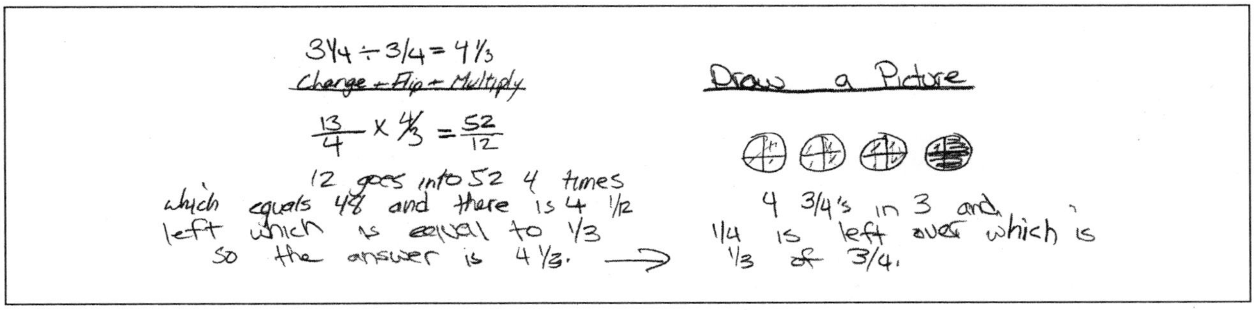

▲▲▲▲▲▲**Figure 7** *Anita explained the two strategies she used—change and flip and multiply, and draw a picture.*

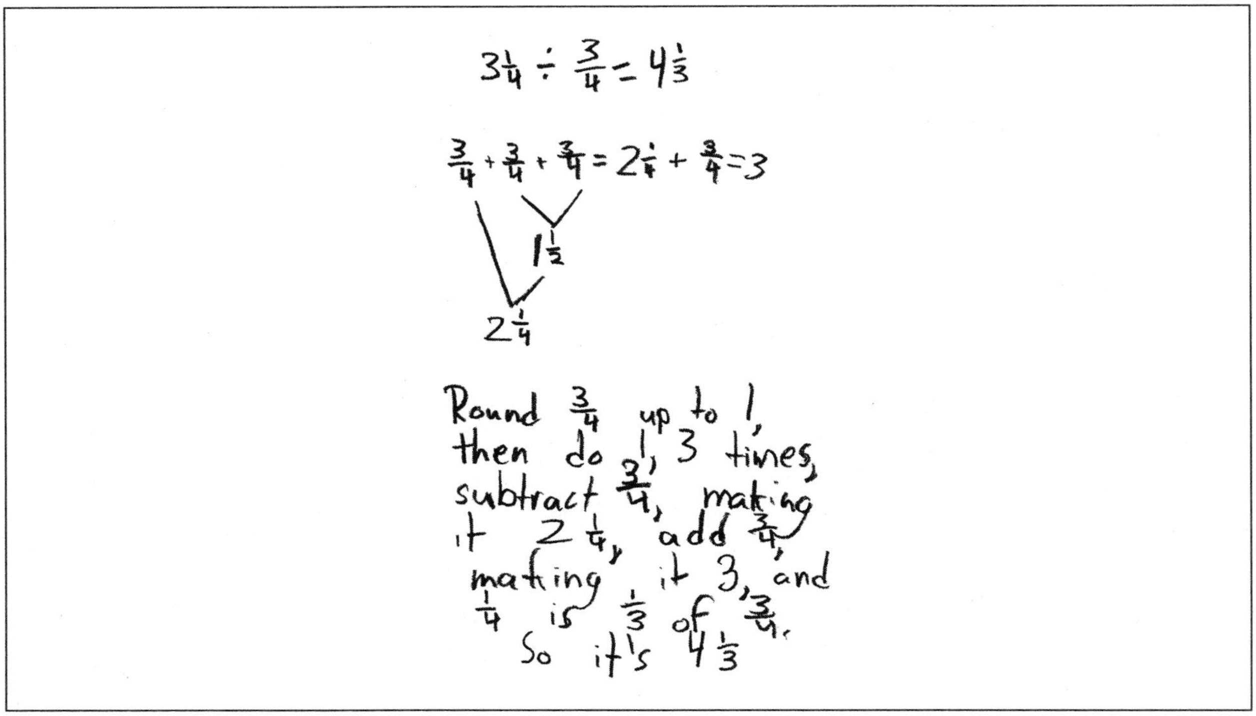

▲▲▲▲▲▲**Figure 8** *Pierre had a unique way of reasoning by first rounding the divisor up to 1 and then adjusting afterward.*

Students learn that they sometimes need to double more than one time to use this strategy. For example:

$\frac{2}{3} \div \frac{1}{4}$

$\frac{4}{3} \div \frac{1}{2}$

$\frac{8}{3} \div 1$

The answer is $\frac{8}{3}$, or $2\frac{2}{3}$.

In both of these problems, the divisor eventually became one. This doesn't always happen, but the strategy can still be useful for some problems. For example:

$1\frac{1}{4} \div \frac{3}{4}$

$2\frac{1}{2} \div 1\frac{1}{2}$

$5 \div 3$

The answer is $\frac{5}{3}$, or $1\frac{2}{3}$.

As with all of the strategies, if a particular one isn't useful, then students learn to choose another. For example, consider the problem $\frac{2}{3} \div \frac{3}{4}$. Doubling twice results in the problem $\frac{8}{3} \div \frac{12}{4}$, or $2\frac{2}{3} \div 3$, which has a whole number divisor; however, this doesn't make the problem easier to think about. For a problem like $\frac{2}{3} \div \frac{3}{4}$, inverting and multiplying is probably the most accessible and efficient strategy.

The standard invert-and-multiply method is useful for *all* division problems, which is why it is viewed as a useful algorithm for dividing fractions and has become the standard algorithm. Why, then, don't I recommend just teaching that method, in a way that helps students understand why it works, as I presented in Chapter 10? Why do I bother with all of the other methods that work for some but not all problems?

While computing efficiently is an important goal of arithmetic instruction, so is developing students' number sense, and considering multiple strategies contributes to developing their number sense. Multiple strategies help students see how ideas connect. They develop students' flexibility in numerical reasoning, help them understand both when procedures are useful and when they are not, and provide them ways to check their computations. Teaching multiple strategies encourages students to be playful with numbers, even inventive. It broadens their mathematical understanding and skills. I can't think of why I would limit their experience to just one method. Read the "Teaching Notes" in Chapter 11 for an elaboration of this idea.

If you're planning to use this book with students who are ready to think about multiplying and dividing fractions but have not had the experiences in my prior Teaching Arithmetic books *Lessons for Introducing Fractions, Grades 4–5* and *Lessons for Extending Fractions, Grade 5*, I strongly suggest that you teach at least the lessons from the first book that engage students with fraction kits, Chapters 2 and 15. Fraction kits are referred to in a number of lessons in this third book; they're an invaluable tool for building students' skills with naming and comparing fractions and for developing an understanding of equivalence that allows students to learn to add and subtract fractions with ease. If your students have not experienced fraction kits, I urge you to start there. If you do not have a copy of the first fraction book, we've put all the information you need about fraction kits in the booklet, *The Fraction Kit Guide*, accompanying this book.

Goals for Fraction Instruction

Our goal in teaching fractions is to give all students the chance to learn how to

▲ name fractional parts of wholes and sets;

▲ represent fractional parts using the standard notation, including proper fractions, improper fractions, and mixed numbers, and also with concrete and pictorial representations;

▲ recognize equivalent fractions and represent fractions and mixed numbers in equivalent forms;

▲ compare and order fractions;

▲ make reasonable estimates with fractions;

▲ compute with fractions;

▲ apply fractions to a variety of problem-solving situations that come from real-world contexts and from other areas of the mathematics curriculum.

This book focuses primarily on the next-to-last bullet—compute with fractions—and addresses how to teach students to multiply and divide fractions. The lessons also address the ideas and skills in the other bullets and assume that students are comfortable naming, comparing, and ordering fractions, understand equivalence, and can add and subtract fractions and mixed numbers.

The Structure of the Lessons

To help you with planning and teaching the lessons in this book, each lesson is organized into the following sections:

Overview   To help you decide if the lesson is appropriate for your students, this is a nutshell description of the mathematical goal of the lesson and what the students will be doing.

Materials   This section lists the special materials needed along with quantities. Not included in the list are regular classroom supplies such as pencils and paper. Worksheets that you need to duplicate are included in the Blackline Masters section at the back of the book.

Time   The number of class periods is indicated for each lesson; nine lessons require one class period and three require two. Seven of the lessons call for additional time for repeat experiences, variations, or extensions.

Teaching Directions   The directions are presented in a step-by-step lesson plan.

Teaching Notes   This section addresses mathematical and pedagogical issues underlying the lesson and, when appropriate, indicates the prior experiences or knowledge students need.

The Lesson   This is a vignette that describes what actually occurred when the lesson was taught to one or more classes. While the vignette mirrors the plan described in the teaching directions, it elaborates with details that are valuable for preparing and teaching the lesson. Samples of student work are included.

Extensions   This section is included for some of the lessons and offers follow-up suggestions.

Questions and Discussion Presented in a question-and-answer format, this section addresses issues that came up during the lesson and/or questions that have been posed by other teachers.

How to Use This Book

Teaching the lessons as described in the twelve chapters requires at least fifteen days of instruction, plus additional time for repeat experiences and practice as recommended for some lessons and for the nine individual assessments suggested. While it's possible to spend a continuous stretch of several weeks on these lessons, in my experience, time is required for students to absorb concepts. You might teach the first six lessons, about multiplying fractions, and then give students time for practice before diving into teaching division.

CHAPTER ONE
WHOLE NUMBER MULTIPLICATION
THE BUILDING BLOCK

Overview

This lesson uses ideas about multiplying whole numbers as a foundation for helping students learn about multiplying fractions. Students discuss six statements about multiplication of whole numbers. For each, they decide if they agree or disagree. If they disagree with all or part of a statement, they edit the statement to make it true. The lesson not only strengthens students' number sense about whole number multiplication but also lays the foundation for subsequent lessons that focus on multiplying fractions.

Materials

▲ none

Time

▲ one class period

Teaching Directions

1. Tell the students that you're going to help them use what they already know about multiplying whole numbers to help them learn about multiplying fractions. Tell them that when they connect new ideas to what they already know, it's easier to learn new ideas and skills.

2. Next, tell the students that you'll present, one by one, six different statements about multiplying whole numbers. For each, they are to decide if they agree or disagree that the statement is true. If they disagree, ask how they might change the statement to make it true. The statements are as follows:

1. Multiplication is the same as repeated addition.
2. *Times* means "groups of."
3. A multiplication problem can be shown as a rectangle.
4. You can reverse the order of the factors and the product stays the same.
5. You can break numbers apart to make multiplying easier.
6. When you multiply two numbers, the product is larger than the factors.

Note: All of the statements above are true except for Statements 1 and 6. For the first statement, a possible clarification is Multiplication is the same as repeated addition *only if you add the same number again and again.* For the last statement, a possible correction is When you multiply two numbers, the product is larger than the factors *unless one of the factors is zero or one.*

3. Write on the board: *1. Multiplication is the same as repeated addition.* Ask the students to first think about the statement by themselves and then discuss their ideas with a neighbor. Then lead a class discussion, asking students to provide specific examples that relate to the statement. For this statement, someone will typically suggest a clarification, that multiplication is the same as repeated addition only if you add the same number again and again. If students do not suggest this, be sure to point out that while 4×3 is the same as $3 + 3 + 3 + 3$, there is no multiplication problem to represent an addition problem like $1 + 5 + 9 + 3$.

4. Continue in the same way for the other five statements. For each, before you lead a class discussion, have students first think about the statement by themselves and then discuss their ideas with a neighbor. **Note:** For Statement 5, ask students to try two problems, first 8×13 and then 42×13. Show students how to represent 42×13 with a rectangle. This will be useful for students' later experience with multiplication of fractions.

100	100	100	100	10	10
10	10	10	10	1	1
10	10	10	10	1	1
10	10	10	10	1	1

5. After class, copy the statements onto chart paper to use in the following lessons.

Teaching Notes

A sound teaching strategy for teaching students something new is to start with what they already know and build on their knowledge in as many ways as possible. This lesson suggests an approach for introducing students to multiplication of fractions by building on what they've learned about multiplication of whole numbers. The goal of the lesson is to build a foundation of understanding that avoids the risk of teaching students rules that either appear arbitrary or have no meaning to them.

To prepare for the lesson, I created the following six statements about multiplication.

1. Multiplication is the same as repeated addition.
2. *Times* means "groups of."
3. A multiplication problem can be shown as a rectangle.
4. You can reverse the order of the factors and the product stays the same.
5. You can break numbers apart to make multiplying easier.
6. When you multiply two numbers, the product is larger than the factors.

To discuss these statements with the students, I planned to write them on the board, one by one, and ask the students to think about if they are true when we think about multiplying whole numbers and, if not, how the statements could be changed to make them true. The class described in the following vignette correctly accepted all but the first and last statements as I had written them. They suggested edits so that the final list looked as follows, with the students' changes in italics:

1. Multiplication is the same as repeated addition *when you add the same number again and again*.
2. *Times* means "groups of."
3. A multiplication problem can be shown as a rectangle.
4. You can reverse the order of the factors and the product stays the same.
5. You can break numbers apart to make multiplying easier.
6. When you multiply two numbers, the product is larger than the factors *unless one of the factors is zero or one*.

It's also true that the product will be smaller if one factor is a negative number. However, since fractions were the context for this exploration, and the students at this grade level typically haven't yet learned about operations that involve negative numbers, I didn't raise that issue. Nor have any students raised the issue when I've taught this lesson.

When you teach this lesson to your class, their suggested changes may not be the same as the wording that my class came up with. That's fine.

Statement 3 relates multiplication to rectangles, an idea that will also be useful in helping students understand multiplication of fractions. Reinforce this idea when you discuss Statement 5 by giving students whole number examples. In the lesson that follows, I asked students to solve 42 × 13, and then I drew a rectangle to illustrate the partial products. You may find this instructive for your class.

100	100	100	100	10	10
10	10	10	10	1	1
10	10	10	10	1	1
10	10	10	10	1	1

If your students' understanding of these ideas about multiplication of whole numbers is weak, then I suggest that you provide more instruction in the area of whole number multiplication before asking them to think about multiplying fractions. (For help with this, see the Teaching Arithmetic book that I wrote with Maryann Wickett titled *Lessons for Extending Multiplication, Grades 4–5* [Math Solutions Publications, 2001].)

The Lesson

▲▲▲

To begin the lesson, I said to the students, "I've been thinking about how to help you learn about multiplying fractions, and I decided that we should start with what you know about multiplying whole numbers. I've written six statements about multiplying whole numbers, and I'm interested in what you think of each of them. I'll start by writing one of them on the board. Please read it and then think quietly to yourself about whether you agree with it or not. Raise a hand when you're ready to share your thinking." I turned to the board and wrote:

1. *Multiplication is the same as repeated addition.*

I waited until about half of the students had raised their hands. Then I asked them to discuss their ideas with their neighbors. After a moment, I asked for their attention and called on Pierre. He said, "Well, I kind of agree and I kind of don't. Multiplying won't help you with some problems, like four plus three. But it works for four times three because that's the same as three plus three plus three plus three." I wrote to the side of the statement:

$4 + 3$
$4 \times 3 = 3 + 3 + 3 + 3$

I said to Pierre, "So you're saying that multiplication doesn't help with a problem like four *plus* three." I pointed to $4 + 3$ on the board as I said this. Pierre and others nodded. I then pointed to $4 \times 3 = 3 + 3 + 3 + 3$ and continued, "But if we think about four *times* three,

then that's a short way of thinking about adding four threes." Again, Pierre and others nodded.

"Or you could go four plus four plus four," Helene added. "You still get twelve." I wrote on the board:

$3 + 3 + 3 + 3 = 4 + 4 + 4$

"Is this what you meant?" I asked Helene. She nodded.

I then said, "So the statement I wrote on the board is sometimes true but sometimes not true. How could we change the sentence so that it's true all of the time?" A few hands shot up.

Rather than call on one of the faster thinkers, I decided to give all of the students more time to think. I said, "Please turn and talk to a neighbor about how to edit the statement." A buzz of noise erupted in the room. After a few moments, I called the students back to attention and asked who had an idea about how to change what I had written. Now more than half the students had their hands raised. I called on Sabrina.

"It's only right if you're adding the same number. I think you should write 'when you add the same number' at the end," she said. I followed her suggestion:

1. *Multiplication is the same as repeated addition when you add the same number.*

I turned back to the class. Some students were nodding their agreement and a few hands were still up. I called on Francis.

"I think you need to say more," he said.

"What else should we say?" I asked.

Francis responded, "Well, it's multiplying when you add the same number again and again. I think you should write 'again and again' on the end." I made the addition:

1. *Multiplication is the same as repeated addition when you add the same number again and again.*

The others nodded and no other hands were raised. I said, "So we all agree that this statement is now true?" The students nodded.

STATEMENT 2

I then said, "OK, here's my next idea. Please think about it for a minute and then talk with your neighbor." I wrote on the board underneath the first statement:

2. *Times means "groups of."*

I called the students to attention and asked what they thought. Most nodded in agreement. They were comfortable thinking of multiplication as groups. I asked, "Can someone explain why this makes sense using the four times three problem that Pierre suggested?"

Annie said, "Four times three is the same as four groups of three, and that's why you can add four threes." The rest of the students seemed to agree.

"And that's the same as three groups of four," Eddie added. I nodded. I thought about whether I should address the difference between 4 × 3 and 3 × 4: 4 × 3 means four groups of three, and 3 × 4 means three groups of four, a difference that's important when we consider multiplication in a context. (For example, four bags with three apples in each is different from three bags with four apples in each.) I decided not to address this idea at this time. Statement 4 addressed commutativity, so I knew that we would talk about this idea.

STATEMENT 3

"Here's another statement," I said and wrote on the board underneath the other two statements:

3. *A multiplication problem can be shown as a rectangle.*

I drew a 3-by-4 rectangle next to the statement.

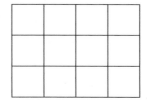

I asked, "What does this rectangle have to do with multiplication? Talk about this with your neighbor." After calling them back to attention, I called on Brendan.

"The rectangle shows three times four," Brendan said.

"And what's the answer?" I asked.

"Twelve," Brendan said.

"And how does the rectangle show the answer?" I probed.

"There are twelve little squares," Brendan said. I nodded and wrote on the board underneath the rectangle:

3 × 4 = 12

"It also shows four times three," Annie added. "That's twelve, too."

"So you're looking first at the side that's four units long," I said, running my finger over the top side, "and then the three-unit side." I ran my finger down the right side. Annie nodded.

"It's like adding if you add up the threes," Hassan said, moving his finger up and down vertically to indicate that he was talking about the columns with three small squares in each. "Three plus three plus three plus three is twelve."

"Or you could add the rows," Julio said. "That's adding four three times, and that works, too." I recorded each of their ideas under the rectangle:

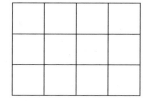

$$3 \times 4 = 12$$
$$4 \times 3 = 12$$
$$3 + 3 + 3 + 3 = 12$$
$$4 + 4 + 4 = 12$$

"Do we need to edit this statement at all?" I asked. No one wanted to change it.

STATEMENT 4

"OK, think by yourself about my next idea," I then said, writing on the board underneath the other statements:

> 4. *You can reverse the order of the factors and the product stays the same.*

After a moment, I asked the students to talk with their neighbors. Then I asked the class, "Does this idea make sense?" Many students were nodding their heads or had raised their hands. I called on Celia.

"You can just look at what you wrote about the rectangle," she said. "Three times four is the same as four times three."

"It works like that for any numbers," Damien added.

"That's like my idea from before," Helene said.

"Do you know a word for this particular property of multiplication?" I asked.

Saul offered, "Yeah, it's called switcheroo." Many students nodded and some giggled.

I responded, "Well, yes, *switcheroo* makes sense because if you switch the factors, the product stays the same. Another word that means the same thing, which mathematicians use, is *commutative*. Multiplication is commutative because you can switch the order of the factors and still get the same product." I wrote *commutative* on the board and asked the class to say it aloud.

STATEMENT 5

"Here's my next idea about multiplication," I said and wrote on the board underneath the other statements:

> 5. *You can break numbers apart to make multiplying easier.*

After the students thought silently for a moment, I said, "How could this idea help us solve a problem like eight times thirteen?" I wrote on the board:

8×13

"Talk to your neighbor about your ideas," I said. After a short time, many students had their hands up, including Clark, who struggled with math and didn't often volunteer. I was pleased to see Clark willing to share, so after I called the class to attention, I began the discussion by calling on him.

He said, "Well, I did eight times ten, and that's eighty. Then I did eight times three, and that's twenty-four. Then I added eighty and twenty-four and I got. . . ." Clark hesitated and I gave him time to think by recording on the board what he had explained so far. Seeing the numbers written down seemed to help him and he completed his thought. "One hundred four," he said.

$$8 \times 13$$
$$13 = 10 + 3$$
$$8 \times 10 = 80$$
$$8 \times 3 = 24$$
$$80 + 24 = 104$$

"I agree with your answer, Clark," I said. I gave Clark this confirmation because I knew that he lacked confidence. Clark grinned, pleased with what he had done. "Which number did you break apart?" I then asked.

Clark responded, "I broke the thirteen into ten and three."

Damien shared his idea next. He said, "I did it another way. I broke the thirteen into six and seven. I did seven times eight, and that's fifty-six. Then I did six times eight and got forty-eight. Then I added fifty-six and forty-eight. I took two from the fifty-six and put it on the forty-eight to make it fifty. That made fifty-four plus fifty, and that's one hundred four, just like Clark got." I wrote on the board:

8×13
$13 = 6 + 7$
$7 \times 8 = 56$
$6 \times 8 = 48$
$56 + 48 = 54 + 50 = 104$

Gloria wanted to report next. "You could break apart the eight," she said.

"What would you break it into?" I asked.

"Four and four," Gloria said. "Then you have to do four times thirteen two times." I wrote on the board:

8×13
$8 = 4 + 4$
$8 \times 13 = (4 \times 13) + (4 \times 13)$

"And how much is four times thirteen?" I asked Gloria.

Gloria sat quietly, then shrugged. "That's a hard one," she said.

I explained, "I know the answer because I know that there are fifty-two cards in a deck. And a deck has four suits—hearts, spades, diamonds, and clubs—each with thirteen cards. So four thirteens must be fifty-two. How much is fifty-two plus fifty-two?"

"Oh, it's a hundred four," Gloria said. "It's the same answer." I wrote on the board:

$52 + 52 = 104$

No one had another way to report, so I posed another multiplication problem with whole numbers, this one with two two-digit factors. Even though I was preparing students for multiplying fractions, I thought this was a good opportunity to reinforce the students' learning about multiplying two-digit numbers. Besides, I know that when multiplying two two-digit numbers using the break-apart method, students often make the error of leaving out some of the partial products. I think this is important to address because the same error can occur when they apply this strategy to multiplying fractions. "How could we solve forty-two times thirteen using the break-apart method?" I asked and wrote the problem on the board. I asked the students to talk with their neighbor about how to solve it.

42×13

When I brought the class back to attention, Anita shared first. She made the error I mentioned above. She said, "I did forty times ten, and that's four hundred. Then I did two times three, and that's six. Then I added four hundred and six and got four hundred six." I recorded on the board:

42×13
$40 \times 10 = 400$
$2 \times 3 = 6$
$400 + 6 = 406$

Some students shook their heads in disagreement, some nodded, and others looked confused.

Kayla said, "Four hundred six can't be big enough. I agree that forty times ten is four hundred, but forty-two times ten is more than four hundred six."

"How much is forty-two times ten?" I asked Kayla.

"It's forty-two with a zero on the end, and that's four hundred twenty," Kayla answered. I wrote on the board:

$42 \times 10 = 420$

Kayla and the others, including Anita, nodded their agreement. If Kayla hadn't made this observation, I would have done so. I then said to the class, "Talk to your neighbor about this problem."

When I called the class back to attention, I called on Celia. She said, "I agree with Kayla. You have to do forty-two times ten. And then you have to do forty-two times three. You can't just multiply two times three." I wrote on the board:

42 × 13
42 × 10 = 420
42 × 3 =

"How much is forty-two times three?" I asked.

Celia answered, "Well, forty times three is one hundred twenty, and two times three is six, so it's one hundred twenty-six. Then you add up the four hundred twenty and the one hundred twenty-six, and you get five hundred forty-six." I completed what I had recorded:

42 × 13
42 × 10 = 420
42 × 3 = 126
420 + 126 = 546

Some students nodded their agreement, while others still looked confused.

Maria wanted to explain another way. She explained that she would do four multiplications to get the same answer as Celia did. I recorded her idea on the board:

42 × 13
40 × 10 = 400
40 × 3 = 120
2 × 10 = 20
2 × 3 = 6
400 + 120 + 20 + 6 = 520 + 20 + 6
= 546

"Oh, I see now what I did wrong," Anita said. A few others still looked unsure.

I said, "Let's use the idea about showing a multiplication problem as a rectangle and see if that helps us." Representing the problem with a rectangle is a way to illustrate the partial products. I continued, "How long would the sides of a rectangle be for this problem?"

Students answered easily. "Forty-two and thirteen." I drew a rectangle on board, marking off the tens on each dimension (see below).

Then I drew lines to divide the rectangle into 10-by-10 sections and also drew lines to show the extra two and three in forty-two and thirteen. (See the first rectangle on the next page.)

Finally, with the students' help, I wrote the value of each section. Now most students were nodding, seeing the connection to partial products. (See the second rectangle on the next page.)

42

13					

100	100	100	100	10	10
10	10	10	10	1	1
10	10	10	10	1	1
10	10	10	10	1	1

STATEMENT 6

"Here's the last statement I have," I said and wrote on the board:

> 6. *When you multiply two numbers, the product is larger than the factors.*

I pointed to "numbers" in the sentence and asked, "Do you know a word that we could use instead of *numbers* if we're talking about multiplication?"

"*Factors,*" several students called out, and I wrote *factors* in parentheses above the word *numbers*.

> *(factors)*
> 6. *When you multiply two numbers, the product is larger than the factors.*

"What do you think about this idea?" I asked. "Think about this quietly on your own." After a moment, I said, "Now talk with your neighbor about what you think."

When I called the class to attention, I first called on Craig. He said, "It doesn't work with one times one because the answer is one, and that's not bigger than

the factors." To be sure that all of the students followed Craig's idea, I wrote on the board to the side:

> *1 × 1 = 1*

"So the product of one isn't bigger than either of the factors," I said.

Sachi then added, "It doesn't work with zeros, either, because zero times one is zero." I recorded on the board:

> *0 × 1 = 0*

"Zero times anything is zero," Eddie added, "so it doesn't work for zero times anything."

"Are there any other factors besides one or zero that don't work?" The students thought for a moment, and most shook their heads "no."

I then said, "So my statement is true sometimes but not all of the time. How can we edit it so that it's true all of the time? Talk with your neighbor about this."

After a moment, I called them back to attention and called on Anita to correct my statement. She said, "I think that since it works for all the numbers except for zero and one, then you should just add 'unless one of the factors is zero or one.'" I edited the sentence:

(factors)
6. *When you multiply two numbers, the product is larger than the factors unless one of the factors is zero or one.*

"Is this OK now?" I asked. The students nodded.

It was nearly the end of the class period. I ended the class by saying, "You've done really good thinking today. Tomorrow we'll look at these statements again and think about them in relation to multiplying fractions."

After class, I copied the statements onto chart paper to use in the next day's lesson.

Questions and Discussion

▲▲

▲ *What do you do about the students who seem confused or who aren't following the discussion?*

I know that it's harder for some students than others to follow other people's reasoning. That's why I ask students first to think on their own and then talk with just one other person before I lead a class discussion. This offers students several ways to engage with ideas.

▲ *I notice that you write students' ideas on the board. Why is this important?*

First of all, it's a way to acknowledge a student's thinking and reinforce for students that you value their ideas. Also, it's difficult to follow someone else's reasoning, and being able to read an explanation is helpful for thinking about an idea. When an idea has only been spoken, some students miss it, others have difficulty interpreting it, and there is no record of it to refer to. Also, recording students' ideas models for them how they can explain their ideas on written assignments.

▲ *The students seemed comfortable with the break-apart method of multiplying. How did you teach that to them?*

We do a great deal of practice with mental computation, and when I ask students to multiply a problem like 14 × 6, someone always comes up with the idea of first multiplying 10 by 6, then multiplying 4 by 6, and combining 60 and 24 to get the answer of 84. This is the break-apart method. (The correct mathematical terminology is *the distributive property of multiplication over addition.*) The process seems natural to students, and it's an essential tool for making sense of multidigit multiplication. Specific lessons to accomplish this understanding and skill are included in the Teaching Arithmetic book that I wrote with Maryann Wickett titled *Lessons for Extending Multiplication, Grades 4–5.*

CHAPTER TWO
INTRODUCING MULTIPLICATION OF FRACTIONS

Overview

This lesson builds on what students know about multiplying whole numbers to develop their understanding of what occurs when we think about multiplying fractions. The students revisit the statements presented in Chapter 1, "Whole Number Multiplication: The Building Block," and investigate whether each statement also applies to multiplying fractions. They solve multiplication problems with fractions in several different ways. The lesson is appropriate both for introducing students to multiplying with fractions and for reinforcing understanding of multiplying with fractions for students who have had previous experience.

Materials

▲ chart of statements from Chapter 1

Time

▲ one class period

Teaching Directions

1. Post the chart of the edited statements from Chapter 1. Tell the students that they're going to revisit the six statements they discussed about multiplying whole numbers to see if they also hold true for multiplying fractions.

1. Multiplication is the same as repeated addition only if you add the same number again and again.
2. *Times* means "groups of."
3. A multiplication problem can be shown as a rectangle.
4. You can reverse the order of the factors and the product stays the same.

5. You can break numbers apart to make multiplying easier.

6. When you multiply two numbers, the product is larger than the factors unless one of the factors is zero or one.

2. Point to the first statement on the chart and ask a student to read it aloud. Then write on the board: $6 \times \frac{1}{2}$. Ask the students to think about how they would solve this problem by thinking about multiplication as repeated addition. Record on the board:

$$6 \times \tfrac{1}{2} = \tfrac{1}{2} + \tfrac{1}{2} + \tfrac{1}{2} + \tfrac{1}{2} + \tfrac{1}{2} + \tfrac{1}{2} = 3$$

3. Continue with Statement 2, again asking a student to read it aloud. Discuss the idea that "six groups of one-half" is represented when you write the problem $6 \times \frac{1}{2}$ as repeated addition.

4. Continue with Statement 3 on the chart. Show the class how to represent $6 \times \frac{1}{2}$ with a rectangle. To do this, first draw a 6-by-1 rectangle, then divide the short side in half to show two 6-by-$\frac{1}{2}$ rectangles. Shade the lower half to indicate that it's not part of the problem, and verify the answer of 3.

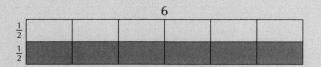

5. Repeat Step 4, this time drawing a rectangle for $\frac{1}{2} \times \frac{1}{2}$. To do this, first draw a 1-by-1 square. Then divide both sides in half, label each side of the upper left portion $\frac{1}{2}$, and shade in the rest.

6. Continue with Statement 4 on the chart. This is true. Reversing the factors in $6 \times \frac{1}{2}$ to $\frac{1}{2} \times 6$ gives you the opportunity to talk with the students about why we can read $\frac{1}{2} \times 6$ as "one-half of six." Explain that, referring to Statement 2, you could read $\frac{1}{2} \times 6$ as "one-half groups of six," but that is awkward. More colloquially, we would say "one-half of six." Read the "Teaching Notes" section for a more complete explanation of why we say that *of* means "times" when multiplying fractions and how to present this idea to your class.

7. Continue with Statement 5 on the chart. Discuss with the class how to think about $6 \times \frac{1}{2}$ by breaking apart the 6. For example, if you think about 6 as $2 + 2 + 2$, you can think of the problem as $(2 \times \frac{1}{2}) + (2 \times \frac{1}{2}) + (2 \times \frac{1}{2})$, which is the same as $1 + 1 + 1$ and produces the same answer of 3.

8. Continue with the last statement on the chart. This needs editing in order to be true for fractions. A possible correct edited version is When you multiply two numbers, the product is larger than the factors *unless one of the factors is zero or one or a fraction smaller than one.*

9. As time allows, present a few other problems for students to relate to the statements:

$\frac{1}{2} \times \frac{3}{4}$

$\frac{1}{2} \times \frac{6}{8}$

$\frac{1}{2} \times 8$

Teaching Notes

Chapter 1, "Whole Number Multiplication: The Building Block," is a prerequisite for this lesson. In that lesson, students discussed the following six statements about multiplication.

1. Multiplication is the same as repeated addition when you add the same number again and again.
2. *Times* means "groups of."
3. A multiplication problem can be shown as a rectangle.
4. You can reverse the order of the factors and the product stays the same.
5. You can break numbers apart to make multiplying easier.
6. When you multiply two numbers, the product is larger than the factors unless one of the factors is zero or one.

   In this second lesson, students consider the same ideas for multiplying with fractions. The lesson is appropriate for students who do or do not have previous experience multiplying fractions. The class described in the lesson that follows had no previous experience multiplying fractions but had experienced most of the lessons in my Teaching Arithmetic book *Lessons for Introducing Fractions, Grades 4–5* (Math Solutions Publications, 2001). Most of the students had a firm foundation of understanding about equivalent fractions and were able to compare and combine fractions. Some still used their fraction kits to help them. (See the booklet, *The Fraction Kit Guide*, accompanying this book.)

   The last statement needs further editing to be true for fractions. The students first suggested this change: When you multiply two numbers, the product is larger than the factors unless one of the factors is zero or one *or a fraction.* However, even though the problem $6 \times \frac{3}{2}$ has a fraction for a factor, its product is larger than the factors! Therefore, the students edited the statement again: When you multiply two numbers, the product is larger than the factors unless one of the factors is zero or one *or a fraction smaller than one.*

   When introducing multiplication of fractions, I initially choose problems that have one whole number factor so that students can reason fairly easily to arrive at answers. For example, the first problem I presented to this class was $6 \times \frac{1}{2}$. Because the first factor is a whole number, students are able to solve the problem using repeated addition, thinking of the problem as "six groups of one-half" and adding one-half six times. Also, I choose the factors so that the answer is a whole number, thus avoiding the extra challenge that a problem like $8 \times \frac{1}{3}$ presents.

The lesson also helps students understand why we use *of* to mean "times" when talking about multiplying fractions. It's true, for example, that $\frac{1}{2} \times 6$ is made more accessible by thinking about it as "one-half of six," but it's important for students to understand why this use of language makes sense. To build this understanding, it again helps to think about multiplying whole numbers. For example, 3×2 can be interpreted as "three groups of two." Similarly, 2×3 can be thought of as "two groups of three." These interpretations are different, but they produce the same product.

A problem involving fractions, such as $3 \times \frac{1}{2}$, can be interpreted as "three groups of one-half." But the reversal, $\frac{1}{2} \times 3$, doesn't translate as handily into colloquial English. It neither sounds right nor is it grammatically correct to say "one-half groups of three." It's OK, however, to say "one-half of a group of three" or just "one-half of three." But is it OK just to decide to use *of* for *times* because it sounds right? Yes, because doing so makes logical sense, too. We know that $3 \times \frac{1}{2}$, as three groups of one-half, is equal to $\frac{1}{2} + \frac{1}{2} + \frac{1}{2}$, or $1\frac{1}{2}$. We also know that $\frac{1}{2} \times 3$ is also $1\frac{1}{2}$, since multiplication is commutative. And we know that "one-half of three" is also one and one-half. These are all different ways to think about the same problem, and students should have the flexibility to interpret problems in ways that help them make sense of what's what. While the above may be a wordy rationale for thinking about why *of* and *times* can be used interchangeably, it's worth the effort to present it to students so that they don't think that the decision to do so has been made on a whim for convenience, but rather understand that it is a convenience that has a rationale.

Keep in mind that the purpose of this lesson isn't to develop computational fluency, but rather to build a foundation of understanding. You'll read in the lesson that Celia, one of the students, noticed that for a problem of multiplying two fractions, multiplying the numerators and denominators gave the same answer the students arrived at by reasoning in several other ways. In my experience, students often make this discovery. However, Celia wasn't convinced that this method would work for all problems. This is also a typical reaction. I chose not to resolve the issue at this time. I'd rather spend time helping students develop multiple strategies for making sense of multiplication problems than introduce an algorithm that they can apply but not explain. There's time later to point out a short way to arrive at the answer, after students have a firm base of understanding.

The Lesson

▲▲▲

I asked the students to read over the list of edited statements about multiplication that I had copied onto chart paper. After giving them time to do so, I asked, "Do you think that all of these statements are also true when we think about multiplying fractions?"

"I don't think that we know how to multiply fractions yet," Julio said. Others seemed relieved to hear Julio's comment.

"Well, I think that you can figure out how to multiply them," I said. "Let's start with the first statement." I pointed to the first statement on the chart:

1. Multiplication is the same as repeated addition when you add the same number again and again.

"Who would like to read this statement?" I asked. I called on Helene and she read it aloud.

"Let's think about this statement together with this problem—six times one-half," I said, writing on the board:

$$6 \times \tfrac{1}{2}$$

"Talk with your neighbor about how you might make sense of this problem," I continued. I carefully chose a problem that was a whole number times a fraction and that had a whole number answer. I've learned that problems like these are appropriate for students when they are beginning to learn about multiplying fractions. Students can use repeated addition to figure out the answer, and the whole number answer, unlike the answer to a problem like $8 \times \tfrac{1}{3}$, makes the problem accessible to most students. I called the students to attention and asked if anyone had an idea.

Juanita said, "I think you can do it by adding one-half over and over again. I did one-half plus one-half, like that, six times. I think the answer is three." I wrote on the board:

$$6 \times \tfrac{1}{2} = \tfrac{1}{2} + \tfrac{1}{2} + \tfrac{1}{2} + \tfrac{1}{2} + \tfrac{1}{2} + \tfrac{1}{2} = 3$$

"How did you get the answer of three?" I asked.

Juanita responded, "One-half plus one-half is one whole, and you can do that three times, and you get three." I indicated Juanita's idea on the board:

$$6 \times \tfrac{1}{2} = \underbrace{\tfrac{1}{2} + \tfrac{1}{2}} + \underbrace{\tfrac{1}{2} + \tfrac{1}{2}} + \underbrace{\tfrac{1}{2} + \tfrac{1}{2}} = 3$$
$$1 \quad + \quad 1 \quad + \quad 1$$

"Is that right?" Eddie wanted to know.

"Does it make sense to you?" I asked.

"It kind of does, but I didn't think you could do that with fractions," he said.

"Can you explain what Juanita did?" I probed.

"It's like if you had six times something else, you could add the something else six times, and that's what Juanita did with the one-halves," Eddie explained.

"I agree with that idea, and yes, it's correct," I said.

Several students seemed to breathe more easily once I had confirmed Juanita's idea. A few whispered, "Yes!"

"So, what do you think about this first statement?" I asked. "Does it work for multiplying with a fraction?" Most hands were up.

"It works," Annie said. "That's what Juanita did."

"She added one-half over and over six times," Brendan added. Others agreed. I wrote *OK* next to the first statement.

STATEMENT 2

I then pointed to the second statement:

2. Times means "groups of."

I called on Clark to read it aloud. Then I said, "Does it makes sense to read 'six times one-half' as 'six groups of one-half'?" Most of the students nodded.

Celia said, "That's the same as Juanita's idea."

"It's OK," Saul added. "The answer is still three." Others nodded again. I wrote *OK* next to the second statement.

STATEMENT 3

I then went on to the third statement:

3. A multiplication problem can be shown as a rectangle.

After Sachi read it, I asked, "Do you think we can use rectangles to show multiplication problems when we're multiplying fractions? Can we draw a rectangle to show six times one-half?" Some students shook their heads "no" and the rest sat quietly thinking. No one raised a hand to volunteer an idea.

"Suppose the problem were six times one," I said, writing *6 × 1* on the board. "Watch as I draw a rectangle that matches this problem." I sketched a rectangle, saying as I did so, "One side of the rectangle is six units long and the other side of the rectangle is one unit long." I labeled the sides *6* and *1* and then divided the rectangle into six small squares.

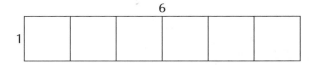

"See if this rectangle helps you think about how I might draw a rectangle to show six times one-half," I said.

There were some murmurs, and a few said, "Oh, I get it!"

Kayla said, in a matter-of-fact tone, "Just cut it in half."

"Which way should I cut the rectangle?" I asked, gesturing with a hand first vertically and then horizontally.

"Sideways," Kayla said. I split the rectangle as Kayla suggested, then erased the 1 and replaced it with $\frac{1}{2}$ written twice. Also, I shaded in the bottom half to indicate that it wasn't part of the problem.

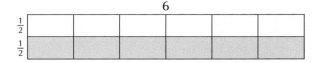

"The top half of the rectangle is six units by one-half unit and shows the problem six times one-half. The bottom shaded half shows the same problem again, but we don't need to consider both. How many squares are there in the unshaded rectangle? Does this still give an answer of three?"

Some students nodded right away while others counted up the halves, some

pointing as they did so. Damien explained, "Two halves make a whole, and you do that three times, so the six halves make three whole squares. Three is still the answer." This seemed to convince the others.

"What about if both the numbers are fractions?" Julio challenged. If Julio hadn't suggested this, I would have brought up the same question. Thinking about a multiplication problem with fractions for both factors can help students see the value of drawing a rectangle.

"Let's try one," I said. "Let's think about drawing a rectangle for the problem one-half times one-half." I wrote on the board:

$$\frac{1}{2} \times \frac{1}{2}$$

The students were quiet. They would face many problems like this one, and rather than give them time to grapple with this example on their own, I decided to show them a way to think about representing the problem with a rectangle. "When I draw a rectangle for a multiplication problem with fractions, I find it easier first to draw a rectangle with whole number sides. So, for this problem, I think about a rectangle that is one by one," I said. I drew a square on the board, labeled each side with a *1*, and continued, "This rectangle is a square because both factors are the same. It shows that one times one is one. Now watch as I draw a rectangle inside this one with sides that each measure one-half." I divided the square, shaded in the part we didn't need to consider to show the $\frac{1}{2}$-by-$\frac{1}{2}$ portion in the upper left corner, and labeled each side $\frac{1}{2}$.

I said, "The part that isn't shaded has sides that are each one-half of a unit. How much of the one-by-one square isn't shaded?"

"One-fourth," several students answered in unison.

Saul was skeptical. "You mean to say that one-half times one-half is one-fourth?" he asked. I nodded.

"I don't get it," he said.

"But do you agree that the unshaded rectangle has sides that are each one-half?" I asked. Saul nodded.

"But you're not sure that the answer of one-fourth is correct?" I asked. Again, Saul nodded. Others, now given some courage by Saul's comment, also nodded.

"Let's go on with the other statements and I think I can help you see why," I said. I knew that if the students thought of the problem "one-half *times* one-half" as "one-half *of* one-half," they would agree with the answer of one-fourth. I planned to develop this idea, and I used the next statement to do so.

STATEMENT 4

I pointed to the next statement:

> 4. *You can reverse the order of the factors and the product stays the same.*

David read it aloud and then Craig commented, "That should work."

"I think so, too," Maria added. Others agreed.

"But it doesn't matter for one-half times one-half," Brendan said. "If you switch them, you still have the same problem."

I said, "Right, so let's think about this statement for the first problem we solved—six times one-half. We already know that the answer is three. What about if we think about the problem one-half times six?" I wrote on the board:

$$\tfrac{1}{2} \times 6$$

I continued, "If we think about the times sign as 'groups of,' then one-half times six should be 'one-half groups of six.' But that doesn't sound quite right." The students agreed.

I then said, "It does make sense, however, to say 'one-half *of* six,' and leave off the 'groups' part. This sounds better, and it's still the same idea. What do you think 'one-half of six' could mean?"

"One-half of six is three," Francis said.

"Ooh, it's the same," Sabrina said. "One-half of six is three, so one-half times six is three, and that's the same as six times one-half."

I said, "Let's think about one-half times one-half the same way. What is one-half of one-half?"

I heard several answers. "A fourth." "A quarter." "One-fourth."

"OK," Saul conceded, "now I see why it can work."

"So what do you think about reversing the order of the factors when the factors are fractions?" I asked.

Again I heard several answers. "It will be the same." "It's OK." "That works." I wrote *OK* next to Statements 3 and 4.

STATEMENT 5

"Let's look at the fifth statement," I said. I pointed to it:

> 5. *You can break numbers apart to make multiplying easier.*

After Hassan read it aloud, I said, "Talk with your neighbor about how you could apply this statement to the problem six times one-half."

After a few moments, hands were raised. I called on Brendan. He said, "It works. You could break the six into twos, and then you do two times one-half three times. Two times one-half is one. One plus one plus one is three. So it works." I wrote on the board:

$6 \times \frac{1}{2}$

$6 = 2 + 2 + 2$

$6 \times \frac{1}{2} = (2 \times \frac{1}{2}) + (2 \times \frac{1}{2}) + (2 \times \frac{1}{2})$
$\quad = 1 + 1 + 1 = 3$

Anita said, "We split the six into four and two. Half of four is two and half of two is one and two plus one is three. It works." I recorded:

$6 = 4 + 2$

$4 \times \frac{1}{2} = 2$

$2 \times \frac{1}{2} = 1$

$2 + 1 = 3$

I wrote *OK* next to the statement.

STATEMENT 6

"We have one statement left," I said. I pointed to it:

> 6. *When you multiply two numbers, the product is larger than the factors unless one of the factors is zero or one.*

Ally read it aloud and I said, "Does this statement hold true for six times one-half?" Hands shot up.

"It doesn't work," Sachi said. "Three is smaller than six, so it doesn't work."

"Could we change the statement so that it does work?" I asked.

Julio had an idea. "I think I know how we could change it," he said. "It should say at the end 'unless the factors are zero or one or a fraction.'" I edited the statement as Julio suggested:

> 6. *When you multiply two numbers, the product is larger than the factors unless one of the factors is zero or one or a fraction.*

I thought about how to respond. If one of the factors is a fraction less than one, then Julio's idea works. But if the fraction is more than one, Julio's idea might not work. I wanted to acknowledge Julio's idea but also give him the chance to refine it. I posed a problem that had a fraction as one of the factors for which the answer was greater than both of the factors. I said, "That's a good idea, Julio, but I think it needs a little more information. Think about this problem—six times three-halves. That's the same as six groups of three-halves." I wrote on the board:

$6 \times \frac{3}{2}$

$\frac{3}{2} + \frac{3}{2} + \frac{3}{2} + \frac{3}{2} + \frac{3}{2} + \frac{3}{2}$

"Talk with your neighbor about what the answer would be to this problem," I said. The room immediately got noisy. As the noise subsided, hands began to go up. In another moment, I asked all of the students for their attention and called on Craig.

"We got nine," he said. "We knew that three-halves is the same as one and a half, and one and a half plus one and a half is three, and three plus three plus three is nine, so the answer is nine." I recorded Craig's idea on the board:

$6 \times \frac{3}{2}$

$\frac{3}{2} + \frac{3}{2} + \frac{3}{2} + \frac{3}{2} + \frac{3}{2} + \frac{3}{2}$

$\frac{3}{2} = 1\frac{1}{2}$

$1\frac{1}{2} + 1\frac{1}{2} + 1\frac{1}{2} + 1\frac{1}{2} + 1\frac{1}{2} + 1\frac{1}{2}$
$\quad\vee \qquad \vee \qquad \vee$
$\quad 3 \quad + \quad 3 \quad + \quad 3$

$\qquad\qquad 9$

Craig continued, "And nine is bigger than six or three-halves. So it doesn't work."

"What doesn't work?" I asked.

"The statement," Craig said. "Well, it works the way it used to be, but it doesn't work the way you changed it."

Anita said, "We got the answer a different way. Can I explain?" I nodded and she continued, "If you add up all the halves, you get eighteen halves. Three plus three plus three, for all six threes, is eighteen. And eighteen halves is the same as nine wholes, so nine is the answer." I recorded Anita's idea:

$$\frac{3}{2} + \frac{3}{2} + \frac{3}{2} + \frac{3}{2} + \frac{3}{2} + \frac{3}{2} = \frac{18}{2}$$

$$\frac{18}{2} = 9 \text{ wholes}$$

Julio's hand was up. "I think I can fix what I said," he said. "The fraction has to be smaller than one. So any number that is zero or one or in between makes an answer that is smaller than the factors."

"So what should I write to change the statement?" I asked.

Julio said, "At the end, write 'zero or one or a fraction that's smaller than one.'" I wrote on the board:

> 6. When you multiply two numbers, the product is larger than the factors unless one of the factors is zero or one or a fraction smaller than one.

Julio and others nodded. I wrote OK next to the revised statement.

ANOTHER PROBLEM

I then said to the class, "OK, now that we've talked about how these statements relate to multiplying fractions, let's try a problem. What is one-half times three-fourths? Take a few moments to talk with your neighbor about this problem. If you're stuck, look at the list of statements to see if any of them can help." I wrote on the board:

$$\frac{1}{2} \times \frac{3}{4}$$

After a minute or so, I called the students back to attention to share their ideas. Hassan shared first. He said, "I think that half of three-fourths is one and a half-fourths because one and a half is half of three. And I think that could be equal to two-sixths or three-eighths."

I responded, "So you think that the answer could be two-sixths or three-eighths, but you're not sure which one?"

Hassan nodded. I wrote these possible answers on the board underneath the problem:

$$\frac{1}{2} \times \frac{3}{4}$$

$$\frac{2}{6}$$

$$\frac{3}{8}$$

I asked, "Does anyone have another idea?"

Julio said, "Well, one times three-fourths is three-fourths, so one-half times three-fourths should be half of that, so that would be one point five-fourths. I don't know what one point five-fourths is equal to, though." I added to the list of possible answers:

$$\frac{1}{2} \times \frac{3}{4}$$

$$\frac{2}{6}$$

$$\frac{3}{8}$$

$$\frac{1.5}{4}$$

"Did anyone use a rectangle to try to solve the problem?" I asked.

Damien said, "I drew a rectangle for three-fourths that was three by four." I drew a rectangle as Damien described. Many of the students looked puzzled.

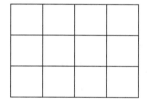

"How did you use the rectangle to solve the problem?" I asked Damien. He looked confused and, after a moment, shrugged.

"I think I can use your idea," I said. "We're trying to show one-half times three-fourths, so I can show a one-half-by-three-fourths rectangle up here in the first small square." I divided the upper left square in halves on one side and in fourths on the other.

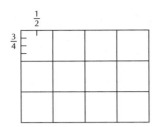

"This is hard to see because it's so small, so I'm going to redraw the small square over here." I redrew the square, outlined a region that was $\frac{1}{2}$ by $\frac{3}{4}$, shaded the rest, and labeled the dimensions of the unshaded area.

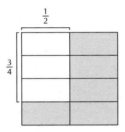

There were lots of murmurs among the students. Several students commented, "Oh, that's three-eighths."

"Who can explain why this unshaded part is three-eighths?" I asked.

Celia answered, "The square is divided into eight pieces, so each piece is one-eighth. And there are three of them."

Craig said, "I got three-eighths in a different way, but I'm not sure I can explain it."

I responded, "Why don't you give it a try, and we'll help you out if you get stuck."

"OK," Craig said. "Well, instead of doing one-half times three-fourths, I did one-half times one-half, and that's one-fourth, like we did before. Then I did one-half times one-fourth and I got one-eighth." I recorded:

$$\frac{1}{2} \times \frac{3}{4}$$

$$\frac{1}{2} \times \frac{1}{2} = \frac{1}{4}$$

$$\frac{1}{2} \times \frac{1}{4} = \frac{1}{8}$$

I realized that Craig had split three-fourths into one-half and one-fourth, but I wasn't sure that others understood. I asked, "Craig, how did you decide to multiply one-half first by one-half and then by one-fourth?"

Craig thought for a moment and then said, "Oh, I know. I split the three-fourths into one-half and one-fourth." I inserted this idea into what I had written on the board:

$$\frac{1}{2} \times \frac{3}{4}$$

$$\frac{3}{4} = \frac{1}{2} + \frac{1}{4}$$

$$\frac{1}{2} \times \frac{1}{2} = \frac{1}{4}$$

$$\frac{1}{2} \times \frac{1}{4} = \frac{1}{8}$$

"Now you have two parts of the answer—one-fourth and one-eighth," I said.

"Oh yeah," Craig said. He paused and looked confused. It's common for students to lose their train of thought when struggling with a new idea. Then Craig brightened and said, "I changed one-fourth into two-eighths so I could add them together. Two-eighths plus one-eighth is three-eighths. So I think that the answer is three-eighths." I completed recording and Craig looked triumphant.

$$\frac{1}{2} \times \frac{3}{4}$$

$$\frac{3}{4} = \frac{1}{2} + \frac{1}{4}$$

$$\frac{1}{2} \times \frac{1}{2} = \frac{1}{4}$$

$$\frac{1}{2} \times \frac{1}{4} = \frac{1}{8}$$

$$\frac{1}{4} + \frac{1}{8} = \frac{2}{8} + \frac{1}{8} = \frac{3}{8}$$

"That's another way to explain why three-eighths can be the answer," I said, pointing to where I had listed that possibility on the board.

Kayla said next, "I think its three-eighths, too, because what Julio said makes sense to me and I think that one point five-fourths is the same as three-eighths. You can change one point five-fourths to fifteen-fortieths, and that's the same as three-eighths." I wrote on the board:

$$\frac{1.5}{4} = \frac{15}{40} = \frac{3}{8}$$

"Why is one point five-fourths the same as fifteen–fortieths?" I asked Kayla.

"You just multiply by ten," she answered.

"What did you multiply by ten?" I asked, pushing Kayla to clarify her thinking.

"I did both the top and the bottom," she replied. "I multiplied one point five by ten and then I multiplied four by ten."

"And how did you then decide that fifteen-fortieths was the same as three-eighths?" I asked.

Julio, now excited, interrupted, "I know! Because you can divide fifteen by five and forty by five, and then you get three-eighths."

I looked back at Kayla. "That's what I did, too," she said.

I then returned to Hassan and asked, "Hassan, I was wondering if you had any more thoughts about your idea that the answer was one and a half-fourths?" Hassan shook his head and shrugged.

"I think we might be able to use a circle to understand your idea better," I said. I drew a circle and divided it into fourths.

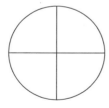

"How can I show one and a half–fourths on this circle?" I asked.

Gloria said, "Put a line to split that fourth in half."

"Which fourth?" I asked.

"The bottom one on the right," Gloria answered. I did as Gloria suggested and then shaded in one-fourth and one-half of a fourth.

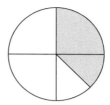

A few students commented, "Oh, that's three-eighths." I drew lines to show the eighths more clearly. Now it was clear to all of the students that three-eighths of the circle was shaded.

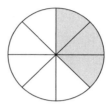

I said, "The shaded area shows half of three-fourths, and that's the same as three-eighths."

Celia then said, "I just noticed something." She had been looking at the numerical problem, $\frac{1}{2} \times \frac{3}{4}$, and said, "I noticed that you can just multiply on the top one times three, and then multiply on the bottom two times four, and that gives you three-eighths."

Some students look surprised. I wasn't, however. I've found that it's typical when I'm teaching multiplication of fractions for a student to notice what Celia did. When it happens, I acknowledge the contribution and ask a question to test the student's awareness of the method.

"Do you think that would work for every problem?" I asked Celia.

Celia responded, "No, probably not."

"Will Celia's idea work for every problem?" Helene wanted to know.

"That's something you might want to think about," I suggested. It was now the end of the period, so with this comment, I ended the discussion. I planned to address it later, after the students had had more experience figuring out answers to multiplication problems with fractions by reasoning.

Questions and Discussion

▲▲

▲ *Why wasn't Celia's idea a good entry for introducing the standard procedure for multiplying fractions?*

It might have been a good idea if Celia had made her discovery after the students had had more experience thinking about multiplying fractions. I prefer to delay discussing the standard algorithm until students have developed a toolbox of strategies for multiplying problems with factors that are fractions, mixed numbers, and whole numbers. Then the method becomes another strategy they can use. Also, when discussing Celia's method, I want to be able to explain to students why the method makes sense, and for that they need more experience with representing multiplication problems as rectangles.

▲ *When you were showing the students how to draw rectangles for the problems $6 \times \frac{1}{2}$, $\frac{1}{2} \times \frac{1}{2}$, and $\frac{1}{2} \times \frac{3}{4}$, each time you started with a larger rectangle. Why did you do this?*

I have found that it's easier for students to draw rectangles with dimensions that are whole numbers. Therefore, I always start with a rectangle that rounds up fractions to the next whole number. Also, students need the reference of a whole square in order to calculate the value of the pieces in the rectangle that represents the problem. For example, if I started by drawing a 6-by-$\frac{1}{2}$ rectangle, the students would have no frame of reference for understanding that each part was worth half of a square.

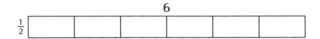

For a more complete discussion about helping students understand how to use rectangles to solve multiplication problems with fractions, see Chapter 4.

CHAPTER THREE
MAKING ESTIMATES

Overview

In this lesson, students estimate answers for problems that involve multiplying fractions, mixed numbers, and whole numbers. Making estimates helps develop students' number sense and also helps them evaluate if the actual answers they calculate are reasonable. In this lesson, the students discuss estimates for six different problems. In a class discussion, the students calculate the exact answer for the last problem. Students then each complete a writing assignment in which they record a solution strategy for the problem and explain their reasoning.

Materials

▲ none

Time

▲ one class period, plus time for additional experiences

Teaching Directions

1. Check that the students understand what an estimate is. Ask several students to give their ideas.

2. Write on the board: $6\frac{1}{3} \times 2\frac{1}{2}$. Ask: "What estimate would you make for the answer to this problem?" Have all students who are interested give an estimate and ask them to explain their reasoning. Record all estimates on the board and draw a wavy circle around each.

$6\frac{1}{3} \times 2\frac{1}{2}$

3. Repeat this procedure for five more problems:

$4\frac{1}{2} \times 2\frac{3}{4}$

$3\frac{1}{2} \times \frac{2}{3}$

$4 \times \frac{3}{4}$

$7\frac{1}{2} \times 2\frac{1}{3}$

$3\frac{3}{4} \times 7$

4. For the last problem, $3\frac{3}{4} \times 7$, ask students for ideas about how to figure out an exact answer. Record their ideas on the board.

5. Ask the students to copy down the last problem and solve it in some way that makes sense to them.

Teaching Notes

The primary focus of this lesson is on having students make estimates for multiplication problems. Not only is making estimates useful for evaluating the accuracy of answers, but asking students to make estimates focuses them on the meaning of the numbers, not on the procedures for calculating. Also, from considering problems to make estimates, students gain familiarity with thinking about multiplying fractions, mixed numbers, and whole numbers without the pressure of figuring out exact answers.

I presented six problems in this lesson:

$6\frac{1}{3} \times 2\frac{1}{2}$

$4\frac{1}{2} \times 2\frac{3}{4}$

$3\frac{1}{2} \times \frac{2}{3}$

$4 \times \frac{3}{4}$

$7\frac{1}{2} \times 2\frac{1}{3}$

$3\frac{3}{4} \times 7$

Students' estimates gave me insights into how they were thinking about fractions. For example, after Anita suggested twelve as an estimate for the first problem, reasoning that six times two was twelve, so twelve would be close, Annie said, "I think eleven is a good estimate. I agree with Anita that six times two is twelve, but then you have to multiply the fractions. And when you multiply fractions, the answer gets smaller." In this instance, Annie erroneously applied the idea that when multiplying fractions, the products can be smaller than the factors. I chose not to comment. Annie was an eager student, willing to participate, and typically needed time for ideas to jell in her mind. I didn't want to discourage her from taking the risk of offering ideas. Also, misconceptions often reflect partial understanding or confusion, and I've come to understand that these are typical to the learning process. In the lesson, Annie asked to change her estimate, and I asked her to explain her reasoning. Annie's idea didn't prevent her from correctly solving the problem I assigned or correctly solving problems on subsequent assignments.

However, when Damien asked to withdraw his estimate of 5 or 6 for the problem $3\frac{1}{2} \times \frac{2}{3}$, I pushed him to explain his thinking. Damien was a strong, thoughtful, and confident student, and I felt it was appropriate to probe his thinking. Making decisions about responding differently to different students is part of the art of teaching.

The Lesson

▲▲

I began the lesson by asking, "Who can explain what an estimate is?"

Eddie answered first. "An estimate is like a guess," he said.

Ally added, "It's something that's close, but it's not exactly right."

"So we can think of an estimate as a close guess," I said. "Does anyone have another idea?"

Hassan said, "It's like a contest."

"How is an estimate like a contest?" I asked.

Hassan responded, "You know how sometimes they have a big jar full of marbles or beans and you get to enter the contest with your estimate?"

"Oh, I see," I said, "and the idea is to make as close a guess as possible." Hassan nodded.

Juanita had an idea to share. She said, "It's kind of like rounding. If you have a number that's near a number, you can round up or down."

"Can you give me an example?" I asked.

Juanita said, "If you have ninety-seven, then you could round it up to one hundred."

Feeling confident that the students knew what an estimate is, I turned to the board and wrote a problem:

$$6\frac{1}{3} \times 2\frac{1}{2}$$

"What estimate would you make for the answer to this problem? About what do you think the answer will be?" I asked. "Raise a hand when you have an idea." After a moment, more than half of the students had their hands raised. I called on Anita.

"I think it could be twelve," she said. I wrote Anita's estimate on the board, putting it in a wavy circle to indicate that it was an estimate, not necessarily the exact answer:

$6\frac{1}{3} \times 2\frac{1}{2}$ ⟨12⟩

"Can you explain why you think that?" I asked.

"Because six times two is twelve, and I think that's close," Anita explained.

Annie had a different idea. "I think eleven is a good estimate," she said. "I agree with Anita that six times two is twelve, but then you have to multiply the fractions. And when you multiply fractions, the answer gets smaller."

Celia shared next. "I think it's fifteen," she said. "I agree with Anita, too. If you multiply six times two, you get twelve. But then you have to multiply the six times one-half, too, and that's three more. So I guess fifteen." I recorded Annie's and Celia's estimates:

$6\frac{1}{3} \times 2\frac{1}{2}$ ⟨12⟩ ⟨11⟩ ⟨15⟩

Annie's hand shot up. "Can I change my mind?" she asked.

"Yes, it's fine to change your mind, but I'm interested in your thinking," I responded.

Annie explained, "I think what Celia said makes sense, so I think fifteen, too. Or maybe fourteen. First I listened to Anita and I thought it should be a little smaller because of the small fractions, but then what Celia said made sense. But maybe it should be a little smaller than that. But I'm not sure. But I think you should erase the eleven." I did as Annie asked.

A SECOND PROBLEM

I then said, "I'm going to write another problem on the board. Please think about an estimate for the answer." I wrote on the board:

$4\frac{1}{2} \times 2\frac{3}{4}$

Conversation broke out and I waited a moment before asking for the students' attention. Then I called on Brendan.

"I think twelve," he said. I recorded *12* in a wavy circle:

$4\frac{1}{2} \times 2\frac{3}{4}$ ⦅12⦆

Brendan explained, "First I thought, 'Four times two is eight,' but then I thought about, 'What is four and one-half times two?' That's four and one-half two times, and that's nine. So the answer is at least nine. Then there is the three-fourths. I think it will be bigger than nine, so I'm guessing twelve."

Helene had a different estimate. "I think ten or maybe eleven," she said. "I get what Brendan said about four and one-half times two is nine, but I don't think it will be that much more. Three-fourths isn't even one."

Juanita used the idea she had shared earlier about rounding to give a different estimate. She explained, "I think thirteen. I rounded two and three-quarters up to three. Then I thought about four and one-half times three. Four times three is twelve, and one-half times three is one and a half. Twelve and one and a half makes thirteen and a half, but that's too big because I rounded up. So I think thirteen." I recorded Helene's and Juanita's estimates:

$4\frac{1}{2} \times 2\frac{3}{4}$

A THIRD PROBLEM

I then wrote a third problem on the board:

$3\frac{1}{2} \times \frac{2}{3}$

More students were eager to offer estimates for this problem. It seemed that they were more comfortable after our discussions of the first two examples. When hands were raised, I said, "I'm going to call on people who haven't yet had a chance to share."

Damien went first. "Five or six," he said.

"Can you explain your idea?" I asked.

"I'm not sure," Damien said. "It just seems right."

"Well, listen to other explanations and see if they can help you explain your idea," I said. I called on Sabrina.

"I think it's one," she said.

"Whoa!" Damien said, surprised by Sabrina's estimate.

"Can you explain?" I asked Sabrina.

Sabrina said, "Well, three times one is three, right?" I nodded. "So when you multiply three by a fraction, it gets smaller. But I'm not really sure." I now had two estimates recorded on the board:

$3\frac{1}{2} \times \frac{2}{3}$ ⦅5 or 6⦆ ⦅1⦆

Students wanted to weigh in with other estimates and hands were waving. I called on Craig. "My estimate is somewhere in between three and three and a half," he said. "I can explain it."

I said, "OK, but let's wait a moment until everyone is listening." The students were sharing ideas among themselves and I wanted all of them to participate in this discussion. When the class settled down, I asked Craig to continue.

"Well, suppose you round the two-thirds up to one whole," Craig began. "Then three and a half times a whole is three and a half, because any time you times something by one, it stays the same. But the whole is too big. It really is only two-thirds. So three and a half is too big. So that's why I said it should be in between three and three and a half." I recorded Craig's estimate:

Hands were still waving. I called on Ally. "I think two," she said. "I think that two-thirds of three is two, and the extra half won't matter so much."

"How do you know that two-thirds of three is two?" I asked.

"If you have three things, then each one is one-third. So two of them has to be two-thirds," Ally explained. I drew three circles on the board and asked Ally to come up and explain. She came to the board, drew lines between the circles, and wrote $\frac{1}{3}$ underneath each.

"So one of them is one-third, two are two-thirds, and all three circles are three-thirds, and that's the same as a whole," Ally explained. She then returned to explaining her estimate. "So three times two-thirds is two, and the extra half won't matter so much." I recorded Ally's estimate:

$3\frac{1}{2} \times \frac{2}{3}$ 〈5 or 6〉 〈between 3 & 3½〉 〈2〉

Damien's hand was up. "I want to change my mind," he said.

"That's fine," I said. "What are you thinking now?"

Damien responded, "I think my estimate is too big. I kind of agree with what Craig said. I think you should erase mine."

"Can you remember what your first idea was that made five or six seem like a better estimate?" I asked.

Damien replied, "I rounded two-thirds up to one whole, and I rounded three and a half up to four, and I think I just added by mistake. I'm not sure what I did, but now I think it has to be less than three and a half." I did as Damien requested and erased his first estimate.

A FOURTH PROBLEM

I wrote the fourth problem on the board:

$4 \times \frac{3}{4}$

Conversations broke out. After a moment, many hands were raised. I called on Julio.

"This one is easy," he said. "The answer is three, because three-fourths of four is three. The best estimate is three."

"How can you explain why three-fourths of four is three?" I asked.

"Like Ally did, but with four circles," Julio said. He came up and drew four circles on the board, then drew lines between them, and then wrote fractions beneath.

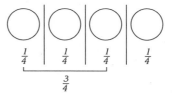

"That one was really easy," David said.

A FIFTH PROBLEM

I wrote the fifth problem on the board:

$7\frac{1}{2} \times 2\frac{1}{3}$

"Ooh, that looks harder," Helene said.

Francis shared first. "I think it's more than fourteen, but I'm not sure how much more. I know that seven times two is fourteen, and so with the extra fractions, it will be more."

"What number should I write?" I asked.

"I'm not sure," Francis said. "Let someone else explain."

Brendan's hand shot up. "I think it's bigger, maybe twenty or more."

"Should I record 'twenty or more' in a wavy circle?" I asked. Brendan nodded and I did so:

$7\frac{1}{2} \times 2\frac{1}{3}$ (20 or more)

Then Brendan explained, "I rounded. First I rounded two and two-thirds up to three. That would be too much. So I rounded seven and one-half down to seven. The rounding up and rounding down should sort of even out. That means I had seven times three, which is twenty-one. But I'm not sure if it will be more or less than that. So I guess twenty or more."

Pierre added, "I think Brendan has a really good idea, but I think a better estimate is twenty-one." Pierre shrugged when I pushed him to explain.

Maria said, "I think only eighteen."

"How did you get that?" Julio asked her.

"OK," she said, "I'm not sure, but I'll try to explain. I know that seven and one-half times two is fifteen, because you can add seven and one-half plus seven and one-half. OK. So then I have to think about seven and one-half times one-third. And I think that would make it maybe three more. So I think eighteen." I recorded Pierre's and Maria's estimates:

$7\frac{1}{2} \times 2\frac{1}{3}$ (20 or more) (about 21) (18)

THE LAST PROBLEM

I presented one last problem. For this problem, after asking the students for estimates, I led a discussion about how to find the exact answer. I wrote the problem on the board:

$3\frac{3}{4} \times 7$

I called on Anita to share first. She said, "I think twenty-three is a good estimate because seven times three is twenty-one. Then three-fourths of seven makes it more, so I think about twenty-three."

David said, "I think twenty-five is better because I think that three-fourths of seven is more than two, so the answer will be more than twenty-one plus two." I recorded these estimates:

$3\frac{3}{4} \times 7$ (23) (25)

No one else volunteered an estimate, so I asked, "How would you figure out the exact answer? Talk with your neighbor about this and raise a hand if you have an idea to share." Conversation broke out. A few students reached for pencil and paper, but most didn't. After a minute or so, I brought them back to attention and called on Kayla.

She said, "First I did the three times seven part, and that was easy. It's twenty-one. So then I did the three-fourths times seven, and that's the same as three-fourths added seven times. I added them up by counting by threes—three, six, nine, twelve, fifteen, eighteen, twenty-one. That's twenty-one–fourths. Then I thought that four times five is twenty, so there are five wholes in twenty-one–fourths and one-fourth left over. So I added twenty-one from the seven times three plus five plus one-fourth. That makes twenty-six and one-fourth." I recorded on the board as Kayla explained:

$3 \times 7 = 21$

$\frac{3}{4} \times 7 = \frac{3}{4} + \frac{3}{4} + \frac{3}{4} + \frac{3}{4} + \frac{3}{4} + \frac{3}{4} + \frac{3}{4}$

$3, 6, 9, 12, 15, 18, 21$

$\frac{3}{4} \times 7 = \frac{21}{4}$

$4 \times 5 = 20$

$\frac{21}{4} = 5 + \frac{1}{4}$

$21 + 5 + \frac{1}{4} = 26\frac{1}{4}$

Francis had another way to explain why twenty-one–fourths was equal to five and one-fourth. He had used pencil and paper. "I wrote the three-fourths like Kayla did," he said, "and then I drew three lines underneath each, like tally marks. And then I knew that four of the tally marks were four-fourths, and that's one, so I circled them in fours and figured it out." Francis came up to show his idea on the board.

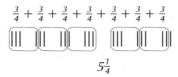

I then modeled for the students how to solve the problem using a rectangle. I explained, "First I round up the fraction and draw a rectangle that is seven units by four units." I drew the rectangle and divided it into squares.

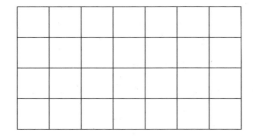

"Then I shorten the side that's four units to three and three-fourths," I said. I divided the bottom row into four slices and shaded in the bottom row of slices to indicate that I didn't need to consider it. Also, I darkened the outline of the 7-by-$3\frac{3}{4}$ rectangle and labeled the dimensions.

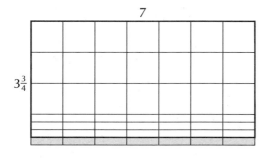

"Let's count the squares in the rectangle that is seven by three and three-fourths," I said.

Saul asked, "Why don't you just subtract the shaded pieces from the twenty-eight?"

"OK," I said. "How much are the shaded pieces worth?"

Saul said, "There are seven of them. Four of them make a whole square, so you have one whole and three-fourths." I wrote on the board:

$28 - 1\frac{3}{4}$

"Who would like to do the subtraction?" I asked.

Gloria said, "Twenty-eight minus one is twenty-seven, and twenty-seven minus three-fourths is twenty-six and one-fourth." I recorded on the board:

$28 - 1 = 27$
$27 - \frac{3}{4} = 26\frac{1}{4}$

"Let's see if we get the same answer by counting up the squares in the unshaded part, the rectangle that is seven by three and three-fourths," I said.

Francis said, "You have twenty-one whole squares and then . . . oh yeah, twenty-one slices, and those are fourths."

"So how much is that altogether?" I asked.

"Well, four of the slices make one whole, so you can color in fours and count them up," Francis said. "Can I come up and do it?" I agreed, and Francis used different colors and counted five wholes and one extra fourth.

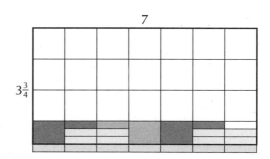

I recorded:
$21 + 5 + \frac{1}{4} = 26\frac{1}{4}$

A WRITING ASSIGNMENT

I then asked the students to copy down the problem we had just discussed and record a solution strategy that made sense to them. "You know what the answer is," I said, pointing to the answer of $26\frac{1}{4}$ on the board. "Choose a way to show how you would figure it out."

Most of the students solved the problem by first multiplying 3×7, then multiplying $\frac{3}{4} \times 7$, and finally combining the partial products. They showed various ways of figuring out the partial product of $\frac{3}{4} \times 7$. On his paper, for example, Brendan used a variation on the method that Francis had described for figuring out that twenty-one–fourths was equal to five and one-fourth. He drew a row of twenty-one tally marks. He crossed out four and made a tally mark above the row, then crossed out four more and made another tally mark, and continued in this way to show five and one-fourth (see Figure 3–1).

Craig drew a rectangle and divided it as I had done on the board. He wrote:

The rectangle is used to count the answer. Visualy count the answer as you see there are 21 full squares and there are 7 squares that resemble $\frac{3}{4}$. $7 \times \frac{3}{4} = 5\frac{1}{4}$. $5\frac{1}{4} + 21 = 26\frac{1}{4}$.

Kayla's method for figuring out the problem was unique. She wrote:

I split $3\frac{3}{4}$ into 3 and $\frac{3}{4}$. Then I multiplied 3×7. After that I divided 7 in half. I divided half of 7 in half to get $\frac{1}{4}$ of 7. I multiplied that by 3 to get $\frac{3}{4}$ of 7. Then I added $\frac{3}{4}$ of 7 to the answer of 3×7 and that was my answer. (See Figure 3–2.)

Even though the answer was on the board, Helene wrote a different one on her paper—$21\frac{21}{4}$! She showed how she added $\frac{3}{4}$ seven times to get $\frac{21}{4}$, and she added that to 21, the product of 3×7. I talked with Helene about how to represent the answer in the more conventional way.

Figures 3–3 through 3–5 show three more ways to solve the problem.

EXTENSIONS

Over the next several days, present the students with a problem, ask them for estimates, discuss different ways to solve it, and then ask students to record a solution strategy that makes sense to them. You also may want to ask them to solve the problems in at least two ways. This sort of practice, done over time, helps reinforce students' understanding and skills.

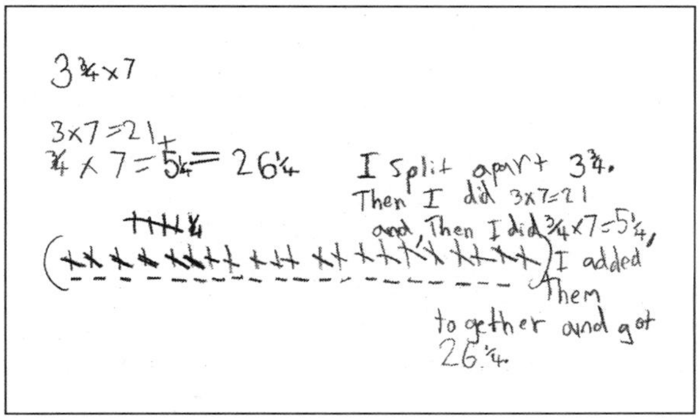

▲▲▲▲▲▲Figure 3–1 *Brendan showed how he used Francis's system of tally marks to figure out the value of $\frac{3}{4} \times 7$.*

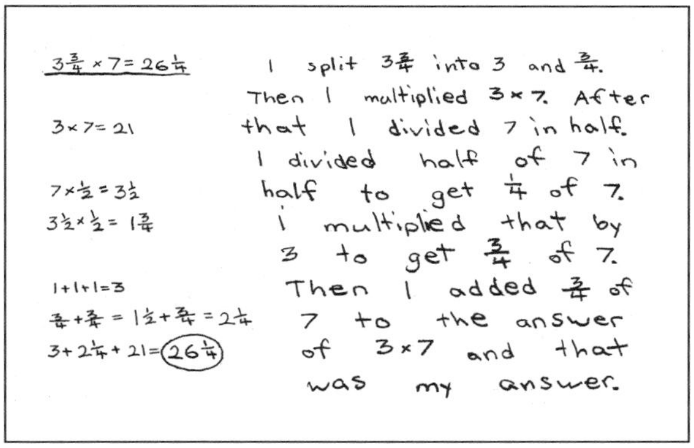

▲▲▲▲▲▲Figure 3–2 *Kayla's paper showed a unique way of figuring out $\frac{3}{4} \times 7$.*

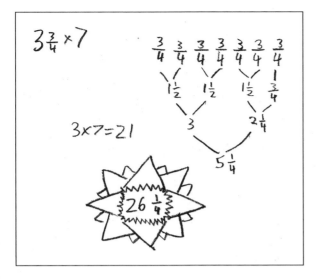

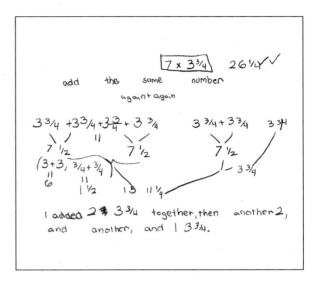

▲▲▲▲▲▲Figure 3–3 *Pierre combined the seven $\frac{3}{4}$s by combining pairs of them. He arrived at the correct answer of $26\frac{1}{4}$.*

▲▲▲▲▲▲Figure 3–4 *Celia solved $3\frac{3}{4} \times 7$ by adding $3\frac{3}{4}+3\frac{3}{4}+3\frac{3}{4}+3\frac{3}{4}+3\frac{3}{4}+3\frac{3}{4}+3\frac{3}{4}$.*

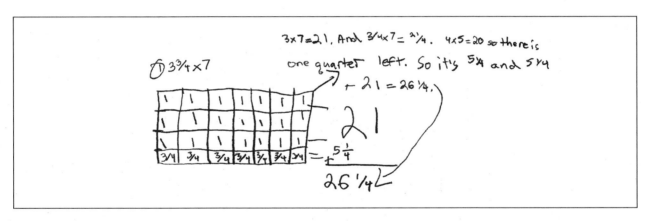

▲▲▲▲▲▲Figure 3–5 *Julio drew a rectangle to show how to find the answer.*

Questions and Discussion

▲▲

▲ **I'd be concerned if a student of mine gave an answer of twenty-one and twenty-one–fourths, as Helene did. It just doesn't seem right. Were you concerned?**

Helene's answer wasn't conventional, for sure, but it was equivalent to twenty-six and one-fourth. When I see an unusual representation such as this, I think it's important to check that the student can figure out alternative ways to express a fraction. Sometimes, a student is trying to be mathematically playful and/or original. In this case, however, Helene wasn't sure how to deal with the twenty-one–fourths, so she just left the fraction as is. By talking with her, I was able to help her see how improper fractions can be changed to mixed numbers or sometimes whole numbers. At the same time, I think that it's valuable for others in the class to consider nonconventional representations as well. In this situation, after talking with Helene, and with her permission, I shared her answer with the class. I wrote it on the board and said, "This is another correct answer to the problem. Who can explain why I think this answer is worth the same as twenty-six and one-fourth?"

▲ *Why do you have the students put their estimates in wavy circles? Do the circles have some mathematical significance?*

The wavy circle has no mathematical significance that I know of. The convention is one that I started using with students several years ago. The wavy circle serves two purposes. One is that it makes it easier for me to find students' estimates on their papers. Also, before introducing this convention, students regularly either forgot or ignored my direction for making estimates. The wavy circles solved this problem because, I think, there is a certain appeal and novelty to using them.

▲ *Why did you ask the students to solve the same problem that they had just discussed? Wouldn't you learn more if you gave them a different problem to solve and explain?*

In this instance, my primary goal wasn't to assess the students' ability to solve a new problem, but rather to give them experience explaining a solution strategy for the answer that they had already thought about. Also, giving them the support of knowing the right answer would help focus them on thinking and explaining. At the same time, however, the assignment served as an assessment of the lesson and revealed to me who was able to follow the discussion and who wasn't, and which explanations seemed to make sense to the students. In that way, the assignment helped guide me in deciding what instructionally made sense to present next.

CHAPTER FOUR
DRAWING RECTANGLES

Overview

This lesson builds on what the students have learned so far about multiplying fractions and focuses specifically on helping them learn how to draw rectangles for figuring out the answers to multiplication problems. This skill is useful both as a check for answers found by other methods and also for helping students later understand why the standard algorithm of multiplying across the numerators and denominators works. After the teacher demonstrates how to draw rectangles for several problems, the students solve other problems on their own, solving each by drawing a rectangle and also by some other method.

Materials

▲ none

Time

▲ one class period, plus time for additional experiences

Teaching Directions

1. Write on the board: $3\frac{1}{2} \times 5$. First ask the students to estimate the answer and then ask for ideas about how to arrive at an exact answer. Establish that the answer is $17\frac{1}{2}$. As students explain their ideas, record on the board or have students come up and record.

2. When no one else has a solution strategy to report, demonstrate for the class how to find the answer by drawing a $3\frac{1}{2}$-by-5 rectangle. Tell them that you'll start by rounding three and a half to four so that both sides of the rectangle will be a whole number. Then follow these steps:

1. Draw a horizontal line, mark off 5 units, and erase any extra.

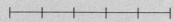

2. Draw a second side 4 units long.

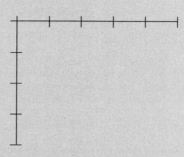

3. Complete the rectangle and divide it into small squares. Check that the students know that there are twenty squares and, therefore, the answer to $3\frac{1}{2} \times 5$ must be smaller.

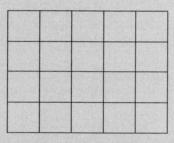

4. Draw a horizontal line to create a $3\frac{1}{2}$-by-5 rectangle. Label the sides and shade the bottom portion to show that it isn't part of the problem. Outline the $3\frac{1}{2}$-by-5 rectangle with a darker line.

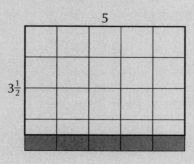

5. Have students help you count the number of squares in the unshaded section. First count the whole squares and then count the partial squares.

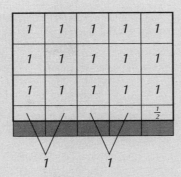

3. Point out that each of the five columns in the rectangle is $3\frac{1}{2}$ units, which shows how you could solve the problem by adding three and a half five times. Also show the partial products of 3×5 (the fifteen whole squares) and $\frac{1}{2} \times 5$ (the five partial squares).

4. Write another problem on the board: $3 \times 2\frac{1}{2}$. Repeat Step 1 and establish the answer of $7\frac{1}{2}$. Then repeat Steps 2 and 3. If appropriate, ask a student to come to the board and draw the rectangle.

5. Write another problem on the board: $2\frac{1}{4} \times 3$. Repeat Step 1 and establish the answer of $6\frac{3}{4}$. Then ask students to each draw the rectangle to represent the problem and figure out the answer. Pose another problem for students who finish early—$\frac{1}{2} \times \frac{3}{8}$. Circulate and observe. Then lead a class discussion about both problems and have students come to the board and draw solutions.

6. End the class by telling students that they will have more opportunity to practice this new skill.

Teaching Notes

Interpreting multiplication problems with rectangles, whether the problems involve whole numbers, mixed numbers, or fractions, offers students another strategy for computing and a way to check answers found through other methods. Drawing rectangles for problems also contributes to students' overall understanding of multiplication and why partial products are sometimes helpful. And this interpretation links multiplication to the area of rectangles, making the connection between numbers and geometry. This lesson is appropriate for students who have experienced the lessons in Chapters 1, 2, and 3.

You'll notice that I recommend the procedure of first drawing a rectangle that is larger than the problem requires, rounding fractions up to whole numbers. For example, for $2\frac{3}{4} \times 3\frac{1}{2}$, it's a good idea first to draw a 3-by-4 rectangle and then to adjust it to the problem, shading the areas that are not under consideration. Doing this makes it easier to figure the value of partial squares since the whole squares are there as a reference.

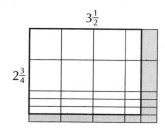

$3\frac{1}{2}$

$2\frac{3}{4}$

In this rectangle, there are six whole squares, two one-half pieces, nine one-fourth pieces, and three one-eighth pieces. Multiplying mixed numbers typically poses problems for students, and having this interpretation is a way for students to check answers.

In this lesson, however, the problems I chose to present avoided the issue of multiplying two mixed numbers. Rather, I chose problems that I knew the students could solve numerically, so that drawing rectangles would be a check on the answers they had already found. (See Chapter 5 for a lesson that addresses multiplication of mixed numbers.)

The Lesson

▲▲

I started class by writing a problem on the board:

$3\frac{1}{2} \times 5$

My plan was to ask the students for an estimate, then talk about figuring out the exact answer, and finally demonstrate how to draw a rectangle to find the product. I had been incorporating rectangles into the instruction over the past several days, but I thought that the students would benefit from more specific instruction.

I stood at the board, pointing at the problem and waiting for the students to settle and focus. "What would be a good estimate for this problem?" I asked, building on the estimation lesson I had taught a few days before.

"I think seventeen," Jake said. "Three times five is fifteen, and the answer should be a little bit bigger." I wrote on the board:

$3\frac{1}{2} \times 5$ ⑰

Sandro raised a hand. He said, "I think I know the exact answer."

"That's just what I was going to ask next," I said. "Tell us your idea."

Sandro said, "Well, I know that three times five is fifteen, like Jake said. And one-half of five is two and a half. So I think it's seventeen and a half."

"How did you get the seventeen and one-half?" I asked.

"I added fifteen plus two and a half," Sandro replied. I recorded Sandro's thinking on the board:

$3\frac{1}{2} \times 5$

$3 \times 5 = 15$

$\frac{1}{2} \times 5 = 2\frac{1}{2}$

$15 + 2\frac{1}{2} = 17\frac{1}{2}$

"It's always good to solve a problem in more than one way," I said. "Who has another way to figure out the answer?"

Carlotta said, "You add three and one-half five times—three and one-half plus three and one-half, like that, five times."

"So you're thinking of the problem as five groups of three and one-half?" I asked. Carlotta nodded. "OK," I said and wrote on the board:

$5 \times 3\frac{1}{2}$

$3\frac{1}{2} + 3\frac{1}{2} + 3\frac{1}{2} + 3\frac{1}{2} + 3\frac{1}{2}$

"Can I come up and show how I can add them?" Carlotta asked.

I agreed. "But please be sure to explain what you're doing," I said. Carlotta came to the board and recorded as follows:

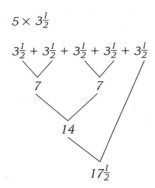

She then explained, "I know that three and a half plus three and a half is seven, and I did that twice. Then seven plus seven is fourteen, and fourteen plus the other three and one-half is seventeen and one-half."

Sadie raised her hand. "I got the same answer, but I did it another way," she said. "I know that five threes make fifteen, and five halves make two and one-half. So fifteen and two and a half makes seventeen and a half." Sadie's idea was the same as Sandro's. Still, I recorded her thinking on the board:

$5 \times 3 = 15$

$5 \times \frac{1}{2} = 2\frac{1}{2}$

$15 + 2\frac{1}{2} = 17\frac{1}{2}$

"Does anyone have another way to share?" I asked. No one volunteered.

"I have a way to share," I then said. "I can draw a rectangle to help me figure out that the answer is seventeen and one-half. I've shown you how to do this for some of the other problems we've talked about, and I'd like you to pay close attention now. In a little while, I'm going ask all of you to try this method for finding answers to problems

like this one." I turned to the board and explained as I began to draw. "I need to draw a rectangle that is five on one side and three and a half on the other. First I'll draw a side that's five units long. That's pretty easy for me to do." I drew a horizontal line and marked off five units, erasing the extra bit at the end.

I continued, "OK, now I need to draw a side that's three and a half units. When there's a fraction in the problem, I like to round the number up and draw a side that's a little bit longer so it's a whole number of units. What is three and one-half rounded up?"

"Four," several students answered in unison.

"I'll make this side four units," I said. I drew the other side.

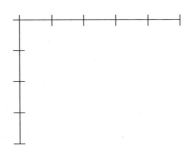

I then completed the rectangle and divided it into small squares.

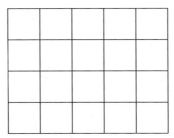

"How many small squares are there?" I asked the class.

"Twenty," several students responded.

I continued my explanation. "I know that this rectangle is too big, so I know that the answer is less than twenty. What I have to do now is make the shorter side measure only three and a half units." I drew a horizontal line to create a $3\frac{1}{2}$-by-5 rectangle inside the original rectangle. I labeled the sides and shaded in the bottom portion to show that we didn't need to consider it for solving the problem. Then I outlined the $3\frac{1}{2}$-by-5 rectangle with a darker line.

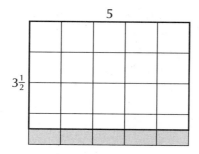

"Who can explain why I shaded in this part of the rectangle?" I asked the class, pointing to the shaded strip at the bottom.

Stella said, "That's the part that isn't part of the problem."

"Who can describe what part of the rectangle shows the three and one-half?" I asked.

Jonathan answered, "It's how long the up-and-down side is. It matches the number in the problem."

"I agree," I responded. "Who can explain why the rectangle that I outlined represents the problem we're trying to solve?"

Jared answered, "It's five on one side and three and a half on the other, and the problem is five times three and one-half."

"So now what should I do with the rectangle?" I asked.

"Count the squares," several students answered together.

"Would someone like to come up and do that?" I asked. I called on Libby and she came up to the board.

"See, there are fifteen whole squares," she began and wrote a *1* in each of them. "And then you put the halves together." Libby pointed to the half-squares as she said, "These two make a whole, these two make a whole, and there's a half left over." She marked these pieces to show what she meant.

"So there are fifteen wholes, then two more wholes to make seventeen, and an extra one-half. That's how you get seventeen and one-half." Others nodded in agreement. I thanked Libby and she returned to her seat.

I then said, "I think that what the rectangle shows also matches what Jake and Sadie were thinking." I pointed to the board where I had recorded Jake's and Sadie's thinking. "See, Jake did three times five first, and Sadie did five times three first, and they got fifteen. There are the fifteen wholes that Libby counted in the five-by-three part of the rectangle." I pointed to the rectangle to help the students make this connection. "Then Jake did one-half times five and Sadie did five times one-half, and that's the same as Libby figuring out how much were the five one-half pieces at the bottom."

"That's cool," Manuel said.

A few students looked confused, so I drew a heavy line dividing the rectangle into two parts, 3-by-5 on the top and $\frac{1}{2}$-by-5 on the bottom. I said, "Here's the three times five part on the top and the one-half times five part on the bottom." This seemed to help.

I then said, "I also think that the rectangle shows Carlotta's idea. Carlotta added three and one-half five times." I pointed to the board where Carlotta's idea was recorded. "The rectangle shows Carlotta's idea, too. There are five columns in the rectangle." I used my finger to show the five columns. "How many squares in each column? Talk to your neighbor about this."

The class broke out into animated conversation. After a moment, I asked for the students' attention and called on Stella.

"Each vertical line has three and a half squares in it," she said. The others agreed.

"Yes, that's right," I said, "and there are five vertical columns." I ran my finger over each column as I said, "That's three and one-half, plus three and one-half, plus three and one-half, plus three and one-half, plus three and one-half. That's the same as Carlotta adding three and a half five times."

ANOTHER PROBLEM

I next wrote on the board:

$3 \times 2\frac{1}{2}$

"About what is the answer?" I asked, reinforcing for the students that they should try to come up with an estimate first.

"Six," Stella suggested. "Three times two is six, and the one-half won't count for much."

"I think seven," Jared said. "Three times two is six, but it's more because of the extra one-half."

"I think seven and a half," Alan said. "Actually, I think that's the exact answer."

"Who is willing to come up and show how you would solve the problem?" I asked. About a third of the class volunteered. I called on Tamika. When she came up to the board, she initially lost her confidence, something that I've often seen happen with students when they face the vastness of the board and realize that they are in front of the class. After a bit, Tamika began with a false start. "You have one-sixth," she said. She wrote $\frac{1}{6}$ on the board and then remained silent.

"Tell us where the one-sixth comes from," I said gently.

"Well, first I broke apart the two and one-half and did three times the one-half," Tamika said. She wrote $3 \times \frac{1}{2}$ on the board and then said, "Oh, no, it's not one-sixth." She erased the $\frac{1}{6}$ and replaced it with $1\frac{1}{2}$. Then she regained her confidence and completed the problem. "And three times the two is six, so you add one and one-half and six to get seven and one-half. Alan was right." Tamika wrote:

$$3 \times \tfrac{1}{2} = 1\tfrac{1}{2}$$
$$3 \times 2 = 6$$
$$1\tfrac{1}{2} + 6 = 7\tfrac{1}{2}$$

Other students were interested in sharing ideas. I called on Jonathan and he came up to the front of the room. "Well, I just did it in my head," he said. "I don't know how to write it." Jonathan was able to figure mentally with a good deal of facility but often had trouble representing his thinking on paper.

"Explain what you did in your head and I'll help you figure out what to record on the board," I said.

In one breath, Jonathan said, "First I thought three twos and that's two, four, six, and then I did three times one-half, and then I added." I realized that Jonathan had done essentially what Tamika had, but he had thought about it in a slightly different way. I pushed Jonathan to write down how he counted to figure out the three twos. And when I pushed him to explain how he knew three times one-half, he reported that he counted by one-halves. Then he wrote:

2, 4, 6
$\frac{1}{2}$, 1, $1\frac{1}{2}$
$6 + 1\frac{1}{2} = 7\frac{1}{2}$

I commented to the students on the importance of learning to represent their thinking. "Then you can communicate how you're thinking with others," I said.

Kendra had another way to share. "I did it by adding three two and a halves," she said.

"Do you want to come up and show your method on the board?" I asked. Kendra nodded and came up. She wrote:

$3 \times 2\frac{1}{2}$

$2\frac{1}{2} + 2\frac{1}{2} + 2\frac{1}{2} = 7\frac{1}{2}$

Then she said, "Two and one-half and two and one-half is five, and five plus two and one-half is seven and one-half."

I then asked, "Would anyone like to come up and try the problem by drawing a rectangle?" Several volunteered and I called on Jake.

Jake came to the board and drew a 3–by-3 rectangle, then inside it a 3-by-$2\frac{1}{2}$ rectangle. He then said, "So there are six whole squares and three half-squares. Two of the half-squares make a whole square, so there are seven whole squares and one extra half-square."

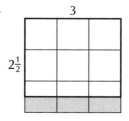

I pointed out to the students how they could see Tamika's and Jonathan's thinking in the rectangle by first looking at the 3-by-2 section and then at the 3–by-$\frac{1}{2}$ section. I also pointed out how each of the three columns in Jake's rectangle had two and a half squares. "And there are three columns, which is why you can add two and one-half three times," I said.

Manuel had a question. "I don't get how Tamika got one and one-half for three times one-half," he said. He had been pondering this for a while and wasn't able to make sense of it.

"Do you want to explain, Tamika?" I asked.

Tamika nodded and said, "Three times one-half is the same as three halves, so you go one-half plus one-half plus one-half." I recorded on the board:

$3 \times \frac{1}{2} = \frac{1}{2} + \frac{1}{2} + \frac{1}{2} = \frac{3}{2} = 1\frac{1}{2}$

"Oh, I see," Manuel said. "One-half and one-half makes one, and a half more makes one and one-half."

Machiko had another way to explain. She said, "If you drew a rectangle with three squares and then cut it in half, you'd have one and a half squares." I drew three squares adjacent to each other to make a rectangle.

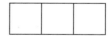

Then I asked Machiko, "Which way did you cut the rectangle, vertically or horizontally?"

"Vertically down the middle," she answered, gesturing with her hand. "That's it," she confirmed after I drew the line.

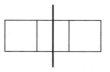

"See, there's a whole square and half of a square in each side of the cut," Machiko added. Manuel nodded to indicate that this also made sense.

Barton had another way to solve $3 \times 2\frac{1}{2}$. He came up and explained, "I doubled both factors, and that's six times five, which is thirty. And then I divided by four." From the whole number work we had done earlier in the year, Barton remembered that doubling both factors results in a product that is four times larger. (For information about that lesson, see Chapter 4 in the Teaching Arithmetic book, *Lessons for Extending Multiplication, Grades 4–5.*) Barton wrote on the board:

$6 \times 5 = 30$

30

$\div 4$

I stopped Barton to correct his representation of the division. I gave him two options for recording thirty divided by four:

$30 \div 4$

$4)\overline{30}$

Sandro didn't understand why Barton divided by four. "Why don't you divide by two?" he asked.

"Because I doubled both factors," Barton said. Sandro was still confused.

"Let's look at an easy problem with whole numbers and see what happens when you double both factors," I said. I wrote on the board:

$2 \times 3 = 6$

$4 \times 6 = 24$

"Oh, I see," Sandro said. "You double twice."

"Let's see what happens if we double just one factor," I said. I wrote on the board:

$2 \times 3 = 6$

$2 \times 6 = 12$

Libby said, "If you just doubled the two and one-half, then the problem would be three times five, and you would only have to divide by two." I wrote on the board:

$3 \times 2\frac{1}{2}$

$3 \times 5 = 15$

$\frac{15}{2} = 7\frac{1}{2}$

"It's easier that way," Jake commented.

A THIRD PROBLEM

I next wrote another problem on the board:

$2\frac{1}{4} \times 3$

"What's a reasonable estimate for this answer?" I asked.

Jonathan answered, "Seven, because two times three is six and there's a little more from the one-fourth."

Sandro said, "I think seven but for a different reason. The answer to the last problem was seven and a half, and they're almost the same, except the one-half is a one-fourth. So this answer should be a little smaller."

I then asked the students to talk with their neighbors and try to figure out the exact answer. "Then raise a hand if you'd like to share a method for figuring out the answer," I said. I had chosen a problem that was similar to the one we had just solved purposely, because after we discussed how to solve it, I planned to have each student draw a rectangle to represent it. Choosing a problem similar to one they had just seen provided some degree of familiarity for them. However, changing one of the factors from $2\frac{1}{2}$ to $2\frac{1}{4}$ gave the extra challenge of figuring the partial product of $\frac{1}{4} \times 3$, which I knew might be more difficult for some of the students than figuring $\frac{1}{2} \times 3$, as they had to do in the previous problem.

When the students were quiet, I called on Alan. He said, "The answer is six and three-fourths. First I did three times two to get six. And then I did three times one-fourth, and that's three-fourths. So the answer is six and three-fourths." I wrote on the board:

$2\frac{1}{4} \times 3$

$3 \times 2 = 6$

$3 \times \frac{1}{4} = \frac{3}{4}$

$6 + \frac{3}{4} = 6\frac{3}{4}$

"How did you know that three times one-fourth was three-fourths?" I asked Alan.

He replied, "Three times one-fourth is one-fourth three times, and that's three-fourths." I recorded on the board:

$3 \times \frac{1}{4} = \frac{1}{4} + \frac{1}{4} + \frac{1}{4} = \frac{3}{4}$

"Raise a hand if you got the same answer as Alan did," I said. Almost all hands were up.

"Who solved the problem in another way?" I asked.

Stella said, "Me and Carlotta added two and one-fourth plus two and one-fourth plus two and one-fourth. We added the twos and we added the one-fourths, and we got the same answer." I wrote on the board:

$2\frac{1}{4} + 2\frac{1}{4} + 2\frac{1}{4} = 6\frac{3}{4}$

"Any other methods?" I asked.

Jared said, "I did it kind of like that but a little different. I knew I needed to do two and one-fourth three times, but first I did it two times in my head, and that got me to four and one-half. Then I added on another two and got six and one-half. And then I had to add on one-fourth, and I know that one-half plus one-fourth is three-fourths. I got six and three-fourths." I wrote on the board:

$2\frac{1}{4} + 2\frac{1}{4} = 4\frac{1}{2}$

$4\frac{1}{2} + 2 = 6\frac{1}{2}$

$\frac{1}{2} + \frac{1}{4} = \frac{3}{4}$

$6\frac{1}{2} + \frac{1}{4} = 6\frac{3}{4}$

No one else had another method to share. I then said to the class, "Take a piece of paper and draw a rectangle to show how to solve this problem. You

already know that the answer is six and three-fourths, so your rectangle should produce that same answer. Check what you've done with your neighbor."

"Can we work together or do we have to do it alone and then check?" Carlotta asked, feeling unsure about whether she could draw a rectangle.

"It's fine for you to work together," I said. "But you should each draw a rectangle for the problem on your own paper. I'll write another problem on the board that you can try if you finish quickly. For the second problem, solve it in two ways, with a rectangle and another way." I wrote a second problem on the board underneath the first one.

$2\frac{1}{4} \times 3$

$\frac{1}{2} \times \frac{3}{8}$

I circulated as the students worked. For some, the task was easy and they finished quickly. Most students first drew a 3-by-3 rectangle and then shortened one side to $2\frac{1}{4}$ as I had shown. Others, however, only drew a $2\frac{1}{4}$-by-3 rectangle. For the few who were stuck, I insisted that they start with the 3-by-3 rectangle.

I called the class to attention after I noticed that everyone had completed the first problem. Alan and Jake came up to the board and drew rectangles as they had done on their papers.

DISCUSSING $\frac{1}{2} \times \frac{3}{8}$

I then led a discussion about the second problem. "Even if you didn't get to it," I said, "I'd like you to think about the problem and listen to others' ideas. Who can explain a way to solve it without drawing a rectangle?"

Barton said, "Well, I knew that I had to find half of three-eighths. I know that half of three is one and one-half, but you need to keep the denominator, so it's one and a half–eighths. Then if you times them both by two, you get three-sixteenths." I wrote on the board:

$$\frac{1}{2} \times \frac{3}{8} = \frac{1\frac{1}{2}}{8} = \frac{3}{16}$$

Carlotta said, "I broke apart three-eighths into one-eighth three times. Then I knew that half of one-eighth was one-sixteenth, so the answer had to be three-sixteenths." I wrote on the board:

$$\frac{3}{8} = \frac{1}{8} + \frac{1}{8} + \frac{1}{8}$$
$$\frac{1}{2} \times \frac{1}{8} = \frac{1}{16}$$
Three $\frac{1}{16s} = \frac{3}{16}$

I then asked for volunteers to come up and draw the rectangle. I called on Libby. She drew the rectangle correctly, explaining, "I made a one-by-one rectangle. I split one side into two pieces and each was one-half. I shaded out one-half because it didn't count. Then I split the other side into eight pieces and I shaded out five of them to leave the three-eighths. Each of the pieces left is one-sixteenth of my first rectangle, so the answer is three-sixteenths."

I ended class and told the students, "You'll have the chance to try some more problems over the next few days." Figures 4–1 through 4–3 show how three students worked on the class assignment.

EXTENSIONS

Whenever you assign practice problems, ask students to find answers in more than one way, including using rectangles. Over time, students become more proficient with this strategy.

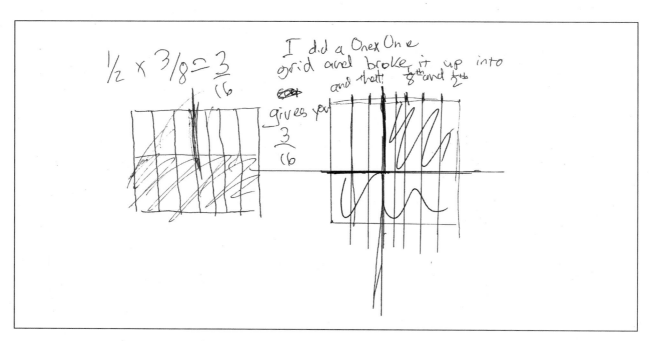

▲▲▲▲▲▲Figure 4–1 *Alan made a false start on the second problem, but he solved it correctly on his second attempt.*

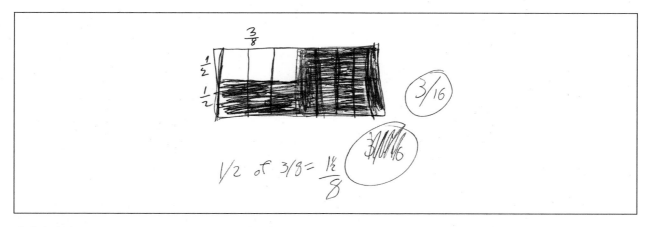

▲▲▲▲▲▲Figure 4–2 *Sandro solved $\frac{1}{2} \times \frac{3}{8}$ the same way that Barton did, by first figuring that the answer was $\frac{1\frac{1}{2}}{8}$. His rectangle helped convince him that the answer could also be $\frac{3}{16}$.*

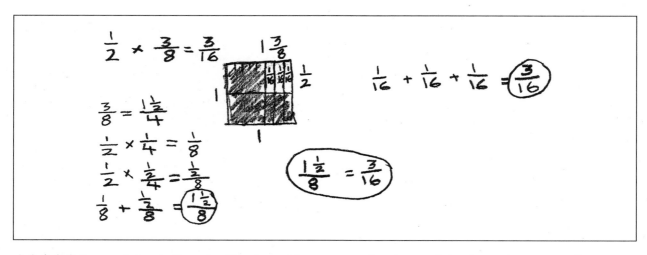

▲▲▲▲▲▲Figure 4–3 *Sadie solved both problems correctly. She explained a unique way of numerically figuring the answer to $\frac{1}{2} \times \frac{3}{8}$.*

Questions and Discussion

▲▲▲

▲ **When Sadie gave the same explanation that Sandro had given for $3\frac{1}{2} \times 5$, why did you write hers on the board as well? Couldn't you have referred to what you had recorded for Sandro?**

There are several reasons I recorded Sadie's reasoning even though it duplicated Sandro's thinking. First of all, I typically record as a student is explaining and, therefore, have no way to be sure that the same explanation has already been given. This was the case with Sadie's explanation. But even if I had been sure ahead of time, I think there are benefits to recording an idea even if it has been given before. One is that it acknowledges the second student's contribution. While I may have noticed that Sadie's explanation was like Sandro's, this may not have been obvious to Sadie. Also, typically there are subtle differences in the students' thinking or wording. In this instance, Sadie reversed the factors and was thinking about

$5 \times 3\frac{1}{2}$, while Sandro had talked about the problem as $3\frac{1}{2} \times 5$. For the second partial product, Sandro thought "one-half of five is two and a half" while Sadie explained "five halves make two and one-half." So while the mathematical recording looked very similar, their thinking was really quite different. Each child's idea was his or her own, wonderful idea. My thinking about this is better explained in the title essay of a book that has long been my favorite—*The Having of Wonderful Ideas,* by Eleanor Duckworth (Teachers College Press, 1996).

▲ *I was surprised at Barton's idea about doubling both factors resulting in a product that is four times larger and then Libby's suggestion to double just one of the factors. Is this important for students to know?*

It's valuable for students to explore the effects on products caused by changes to factors. Doing so both helps develop students' number sense and strengthens their understanding of relationships between factors and products. Chapter 4 in *Lessons for Extending Multiplication* suggests an activity for introducing this exploration, which focuses, along with other ideas, on what happens when one factor is doubled, when both factors are doubled, when one factor is halved, and so on. The lesson presents students with sequences of accessible problems. For example, students investigate what happens to the products of problems like the following:

Doubling One Factor	Doubling Two Factors	Halving One Factor
1×3	3×5	4×20
2×3	6×10	4×10
4×3	12×20	4×5
8×3	24×40	$4 \times 2\frac{1}{2}$
16×3		
16×6		

▲ *Sometimes you record students' ideas on the board and sometimes you have the students come up and record themselves. How do you decide?*

I know that students learn more when they have to do the recording themselves, so as much as possible, I have students come up and do so. Recording requires students to represent their thinking mathematically, and this experience is extremely valuable for them. However, at times I make the decision to record for students so that I can provide them models for what I expect them to do on their own. This is especially helpful when students are first learning how to represent their thinking or need reinforcement. At other times, I make the decision to record for the purpose of pacing a lesson and keeping it moving.

CHAPTER FIVE
MULTIPLYING MIXED NUMBERS

Overview

This lesson focuses specifically on multiplying two mixed numbers. While problems like these have appeared in previous chapters, they typically need extra attention because they provide more of a challenge for most students. A typical error that students make on multiplication problems with mixed numbers—for example, $2\frac{1}{2} \times 3\frac{3}{4}$—is to multiply the whole numbers, 2×3, and then the fractions, $\frac{1}{2} \times \frac{3}{4}$, and then combine these partial products. This lesson helps students see why this strategy is incorrect and helps them find correct ways to solve problems like these.

Materials

▲ none

Time

▲ one class period, plus time for additional experiences

Teaching Directions

1. Write on the board: $2\frac{1}{2} \times 5\frac{1}{4}$. Ask the students for an estimate.

2. Present how a student in another class solved the problem to get the answer of $10\frac{1}{8}$. Record on the board and explain as you do so:

$2 \times 5 = 10$

$\frac{1}{2} \times \frac{1}{4} = \frac{1}{8}$

$10 + \frac{1}{8} = 10\frac{1}{8}$

3. Ask students to talk with a neighbor about this solution.

4. Call the class to attention and, to get a sense of the students' thinking, ask for a show of hands first for who agrees with the solution on the board, then for who disagrees, and finally for who isn't sure.

5. Lead a class discussion for students to explain their ideas for solving $2\frac{1}{2} \times 5\frac{1}{4}$. List them on the board. If any of the following aren't offered, present those that students haven't thought of themselves. List the interpretations as shown:

$$
\begin{array}{llll}
2 \times 5 & 2 \times 5 & 2\frac{1}{2} \times 5 & 2 \times 5\frac{1}{4} \\
2 \times \frac{1}{4} & \frac{1}{2} \times \frac{1}{4} & 2\frac{1}{2} \times \frac{1}{4} & \frac{1}{2} \times 5\frac{1}{4} \\
\frac{1}{2} \times 5 & & & \\
\frac{1}{2} \times \frac{1}{4} & & &
\end{array}
$$

6. Ask students to work in pairs to figure out the answer for each interpretation. Then have students present the answers.

7. Ask students for their ideas about why the second method is incorrect.

8. Represent the problem by drawing a rectangle or having a student volunteer draw a rectangle.

9. Present a second problem—$1\frac{1}{2} \times 1\frac{3}{4}$—and have students solve it on their own in two ways. Circulate as they work and then lead a class discussion.

Teaching Notes

When multiplying $2\frac{1}{2} \times 5\frac{1}{4}$, Jonathan, a fifth grader in a class I was teaching several years ago, reasoned, "Two times five is ten and one-half times one-fourth is one-eighth, so the answer is ten and one-eighth." He wrote:

$$
2\frac{1}{2} \times 5\frac{1}{4}
$$
$$
2 \times 5 = 10
$$
$$
\frac{1}{2} \times \frac{1}{4} = \frac{1}{8}
$$
$$
10 + \frac{1}{8} = 10\frac{1}{8}
$$

Jonathan's reasoning reflects the typical error students make when multiplying two mixed numbers, and I've found that special attention to problems like these is necessary in order to help students learn to reason correctly.

I made time to talk with Jonathan individually, and our conversation was extremely useful for helping me plan this lesson. Jonathan explained that he first estimated the answer. He said, "I know that five times two is ten, and since there are extra fractions, the answer has to be a little more than ten." So the answer of ten and one-eighth seemed reasonable.

I asked Jonathan to look at another problem: $2\frac{1}{2} \times 5$. He was able to figure the exact answer to this problem easily. He told me, "Two times five is ten, and one-half of five is two and a half, so the answer is ten plus two and a half, which is twelve and a half." I recorded Jonathan's thinking next to what he had written for the first problem:

$2\frac{1}{2} \times 5\frac{1}{4}$ $2\frac{1}{2} \times 5$

$2 \times 5 = 10$ $2 \times 5 = 10$

$\frac{1}{2} \times \frac{1}{4} = \frac{1}{8}$ $\frac{1}{2} \times 5 = 2\frac{1}{2}$

$10 + \frac{1}{8} = 10\frac{1}{8}$ $10 + 2\frac{1}{2} = 12\frac{1}{2}$

Jonathan agreed with what I had recorded. I then covered up the calculations to focus Jonathan just on the two problems:

$2\frac{1}{2} \times 5\frac{1}{4}$ $2\frac{1}{2} \times 5$

"Do you think these two problems should have the same answer?" I asked him.
"No," Jonathan said, shaking his head.
"Which of these two problems do you think should have the larger answer?" I asked.
Jonathan quickly pointed to the first one and said confidently, "That one."
"Why do you think that?" I asked.
"Well," Jonathan said, "the first numbers are the same, but it has a bigger second number, so the answer should be a little bit more. Hey, wait!" Jonathan moved my hands to look at what was recorded underneath.
"Something's wrong here," he said. He looked over the calculations for both problems and was now confused.
I knew that Jonathan was confident with multiplying whole numbers, so I then asked him to write down the problem 14 × 23. He did so, first writing the problem horizontally. When I asked him to solve it, Jonathan rewrote the numbers vertically and figured out the answer correctly, showing four partial products. I then asked him to write the first fraction problem vertically. He did so and figured out the answer by finding four partial products and adding them, the same way he had solved the problem with whole numbers. This time he got the answer of $13\frac{1}{8}$. (See Figure 5–1.)
"Why do you think you got a different answer this time?" I asked Jonathan.
"I don't know," Jonathan said. "Is this one right?" He pointed to the second answer he got.
Rather than confirm that the answer was correct, I asked Jonathan, "How about we talk about this problem with the class? If we all think together, maybe we can figure out what's going on. Would that be OK with you?"
"Sure," Jonathan agreed.
The next day, I talked with the students about how valuable mistakes can be for helping us learn and how much I appreciated them being willing to share their thinking even when they weren't sure that they were correct. I reinforced these ideas regularly, always encouraging students to take the risk of explaining an idea, even when they were unsure, and assuring them that their ideas would be treated with respect by the others. Then I told the class that Jonathan was willing to have me present an idea of his that was confusing so that together we could try to make sense of it.
Since that conversation with Jonathan, which occurred several years before writing this book, I've had similar conversations with other students, and I've taught this lesson to several classes. Except for that first year when I had Jonathan's permission to discuss his dilemma with the class, I've not used a particular student from the class (even though the error always comes up). Rather, I refer to Jonathan anonymously as a student from another class and I present his thinking to begin this lesson.

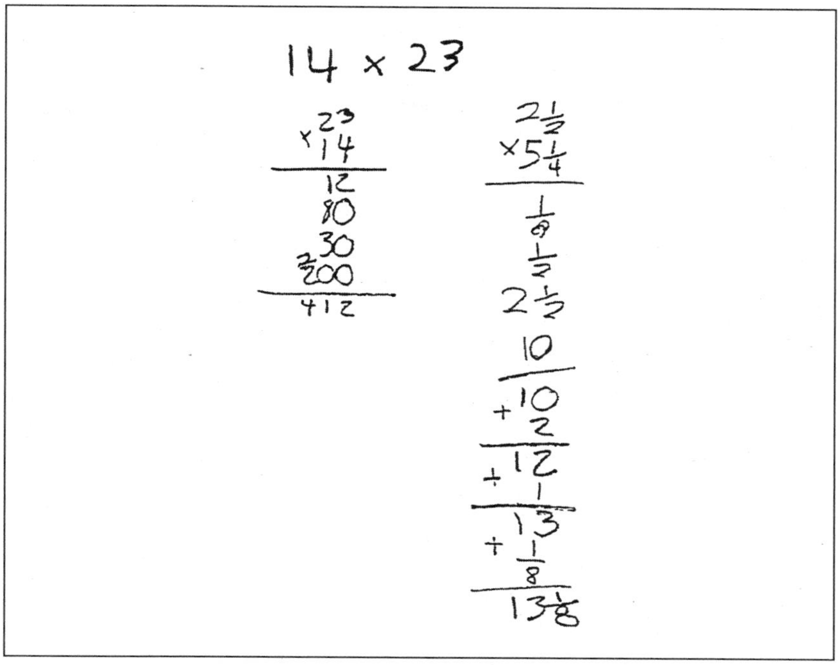

$$14 \times 23$$

$$
\begin{array}{r}
23 \\
\times\,14 \\
\hline
12 \\
80 \\
30 \\
200 \\
\hline
412
\end{array}
\qquad
\begin{array}{r}
2\frac{1}{2} \\
\times\,5\frac{1}{4} \\
\hline
\frac{1}{8} \\
\frac{1}{2} \\
2\frac{1}{2} \\
10 \\
\hline
+10 \\
2 \\
\hline
+12 \\
1 \\
\hline
13 \\
+\frac{1}{8} \\
\hline
13\frac{1}{8}
\end{array}
$$

▲▲▲▲▲▲**Figure 5–1** *Jonathan was able to apply the method he used for whole number multiplication to make sense of multiplying two mixed numbers.*

The vignette that follows describes how the conversation went with one class of fifth graders. My plan was to present Jonathan's dilemma and then ask the students for their ideas for interpreting $2\frac{1}{2} \times 5\frac{1}{4}$. My goal was to compare four different possible interpretations to help them see why the second one in the list below was incorrect.

2×5	2×5	$2\frac{1}{2} \times 5$	$2 \times 5\frac{1}{4}$
$2 \times \frac{1}{4}$	$\frac{1}{2} \times \frac{1}{4}$	$2\frac{1}{2} \times \frac{1}{4}$	$\frac{1}{2} \times 5\frac{1}{4}$
$\frac{1}{2} \times 5$			
$\frac{1}{2} \times \frac{1}{4}$			

Finally, we would draw a rectangle to check the answer and so that I could point out the partial products.

I did not use the example of multiplying whole numbers with this class. If you think it would be appropriate for your students, then incorporate it into the discussion.

The Lesson

▲▲

To begin the lesson, I wrote on the board:

$2\frac{1}{2} \times 5\frac{1}{4}$

"What's an estimate for the answer to this problem?" I asked the students.

"Ten," Annie said. "Two times five is ten, and the fractions will make it a little bit bigger but not much."

"Eleven," Helene offered. "I agree with Annie that it has to be bigger than ten, so I think eleven is a better estimate."

"I think more," Craig said. "I mean, two and a half times five is ten plus another two and a half, and that's more than twelve, so I think maybe thirteen or fourteen."

"I think that, too," Brendan added. I recorded the estimates and drew wavy circles around them.

$2\frac{1}{2} \times 5\frac{1}{4}$ (10) (11) (13 or 14)

"I'd like you to consider how a student in another class solved this problem. Watch as I write and then listen to how he explained." I recorded on the board first:

$2\frac{1}{2} \times 5\frac{1}{4}$

$2 \times 5 = 10$

$\frac{1}{2} \times \frac{1}{4} = \frac{1}{8}$

$10 + \frac{1}{8} = 10\frac{1}{8}$

Then I said, "Here's what the student said." I pointed to what I had recorded as I explained, "First I multiplied two times five to get ten, and then I multiplied one-half times one-fourth, and that's one-eighth. So I added ten and one-eighth, and the answer is ten and one-eighth." Some students sat quietly, others nodded their agreement, others raised their hands to disagree, and Craig jumped up, waving his hand and shaking his head "no."

"Please turn and talk with your neighbor about your thinking," I said. The room burst out in conversation. After a few moments, I interrupted the students and said, "I noticed that some of you were talking and others of you were listening. Now I want you to switch. If you were doing the talking, please listen to your partner without saying anything; if you were listening, now you get to talk. And if both of you were talking, you can practice saying your ideas again so that you'll be ready to present them to the class." The room got noisy again. After a minute or so, I called the class to attention. Lots of the students raised their hands.

Before calling on anyone to share an idea, I asked for a show of hands. "Who agrees with how the student was thinking?" About a third of the students raised their hands. "Who disagrees?" About half of the students raised their hands. "And who isn't sure?" Again, about half of the

students raised their hands, including some who had already raised their hands.

My next goal was to have four different interpretations on the board for the students to consider. I hoped that students would offer them, but if not, I was prepared to present them.

"Who would like to share your thinking?" I asked. "First tell us if you agree or disagree with the student, and then explain how you reasoned." I called on Anita first. I had noticed on her papers that Anita had made this same error for similar problems. I was curious about what she would say now. She was a confident student, comfortable with explaining her thinking and willing to take risks in class discussions.

Anita said, "Well, I sort of agree but I sort of disagree, too. I mean, I used to think that, but Maria showed me that I left out part of the problem."

"Can you explain what you think now?" I asked.

"You have to multiply all of the parts," Anita said. "You have to do two times five, then two times one-fourth, then one-half times five, and then one-half times one-fourth." I recorded on the board.

$2\frac{1}{2} \times 5\frac{1}{4}$

2×5

$2 \times \frac{1}{4}$

$\frac{1}{2} \times 5$

$\frac{1}{2} \times \frac{1}{4}$

"What was your idea before you talked to Maria?" I asked.

"I just did two times five and one-half times one-fourth," Anita answered. I wrote on the board next to Anita's first idea:

$2\frac{1}{2} \times 5\frac{1}{4}$

2×5 2×5

$2 \times \frac{1}{4}$ $\frac{1}{2} \times \frac{1}{4}$

$\frac{1}{2} \times 5$

$\frac{1}{2} \times \frac{1}{4}$

"That's what I think," Clark said. A few others nodded.

"Does someone else have something to add about either of these methods or another method?" I asked.

Kayla said, "I think that the first way is right, but I have a different way to explain. I think that first you have to do two and one-half times five, and then you have to do two and one-half times one-fourth." I added Kayla's idea to the board:

$2\frac{1}{2} \times 5\frac{1}{4}$

2×5	2×5	$2\frac{1}{2} \times 5$
$2 \times \frac{1}{4}$	$\frac{1}{2} \times \frac{1}{4}$	$2\frac{1}{2} \times \frac{1}{4}$
$\frac{1}{2} \times 5$		
$\frac{1}{2} \times \frac{1}{4}$		

Julio said, "I think Kayla is right and I think I can explain why Anita's first way doesn't work. It's OK to multiply the two by the five, but you left out the one-half times five. You can't just throw away that part of the problem. And you threw away the two times the one-fourth, too. It just isn't right."

Pierre said, "I have another way. You can do two times the five and one-fourth and then one-half times the five and one-fourth. I think that works." I recorded:

$2\frac{1}{2} \times 5\frac{1}{4}$

2×5	2×5	$2\frac{1}{2} \times 5$	$2 \times 5\frac{1}{4}$
$2 \times \frac{1}{4}$	$\frac{1}{2} \times \frac{1}{4}$	$2\frac{1}{2} \times \frac{1}{4}$	$\frac{1}{2} \times 5\frac{1}{4}$
$\frac{1}{2} \times 5$			
$\frac{1}{2} \times \frac{1}{4}$			

I was fortunate to have all of these ways suggested. If one or more were missing, I would have presented them so that all of these possibilities were written on the board.

I then said, "Turn and talk with your neighbor about these possibilities. Try to figure out what the answer would be for each. Then we'll talk some more." Asking the students to consider these problems would get them all involved again. Even if they couldn't follow the reasoning, they could do the calculations.

The room got noisy as students got to work. When I called them back to attention, I had volunteers come up and record the partial products and answers for each interpretation (see box below).

Craig said, "That proves that the student was wrong."

Kara wasn't so sure. She said, "I sort of follow what everyone else did, but I still don't get why it isn't OK just to do two times five and one-half times one-fourth."

"Who else has the same question that Kara does?" I asked. Helene, Eddie, and Clark raised their hands. I suspected that Carla, Hassan, and a few others were also confused.

DRAWING A RECTANGLE

"Maybe a rectangle can help you see why your idea leaves out part of the problem," I said. "Who would like to come up and draw a rectangle to check the answer?" There were several volunteers and I called on David. I chose David because I knew

---

$2\frac{1}{2} \times 5\frac{1}{4}$

$2 \times 5 = 10$	$2 \times 5 = 10$	$2\frac{1}{2} \times 5 = 12\frac{1}{2}$	$2 \times 5\frac{1}{4} = 10\frac{1}{2}$
$2 \times \frac{1}{4} = \frac{1}{2}$	$\frac{1}{2} \times \frac{1}{4} = \frac{1}{8}$	$2\frac{1}{2} \times \frac{1}{4} = \frac{1}{2} + \frac{1}{8}$	$\frac{1}{2} \times 5\frac{1}{4} = 2\frac{1}{2} + \frac{1}{8}$
$\frac{1}{2} \times 5 = 2\frac{1}{2}$	$10 + \frac{1}{8}$	$12\frac{1}{2} + \frac{1}{8}$	$10\frac{1}{2} + 2\frac{1}{2} + \frac{1}{8}$
$\frac{1}{2} \times \frac{1}{4} = \frac{1}{8}$	$\mathbf{10\frac{1}{8}}$	$\mathbf{13\frac{1}{8}}$	$\mathbf{13\frac{1}{8}}$
$10 + \frac{1}{2} + 2\frac{1}{2} + \frac{1}{8}$			
$\mathbf{13\frac{1}{8}}$			

from previous assignments that he could do this easily and correctly. David came up, carefully drew a 3-by-6 rectangle, and divided it into eighteen squares.

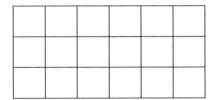

David then divided the bottom row of squares in half, shaded in the bottom strip, and labeled the left side $2\frac{1}{2}$. Then he divided the far right column into fourths, shaded in three-fourths, and labeled the top of the rectangle $5\frac{1}{4}$. He drew Xs in the whole squares.

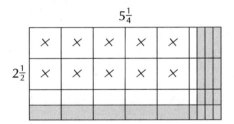

David then explained, "So there are ten whole squares, and that's the two times five part. The bottom pieces are all halves." David stopped to write $\frac{1}{2}$ in each of them, but he got confused when he got to the last piece in the bottom row. "Wait, this is too small. Oh, I know, it's not one-half. I'll save that for later." He wrote $\frac{1}{4}$ in the pieces in the right column, and then said, "The little piece in the corner is half of one of the fourths, so it's one-eighth." He labeled that, too, and then wrote the numbers to add them.

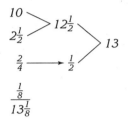

David explained how he added. He said, "Ten plus two and one-half is twelve and one-half. Then two-fourths is one-half, so I put the one-half onto the twelve and one-half, and I have thirteen. Now I have one-eighth left." David's reasoning was impressive, but he now lost track of where he had been.

"Maybe you can keep track of what you're thinking on the board," I suggested. David did so in a rather unconventional way:

$$10 \searrow \atop 2\frac{1}{2} \nearrow 12\frac{1}{2} \searrow \atop \frac{2}{4} \longrightarrow \frac{1}{2} \nearrow 13$$

$$\frac{1}{8}$$
$$13\frac{1}{8}$$

The class cheered for him. I pointed to the second problem in the list, which showed multiplying only 2×5 and $\frac{1}{2} \times \frac{1}{4}$. Then I pointed at the rectangle and said, "The ten from two times five is represented by the whole squares, and the one-eighth from multiplying one-half times one-fourth is represented in this bottom corner by the little one-eighth piece. But the pieces that are halves and fourths aren't accounted for. They're missing, and that's why the student was wrong." Kara nodded, but I still wasn't sure that this was clear yet to her and the others who were unsure.

"Could you do the problem by adding instead of breaking apart?" Annie wanted to know. The students were quiet, thinking about Annie's question. Some were shaking their heads "no."

"Not all methods are good for all problems," I said.

But then Francis came to life. "I know," he said. "You could make the five and one-fourth into five plus one-fourth. I know that sounds like breaking apart, but listen. I want to add five and one-fourth two and a half times. First I can add it two times, and then I can add it another half of a time. It works!"

"Let me try to record your idea, Francis," I said. "You're trying to add five and one-fourth two and a half times?" Francis nodded. I wrote:

$$2\tfrac{1}{2} \times 5\tfrac{1}{4} = 5\tfrac{1}{4} + 5\tfrac{1}{4} + (\tfrac{1}{2} \text{ of } 5\tfrac{1}{4})$$

I used the parentheses to try to make Francis's idea clearer. Francis nodded his agreement with what I had written and then said, "So I add the five and one-fourth two times and that's ten and a half." I added to what I had written:

$$2\tfrac{1}{2} \times 5\tfrac{1}{4} = \underbrace{5\tfrac{1}{4} + 5\tfrac{1}{4}}_{10\tfrac{1}{2}} + (\tfrac{1}{2} \text{ of } 5\tfrac{1}{4})$$

"And now what?" I asked.

"OK," Francis said, "then you have to do half of five and one-fourth. Half of five is two and one-half, and half of one-fourth is one-eighth." I recorded this idea:

$$2\tfrac{1}{2} \times 5\tfrac{1}{4} = \underbrace{5\tfrac{1}{4} + 5\tfrac{1}{4}}_{10\tfrac{1}{2}} + \overbrace{(\tfrac{1}{2} \text{ of } 5\tfrac{1}{4})}^{\tfrac{1}{2} \text{ of } 5 = 2\tfrac{1}{2}}$$
$$\tfrac{1}{2} \text{ of } \tfrac{1}{4} = \tfrac{1}{8}$$

Francis then said, "Then you add them all together. You have to add ten and one-half plus two and one-half plus one-eighth. Ten and one-half plus two and one-half is twelve and two-halves, and that's thirteen, plus one-eighth is thirteen and one-eighth." I recorded:

$$10\tfrac{1}{2} + 2\tfrac{1}{2} + \tfrac{1}{8}$$
$$10\tfrac{1}{2} + 2\tfrac{1}{2} = 13$$
$$13 + \tfrac{1}{8} = 13\tfrac{1}{8}$$

"I don't get how that works," Clark complained.

"It works, I think, but it's too complicated," Maria said.

"It's too hard that way," Pierre said.

"I get it," Julio said. "I think it's cool."

"That was really good, Francis," Celia said.

I commented, "Not every method makes sense for every person. Francis's reasoning is correct and produces the correct answer, but it may not be a way that makes sense for you to use. What's important is that you have a way to make sense of a problem, represent it mathematically, and be able to explain it to someone else."

A SECOND PROBLEM

I wrote another problem on the board:

$$1\tfrac{1}{2} \times 1\tfrac{3}{4}$$

I said to the class, "Please solve this problem on your paper. When you have an answer, talk with your neighbor about it. In a few minutes, we'll talk about what you think."

"Can we talk to our partner if we get stuck?" Hassan asked.

"That's fine," I said. "Or raise a hand and I'll come and help."

"Can we do a rectangle?" Juanita asked.

"That would be fine," I said. "Then, as a check, see if you can figure it out another way. And if you do another way first, try checking with a rectangle."

"I don't like using rectangles," Pierre said.

I responded, "I know that some people find one way easier than another way, but it's good to have at least two ways to do the same problem so that you can check your work. Maybe you can find two ways without drawing a rectangle. That would be OK, too."

The students got to work. I circulated and checked on what they were doing. I noticed that Kara had first written: $1 + 1 = 2$, then $\tfrac{1}{2} \times \tfrac{3}{4} = \tfrac{3}{8}$, and figured the answer to be $2\tfrac{3}{8}$. "I'm confused about why you added the two ones," I said.

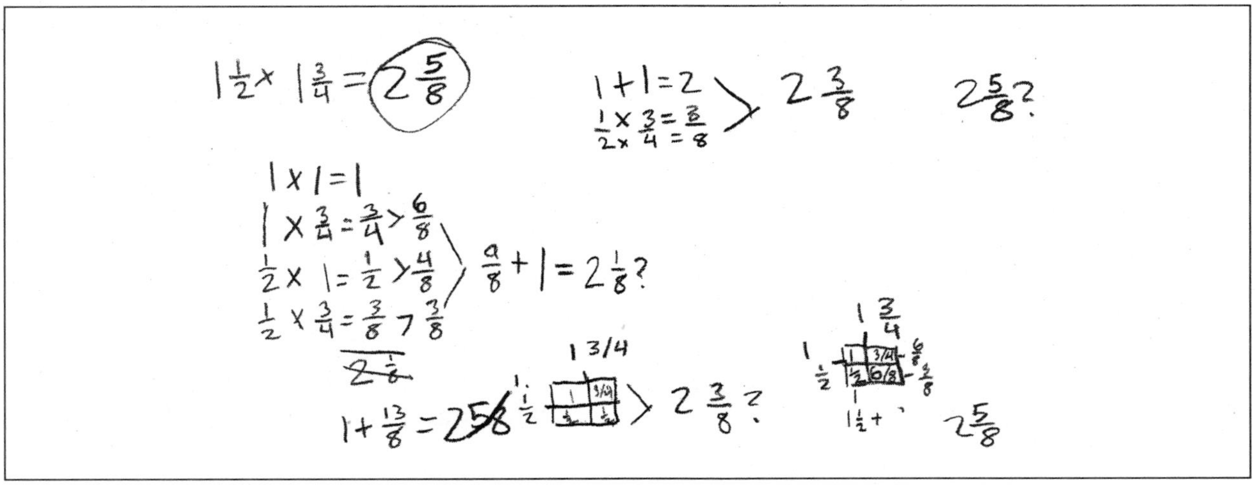

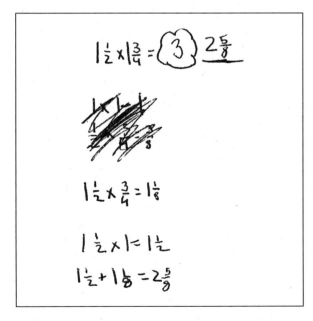

$$1\frac{1}{2} \times 1\frac{3}{4} = \boxed{2\frac{5}{8}}$$

$$1+1=2$$
$$\frac{1}{2} \times \frac{3}{4} = \frac{3}{8}$$ $2\frac{3}{8}$ $2\frac{5}{8}?$

$$1 \times 1 = 1$$
$$1 \times \frac{3}{4} = \frac{3}{4} > \frac{6}{8}$$
$$\frac{1}{2} \times 1 = \frac{1}{2} > \frac{4}{8}$$ $\frac{9}{8} + 1 = 2\frac{1}{8}?$
$$\frac{1}{2} \times \frac{3}{4} = \frac{3}{8}$$ $7\frac{3}{8}$
$$2\frac{1}{8}$$

$$1 + \frac{13}{8} = 2\frac{5}{8}$$ $1\frac{1}{2}$ $> 2\frac{3}{8}?$ $1\frac{1}{4} +$ $2\frac{5}{8}$

▲▲▲▲▲▲**Figure 5–2** *After a few false starts and with some help from her partner, Kara stuck with the problem and was finally able to solve it correctly.*

"Oops," Kara said, "I should multiply. But that can't be right, the answer would be way too small. Oh, I know, I left out the other parts." She checked her partner's paper and then went back to work. In her second attempt, Kara listed all four partial products, but made an addition error and came up with $1\frac{9}{8}$ when she should have gotten $\frac{13}{8}$, giving her an answer of $2\frac{1}{8}$. Then she drew a rectangle but got confused again. Finally, she checked with her partner again. (See Figure 5–2.)

Helene first did the problem incorrectly by multiplying 1×1 and $\frac{1}{2} \times \frac{3}{4}$. Helene

hadn't asked for help, and I was busy with others, so I didn't catch her error. However, when she drew a rectangle, she figured out the correct answer of $2\frac{5}{8}$. (See Figure 5–3.) After our class discussion, she seemed more willing to give up her initial incorrect strategy.

To solve the problem, Ally estimated 3 and then wrote:

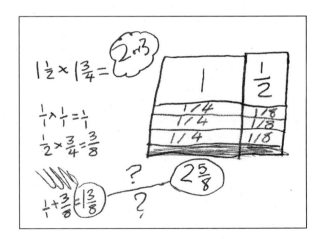

▲▲▲▲▲▲**Figure 5–3** *Helene's paper showed her confusion through her two different answers—$1\frac{3}{8}$ and $\frac{5}{8}$.*

▲▲▲▲▲▲**Figure 5–4** *Ally figured out the answer to $1\frac{1}{2} \times 1\frac{3}{4}$ by figuring $1\frac{1}{2} \times \frac{3}{4}$ and $1\frac{1}{2} \times 1$, and then combining the partial products.*

54   Lessons for Multiplying and Dividing Fractions

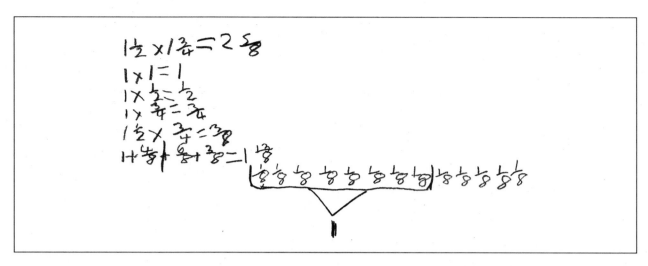

▲▲▲▲▲▲Figure 5–5   *On his paper, Josh wrote $\frac{1}{8}$ thirteen times to figure out how much it was worth. He got the correct answer.*

$1\frac{1}{2} \times 1\frac{3}{4}$

$1\frac{1}{2} \times \frac{3}{4} = 1\frac{1}{8}$

$1\frac{1}{2} \times 1 = 1\frac{1}{2}$

$1\frac{1}{2} + 1\frac{1}{8} = 2\frac{5}{8}$

She had gotten stuck on the second step, however, when she tried to figure out $1\frac{1}{2} \times \frac{3}{4}$. She tried figuring $1 \times \frac{3}{4}$ and then $\frac{1}{2} \times \frac{3}{4}$. She knew that $1 \times \frac{3}{4}$ was $\frac{3}{4}$, but she wasn't sure about how to figure out $\frac{1}{2} \times \frac{3}{4}$. She came to me at that time for help.

"Do you know what one-half times one-fourth is?" I asked her.

Ally thought for only a moment and said, "Half of a fourth is an eighth."

"So, how much do you think is half of three-fourths?" I then asked. Ally saw immediately that it had to be three-eighths. (I tried this reasoning with several other students and it seemed to make sense to them also.)

"Can you add that to your paper?" I asked her. She nodded and then wrote:

$\frac{1}{2} \times \frac{1}{4} = \frac{1}{8}$

$\frac{1}{8} \times 3 = \frac{3}{8}$

$1 \times \frac{3}{4} = \frac{3}{4}$

$\frac{3}{4} + \frac{3}{8} = \frac{9}{8} = 1\frac{1}{8}$

(See Figure 5–4.)

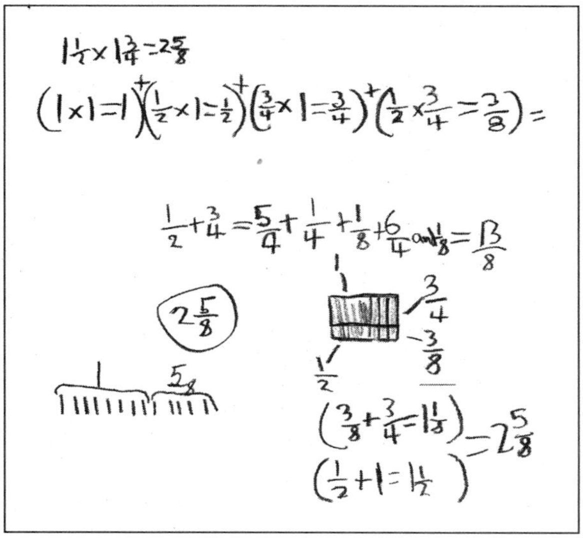

▲▲▲▲▲▲Figure 5–6   *Brendan solved the problem numerically and then with a rectangle.*

I called the class to attention and spent the rest of the class talking about the students' strategies and solutions. It was a productive conversation.

Figure 5–5 and 5–6 show how two other students solved the problem.

EXTENSIONS

On subsequent days, give students additional practice with similar problems.

Multiplying Mixed Numbers   55

Questions and Discussion

▲▲▲

▲ *Since the mixed number problems are consistently difficult for students, wouldn't it be easier to have them use the algorithm?*

It may seem more efficient merely to teach children to convert mixed numbers to improper fractions and then multiply the numerators and denominators. However, this approach circumvents making sense of problems like these and, instead, focuses students on following a particular procedure. In my experience, learning the standard algorithm doesn't result in fewer errors. Students make careless mistakes and often get confused when converting mixed numbers to fractions. Also, it doesn't support the all-important idea that they are to make sense of all that they do in mathematics. My preference is to equip students with ways to reason first. Showing them the standard algorithm can then give them another way to solve problems like these, but I want the algorithm to be an addition to their toolbox of strategies, not the only tool.

▲ *When the students learn to calculate the four partial products, aren't you just teaching them a different algorithm? Won't they still make mistakes?*

Some students are more careful than others, but I've come to accept that all of them make mistakes when calculating. We all do. Some mistakes are careless computation errors while others indicate confusion or misunderstanding. The method I teach in this lesson—the break-apart method (that is, the distributive property)—gives me a way to rely on students' reasoning and number sense. To me, this seems a better approach than the "multiply across the tops and bottoms" rule. While that rule does have its roots in mathematical logic, I don't find it accessible to students the way that considering partial products is.

CHAPTER SIX
THE MULTIPLYING GAME

Overview

The Multiplying Game is a two-person game that combines luck and strategic thinking to give students practice multiplying and comparing fractions. To play, students take turns rolling a die, writing the numbers that come up in the numerators and denominators of two fractions, and then multiplying their fractions. Their goal is to get the smallest possible answer. After multiplying their fractions, students compare the products to decide which is smaller and describe how they reasoned.

Materials

▲ dice, 1 per pair of students
▲ *The Multiplying Game* record sheet, at least 1 per pair of students (see Blackline Masters)
▲ optional: *The Multiplying Game* rules (see Blackline Masters)
▲ optional, for Extension 4: 1–10 die or spinner, 1 per pair of students

Time

▲ one class period to introduce the game, plus additional time for playing and discussion

Teaching Directions

1. On the chalkboard, draw a game board for one round of *The Multiplying Game*.

$$\frac{\square}{\square} \times \frac{\square}{\square} = \qquad \frac{\square}{\square} \times \frac{\square}{\square} =$$

$$\square \qquad\qquad\qquad \square$$

2. Ask for a volunteer to play with you. Play a round, explaining the rules as you do so. You may want to post the rules so that there is a reference for the students when they play in pairs.

The Multiplying Game

You need:
  a partner
  a die

Rules
1. You need a game board with three rounds like this.

$$\frac{\square}{\square} \times \frac{\square}{\square} = \qquad \frac{\square}{\square} \times \frac{\square}{\square} =$$

$\square$ $\qquad\qquad\qquad\qquad\qquad$ $\square$

2. Players take turns rolling the die and writing the number in one of their spaces for that round. Once a number is written, it cannot be changed. The boxes to the side are reject boxes that give one chance to write a number that you don't want to use in the problem.

3. After writing a number, pass the die to the other player.

4. Play until both players have recorded two fractions. (Your reject box may be empty if you used your first four numbers for the fractions.)

5. Multiply your two fractions. Check each other's answers.

6. The winner of the round is the player with the smaller product. Explain how you know which answer is smaller.

7. Play three rounds.

3. Model for the students how to write an explanation of which fraction is smaller.

4. Organize the students to play in pairs. Distribute a record sheet and die to each pair and, if you think it's necessary, distribute a copy of the rules to each pair. Circulate and offer help as needed. Also, look for students who are having difficulty comparing fractions, or students who compare fractions in unique ways.

5. Interrupt the students so that there is time for a whole-class discussion. Ask students for their reaction to the game, and then discuss fractions that were particularly problematic or unusual for students to compare.

6. Optional: Ask students to play the game for homework with someone at home. The next day, have them report about their experiences and discuss fractions that were hard for them to compare.

Teaching Notes

This game is appropriate when students are comfortable comparing fractions and after they have learned to multiply fractions. The more difficult version of the game suggested in Extension 2 provides students practice subtracting fractions.

It's important to model for students how they should explain their reasoning when comparing fractions. In the lesson described, when I introduced the game by playing with a student volunteer, the two fractions that resulted—three-fifths and four-fifths—were trivial for the students to compare. However, this class had had a good deal of experience comparing fractions and, therefore, I didn't feel the need to play another round. In other classes, I've either played another round or have given the students other pairs of fractions to compare in order to model how to write explanations.

The elements of strategy and luck contribute to making the game engaging for students. The strategic thinking that students use about where to place numbers helps them think about what can result when multiplying fractions, rather than merely on the process of multiplying and arriving at an answer. Also, using a die gives them some experience with thinking about the probabilities of the numbers that come up when rolling one die. Students often think that if a certain number hasn't come up for a while, then somehow it's that number's "turn." They are often surprised at the randomness that results in rolls, and this experience can help them realize that each roll of the die is an event independent of all previous rolls—that it's equally likely for each of the numbers to come up on each roll.

The Lesson

▲▲

I wrote on the board *The Multiplying Game* and drew a game board of one round for each of two players.

$$\frac{\square}{\square} \times \frac{\square}{\square} = \qquad \frac{\square}{\square} \times \frac{\square}{\square} =$$
$$\square \qquad\qquad\qquad\qquad \square$$

To introduce the game to the class, I said, "I'm going to teach you how to play a game. First I'd like a volunteer to play with me and help everyone learn the rules. Then you'll play in pairs." Hands shot up of volunteers willing to play. I called on Fanny and she joined me at the chalkboard. I wrote our names above the game board to indicate where we each would write our numbers.

I explained, "We'll take turns rolling the die. Each time we roll, we have to write our number in one of our five boxes. Once you write a number in a box, it has to stay there; you can't erase it and write in another box. The idea is to place the numbers so that you'll have the smaller answer when we each multiply our fractions." Fanny nodded to indicate that she understood.

"Would you like to go first or would you like me to go first?" I asked her.

"You go first," Fanny responded.

I rolled the die. "It's a two," I said and then thought aloud about where I might place it. "I'm not really sure what the best strategy is. I know that the possible numbers I can get on the die are one, two, three, four, five, and six, and I think that if I want a small answer, I'd like the two fractions to be as small as possible. I think I'll write a two in the numerator of the first fraction."

I then gave the students another rule of the game. "When it's your turn, hold onto the die until you're sure you've written the number where you want it. Then pass the die to your partner to take a turn. The other player shouldn't roll the die until the first player has written his or her number. " I handed the die to Fanny and she rolled it.

"Tell the class what number came up," I said.

Fanny responded, "It's a three. I'm not sure where to write it." Some hands shot up of students who were interested in giving their suggestions.

"Would you hear some ideas from others?" I asked. Fanny nodded. She turned to the class and called on several of her classmates.

"I think that the smallest possible numbers should go on top," Alicia said. "The fractions will be smaller that way."

"Do you remember what we call the number in a fraction that's on the top?" I asked Alicia to reinforce the proper terminology.

"The numerator," she responded.

Taber disagreed. "I think you want the small numbers on the bottom. That's the denominator."

He didn't offer an explanation, so I probed, "Can you explain your idea?"

Taber was quiet for a moment, then shrugged and said, "I'm not sure. It just seems better."

Maddy then said, excitedly, "The bigger numbers *have* to go on the bottom. Oops, I mean the denominator. The bigger the denominator, the less the number on the top counts."

Fanny next called on Max. He said, "If I rolled a three . . . well, I'd reject anything under a three, but I'd write a three on top and anything over a three on the bottom. Wait, I'm not sure. It's hard to think about this."

Other hands were still raised, but I then said, "It hard to be sure about a strategy when you're first learning a game. I appreciate that you're willing to help Fanny. As we play, keep thinking about what makes sense. Fanny, are you ready to write your number?"

Fanny responded, "I'll write it where you wrote yours, for the numerator of my first fraction."

$$\text{Ms. Burns} \qquad\qquad \text{Fanny}$$
$$\frac{\boxed{2}}{\Box} \times \frac{\Box}{\Box} = \qquad \frac{\boxed{3}}{\Box} \times \frac{\Box}{\Box}$$
$$\Box \qquad\qquad\qquad\qquad \Box$$

Fanny gave me the die and I rolled a 5. I said, "I'm going to write a five in the denominator of the first fraction so I have two-fifths. I know that two-fifths is less than one-half, so I think that's pretty small." I handed the die to Fanny.

Fanny rolled a 1 and said, "I'm writing it in the numerator of the second fraction. It's like Alicia's idea."

$$\text{Ms. Burns} \qquad\qquad \text{Fanny}$$
$$\frac{\boxed{2}}{\boxed{5}} \times \frac{\Box}{\Box} = \qquad \frac{\boxed{3}}{\Box} \times \frac{\boxed{1}}{\Box} =$$
$$\Box \qquad\qquad\qquad\qquad \Box$$

"You better not roll a one again!" Paolo said.

"A two wouldn't be so good, either," Sandra added.

Fanny gave me the die and I rolled a 4. The students were now very animated and many had suggestions, but to keep the game moving, I quieted them, wrote the 4 in my reject box, and handed the die to Fanny. Fanny rolled a 2, wrote it in her reject box, and gave me the die.

$$\text{Ms. Burns} \qquad\qquad \text{Fanny}$$
$$\frac{\boxed{2}}{\boxed{5}} \times \frac{\Box}{\Box} = \qquad \frac{\boxed{3}}{\Box} \times \frac{\boxed{1}}{\Box} =$$
$$\boxed{4} \qquad\qquad\qquad\qquad \boxed{2}$$

I then rolled a 2 and said, "Let's see. I can write the two either in the numerator or in the denominator of my second fraction. I'd like this fraction to be as small as possible. I think I'll write it in the numerator and hope for a five or six on my last roll. Even a four wouldn't be bad." I recorded the 2 and gave Fanny the die.

Fanny rolled a 5. Her choices were either of the two denominators, and she said, "Ooh, I'm not sure where to write it." She again turned to the class for help.

"Write it under the three so you have three-fifths," Kamila said. "Then you have a chance for a six, and one-sixth is the smallest fraction you can get."

Manjit said, "I'd write it under the one. One-fifth is smaller than three-fifths."

"Hey," Max said, "it doesn't matter where you put it." Max realized that the product wouldn't be affected by which denominator had the five, but none of the other students had this realization, and even after Max said it, no one was convinced. (I hadn't thought of this either until Max pointed it out, but now I realized that applying the algorithm of multiplying the numerators and denominators would result in the same answer no matter where the five was located!)

Fanny decided to place the 5 under the 3. We now each had one roll left, and Fanny gave me the die.

Ms. Burns   Fanny

$$\frac{\boxed{2}}{\boxed{5}} \times \frac{\boxed{2}}{\boxed{}} = \qquad \frac{\boxed{3}}{\boxed{5}} \times \frac{\boxed{1}}{\boxed{}} =$$

$$\boxed{4} \qquad\qquad\qquad \boxed{2}$$

"Whatever I roll now I have to write in the denominator of my second fraction," I commented before rolling. I got a 1 and groaned as I recorded it.

"That's too bad," Lydia sympathized.

I gave the die to Fanny. She rolled it and said, "Oh no! I got a one!" She recorded it in the denominator of her second fraction.

Ms. Burns   Fanny

$$\frac{\boxed{2}}{\boxed{5}} \times \frac{\boxed{2}}{\boxed{1}} = \qquad \frac{\boxed{3}}{\boxed{5}} \times \frac{\boxed{1}}{\boxed{1}} =$$

$$\boxed{4} \qquad\qquad\qquad \boxed{2}$$

Conversation broke out as the students tried to figure out who had won. I quieted them so that I could explain what they were to do next when they played. "Now we each figure out our products, and then we have to agree with each other's answers. My problem is two-fifths times two, which is the same as two-fifths two times. That's four-fifths."

"Mine is easy," Fanny said. "It's three-fifths times one, and that's three-fifths." We both recorded our answers.

Ms. Burns   Fanny

$$\frac{\boxed{2}}{\boxed{5}} \times \frac{\boxed{2}}{\boxed{1}} = \frac{4}{5} \qquad \frac{\boxed{3}}{\boxed{5}} \times \frac{\boxed{1}}{\boxed{1}} = \frac{3}{5}$$

$$\boxed{4} \qquad\qquad\qquad\qquad \boxed{2}$$

Fanny then said, "My answer is smaller. Does that mean I win?"

I responded, "Yes, whoever has the smaller product wins the round. Then there's one more thing you have to do before going on to the next round. You have to explain in writing how you compared the fractions. Fanny, how did you know that your answer of three-fifths was smaller than my answer of four-fifths?"

"It's easy," Fanny replied. "Four-fifths is one more than three-fifths, so three-fifths has to be smaller." I knew that Fanny's explanation wasn't accurate, but the error was one commonly made by students. Fanny meant that four-fifths was *one more fifth* than three-fifths, not simply *one more* than three-fifths. I handled this by recording on the board verbatim what Fanny had said:

Four-fifths is one more than three-fifths, so three-fifths has to be smaller.

Then I said, "I think you understand, but I don't think that your explanation is correct. I think that *one-fifth* more than three-fifths is four-fifths, but *one* more than three-fifths is one and three-fifths." As I said this, I wrote on the board:

$$\frac{3}{5} + \frac{1}{5} = \frac{4}{5}$$

$$\frac{3}{5} + 1 = 1\frac{3}{5}$$

"Oh, that's what I meant," Fanny said.

"How should I correct your sentence?" I asked.

While Fanny read the sentence quietly to herself, other hands shot up. But I waited to give Fanny the chance to make the correction on her own. In a moment, she said, "Oh, I know, just change the 'one' to 'one-fifth'." I made the correction:

Four-fifths is one-fifth more than three-fifths, so three-fifths has to be smaller.

Nick had a question. "Can we write the sentence with fractions, or does it have to be all words?"

"Do you mean like this?" I asked, writing on the board:

$\frac{4}{5}$ *is* $\frac{1}{5}$ *more than* $\frac{3}{5}$, *so* $\frac{3}{5}$ *has to be smaller.*

Nick nodded and I said, "It's fine to use numbers or any other symbols in your explanations as long as what you write is clear."

I gave the class one more direction. "For a complete game, you play three rounds," I said. "But Fanny and I won't continue our game. Instead, you'll all get a chance to play now." I thanked Fanny for playing and she returned to her seat.

"What questions do you have?" I asked the class. There were no questions, so I organized the students into pairs and distributed the dice and record sheets.

OBSERVING THE CLASS

The products that Fanny and I had were easy to compare since the denominators were the same, but I knew that this wouldn't be true most of the time. For example, Kamila and Sandra had the following results in their first round:

Kamila	Sandra
$\frac{1}{3} \times \frac{5}{4} = \frac{5}{12}$	$\frac{2}{5} \times \frac{3}{2} = \frac{6}{10}$

They correctly identified five-twelfths as smaller and wrote: *Because $\frac{5}{12}$ is under $\frac{1}{2}$ and $\frac{6}{10}$ is over.*

Aviva and Lydia's first round produced the following results:

Aviva	Lydia
$\frac{3}{5} \times \frac{3}{2} = \frac{9}{10}$	$\frac{3}{6} \times \frac{1}{4} = \frac{3}{24}$

However, instead of noticing that one fraction was larger than one-half and the other was smaller, they wrote: *$\frac{3}{24}$ is smaller than $\frac{9}{10}$ because $\frac{9}{10}$ is $\frac{1}{10}$ away from $\frac{1}{1}$ and $\frac{3}{24}$ is $\frac{21}{24}$ away from $\frac{1}{1}$.*

Some students found comparing their products to be more challenging. On their second round, Amalia and Max had the following results:

Amalia	Max
$\frac{4}{5} \times \frac{2}{4} = \frac{8}{20}$	$\frac{1}{4} \times \frac{5}{4} = \frac{5}{16}$

They called me over. "We're not sure we're right, but we think that five-sixteenths is smaller," Amalia said.

"Why do you think that?" I asked.

Amalia replied, "Well, first I noticed that they were both smaller than one-half. Then we figured that eight-twentieths was two-twentieths away from one-half and five-sixteenths was three-sixteenths away. But that didn't help."

"But then I got an idea," Max said. "I realized that five-sixteenths wasn't even one-third, because five-fifteenths is one-third and five-sixteenths is smaller than five-fifteenths. But eight-twentieths is more than a third because eight–twenty-fourths is a third. So five-sixteenths has to be smaller."

I was impressed with their reasoning. "Would you be willing to explain how you compared those fractions later in our class discussion?" I asked. They nodded, pleased to be asked. "But first, record your reasoning on your paper," I reminded them. When I checked back later, I saw that their written explanation wasn't as complete as their verbal explanation: *Because $\frac{8}{20}$ is almost $\frac{1}{2}$ and $\frac{5}{16}$ isn't even $\frac{1}{3}$.* I often find that what students write isn't as detailed or complete as what they explain verbally.

Taber then came to me with a question. "If the fraction numbers are all filled in and the reject boxes are still empty, do we have to keep rolling the dice to fill in the reject boxes?" I came over to where Taber and Gabe were playing and looked at their paper. Gabe had completed his five rolls and Taber had rolled the die only four times, but he had used the numbers in the fractions, leaving his reject box still open.

"What do you think?" I asked.

"It doesn't matter what he rolls, so I don't think he should have to," Gabe said. Taber nodded his agreement, and I confirmed that the last roll wasn't necessary.

"Just figure your products and see who has the smaller answer," I said, leaving them so I could continue circulating around the room. In a few moments, however, Taber came to get me again.

"Now we're really stuck," he said. "We can't figure out who wins." I returned to their table and saw that the boys had figured their products correctly.

Gabe	Taber
$\frac{2}{6} \times \frac{2}{5} = \frac{4}{30}$	$\frac{3}{6} \times \frac{1}{4} = \frac{3}{24}$

Gabe said, "We know that thirtieths are smaller pieces than twenty-fourths, but there are more thirtieths than there are twenty-fourths, so we don't know which fraction is smaller."

"How about changing the fractions into other equivalent fractions?" I suggested.

"We did that," Taber said. He showed me another piece of paper on which he had written:

$$\frac{4}{30} = \frac{2}{15}$$
$$\frac{3}{24} = \frac{1}{6}$$

"Hey, that's not right," Gabe said. "Three–twenty-fourths is one-eighth, not one-sixth."

"Oh yeah," Taber said, making the correction.

$$\frac{4}{30} = \frac{2}{15}$$
$$\frac{3}{24} = \frac{1}{8}$$

"But that still doesn't help," Gabe said.

"How about going on to play another round and we'll use your problem for a class discussion," I said. The boys were satisfied with that suggestion and I left them to continue playing.

A CLASS DISCUSSION

I let the students play until fifteen minutes remained in the class, and then I asked for their attention to begin a class discussion. Typically in a class discussion after students have learned to play a new game, I first ask them for their general reaction to the game. In this case, their responses were positive.

"I like getting to roll the die and write the numbers," Paolo said.

"It kind of has a strategy, but there's also luck," Kamila added.

"Some of the problems were challenges," said Alec, always interested in being challenged.

After the students reacted, I then brought to their attention Max and Amalia's example. I had them tell me the problems from their second round and I wrote them on the board:

Amalia	Max
$\frac{4}{5} \times \frac{2}{4} = \frac{8}{20}$	$\frac{1}{4} \times \frac{5}{4} = \frac{5}{16}$

I said to the class, "Amalia and Max figured out a way to compare their answers, but first I'd like you to talk with your partner and see how you might compare them." Animated conversation broke out and some students reached for pencil and paper to figure. While the students were talking, I conferred with Amalia and Max about how they wanted to present their ideas. After they chatted for a moment, Amalia said, "Max is going to do it."

I brought the class to attention. I asked for a show of hands from students who thought that eight-twentieths was smaller, then who thought that five-sixteenths was smaller, and then who wasn't sure. About half of the students weren't sure.

"Please listen to how Amalia and Max reasoned," I said.

Max said, "Well, we knew that they were both less than a half, so that didn't help. But then we figured that five-sixteenths is a little smaller than five-fifteens, so then we knew that five-sixteenths is a little smaller than one-third." I interrupted Max so that I could record on the board, not only to provide a visual record of his reasoning but also to slow down the explanation:

$\frac{8}{20}$ is less than $\frac{1}{2}$ ($\frac{8}{20} < \frac{1}{2}$)

$\frac{5}{16}$ is less than $\frac{1}{2}$ ($\frac{5}{16} < \frac{1}{2}$)

$\frac{5}{15} = \frac{1}{3}$

$\frac{5}{16}$ is less than $\frac{5}{15}$ ($\frac{5}{16} < \frac{5}{15}$)

$\frac{5}{16}$ is less than $\frac{1}{3}$ ($\frac{5}{16} < \frac{1}{3}$)

"Did I record correctly what you explained?" I asked Max. He agreed and I asked him to continue.

"Well," he said, "I knew that eight-twentieths was more than a third. It's almost a half. It's just two-twentieths from a half."

Amalia piped up, "And eight-twenty-fourths is exactly one-third, so eight-twentieths is more than eight-twenty-fourths because twentieths are bigger pieces than twenty-fourths." Again, I interrupted and recorded:

$\frac{8}{20}$ is almost $\frac{1}{2}$ because it is $\frac{2}{20}$ from $\frac{1}{2}$

$\frac{8}{24} = \frac{1}{3}$

$\frac{8}{20}$ is more than $\frac{8}{24}$, so $\frac{8}{20}$ is more than $\frac{1}{3}$

Some of the students understood Max and Amalia's reasoning and others weren't sure. I asked the students to talk with their partners about what they had explained and I had written.

After students had a chance to talk in pairs, I didn't spend more time on this problem but instead moved on to the problem that Taber and Gabe weren't able to solve. As I did with Max and Amalia, I asked the boys to report their problems and I recorded them on the board:

Gabe   Taber

$\frac{2}{6} \times \frac{2}{5} = \frac{4}{30}$ $\frac{3}{6} \times \frac{1}{4} = \frac{3}{24}$

I gave the class time to talk in pairs, and this time a show of hands revealed that only three pairs of students were able to figure out which was smaller.

Julia reported for her and Maddy, "Four-thirtieths is bigger. I got my idea from what Max and Amalia did by saying that five-sixteenths was almost the same as five-fifteenths. Can I come up and show?" I agreed. Julia came to the board and wrote:

$\frac{4}{30} = \frac{2}{15}$

$\frac{3}{24} = \frac{1}{8}$

$\frac{2}{15}$ is just a little bigger than $\frac{2}{16}$

$\frac{1}{8} = \frac{2}{16}$

Julia then said, "So if two-fifteenths is bigger than two-sixteenths, then it's bigger than one-eighth, and that's the same as three–twenty-fourths." Julia then got confused for a minute but recovered quickly. "So—I know—so four-thirtieths has to be bigger, too, so three–twenty-fourths is littler."

Alicia and Althea had a different idea. Alicia came up and wrote:

$\frac{4}{30} = \frac{2}{15}$

$\frac{3}{24} = \frac{1}{8} = \frac{2}{16}$

"See, that makes it easy," she explained. "Two-sixteenths is smaller than two-fifteenths, so that makes three–twenty-fourths smaller than four-thirtieths."

It was now the end of class, and I concluded the lesson by assuring the students that they would have additional time to play the game and think about how to compare their answers. I've learned that over time with this game, students come to think flexibly about comparing fractions while they also practice multiplying fractions and think about strategies for where to place numbers in the fractions. See Figures 6–1 through 6–3 for three pairs' games.

EXTENSIONS

1. As well as writing explanations about how they compared the fractions, ask students to record a number sentence. For example, if they were comparing two-twelfths and two-eighths, they could write either $\frac{2}{12} < \frac{2}{8}$ or $\frac{2}{8} > \frac{2}{12}$.

2. For a more difficult version of the game, instead of scoring 1 point for having the smaller answer in each round, the winner of the round scores the difference between the two answers. For example, in the initial game that I played with

Fanny, she would have scored $\frac{1}{5}$ for the first round, the difference between four-fifths and three-fifths. A caution: Figuring the differences between the two scores

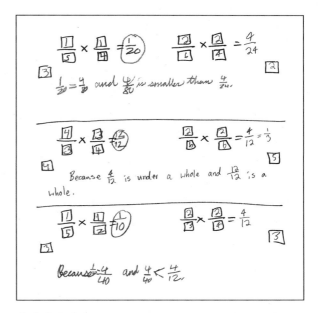

▲▲▲▲▲▲Figure 6–2 *Nick and Angelo compared fractions in their first and third rounds by converting them to equivalent fractions with common numerators.*

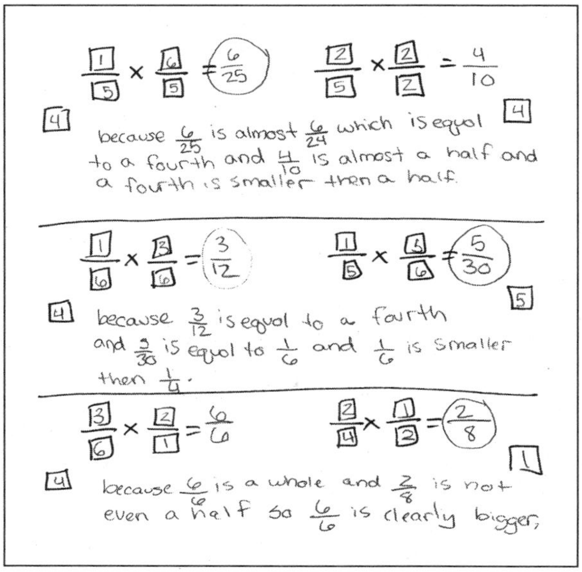

▲▲▲▲▲▲Figure 6–1 *For their first round, Fanny and Eliana estimated that $\frac{6}{25}$ was almost equal to $\frac{6}{24}$ and, therefore, almost equal to $\frac{1}{4}$.*

▲▲▲▲▲▲Figure 6–3 *Maddy and Julia used $\frac{1}{2}$ as a benchmark for comparing their products.*

can present challenging subtraction problems. For example, when Tomo and Bjorn tried this version, in their first round, Tomo got nine-twenty-fifths and Bjorn got three-sixteenths, and they were stumped about how to do the subtraction. I suggested that they revert to the former version of the game.

3. To vary the game, change the rules so that the larger answer wins the round. Then have students play either the first or second version.

4. Have students play with a 1–10 die or spinner for experience with more numbers.

Questions and Discussion

▲▲

▲ *What do you do to help students who aren't able to write explanations for how they compared fractions?*

Learning to explain their reasoning in writing can be difficult for students. It helps, I find, to have students work in pairs. My first step is to have one student tell me his or her idea about how to compare two fractions and then repeat it while his or her partner records the idea in writing, verbatim. Then they switch roles for another pair of fractions, with the first student being the scribe. I find that this helps students see how writing provides a record of their thinking.

▲ *How much time do you provide for students to play the game?*

I vary the way I use the game after the initial introduction. This game, and others like it, is a good option for students who finish another assignment quickly when time is still left in math class. Also, sometimes I devote a class period to the game, having the children play the game for half the time and then having a discussion, such as the one described, in which students present to the class fractions that they found difficult to compare.

CHAPTER SEVEN
WHOLE NUMBER DIVISION
THE BUILDING BLOCK

Overview

This lesson addresses division with whole numbers for the purpose of preparing students for learning about division of fractions. Students discuss ten statements about dividing whole numbers and give examples to explain them. The lesson not only strengthens students' number sense about division but also lays the foundation for subsequent lessons in which they learn to reason about dividing fractions.

Materials

▲ chart of multiplication statements from Chapter 1

Time

▲ one class period

Teaching Directions

1. Tell the students that you're going to help them learn about dividing fractions, but for today, you'll ask them only about dividing whole numbers. Revisit the multiplication statements from Chapter 1 by asking students to read each one aloud.

2. Next tell them that you'll present, one by one, ten different statements that relate to dividing whole numbers. Also tell them that all but the last statement are true. For each, they are to think of examples to illustrate the idea.
1. You can solve a division problem by subtracting.
2. To divide two numbers, $a \div b$, you can think, "How many bs are in a?"
3. You can check a division problem by multiplying.
4. The division sign ($\div$) means "into groups of."

5. The quotient tells "how many groups" there are.
6. You can break the dividend apart to make dividing easier.
7. Remainders can be represented as whole numbers or fractions.
8. If you divide a number by itself, the answer is one.
9. If you divide a number by one, the answer is the number itself.
10. You can reverse the order of the dividend and the divisor, and the quotient stays the same.

Note: None of the statements addresses the sharing, or partitioning, model of division. See the "Questions and Discussion" section at the end of this chapter for information about this.

3. Write on the board: *1. You can solve a division problem by subtracting.* Ask the students to read the statement to themselves and think of an example that illustrates it. Lead a class discussion. If students do not have ideas, show several examples, such as 42 ÷ 6, 8 ÷ 2, 276 ÷ 12. (These examples are discussed in "The Lesson" section.)

4. Continue in the same way for the other nine statements. For each, have students read the statement to themselves and think of an example to illustrate it. For Statement 10, ask students for suggestions about rewording it so that it is true.

5. After class, copy the statements onto chart paper to use in the following lessons. Reword Statement 10 so that it is correct. For example, you could write:

If you reverse the order of the dividend and the divisor, the quotient will be different, unless the dividend and divisor are the same number.

Teaching Notes

This lesson suggests an approach for introducing students to division of fractions that is similar to the approach taken for introducing students to multiplication of fractions (see Chapter 1). The goal of the lesson is to establish ideas about dividing whole numbers to serve as a foundation on which to build understanding of dividing by fractions.

Students should have experienced the lessons about multiplication (Chapters 1–6) before you teach this lesson. Also, at the beginning of this lesson, it's helpful to review briefly with the students the statements that the students have previously discussed about multiplication of whole numbers. The students' familiarity with the multiplication statements helps prepare them to think about these division statements.

Following are the ten statements for the students to consider:

1. You can solve a division problem by subtracting.
2. To divide two numbers, $a \div b$, you can think, "How many bs are in a?"
3. You can check a division problem by multiplying.
4. The division sign (÷) means "into groups of."
5. The quotient tells "how many groups" there are.
6. You can break the dividend apart to make dividing easier.

7. Remainders can be represented as whole numbers or fractions.

8. If you divide a number by itself, the answer is one.

9. If you divide a number by one, the answer is the number itself.

10. You can reverse the order of the dividend and the divisor, and the quotient stays the same.

In this lesson, I write these statements on the board, one by one, and ask the students to come up with examples to illustrate the idea. When you teach this lesson to your class, if your students' understanding of any of these ideas is weak, then I suggest that you provide more instruction in the area of whole number division before asking them to think about dividing fractions.

There is a potential problem with Statement 2: To divide two numbers, $a \div b$, you can think, "How may bs are in a?" The problem is that it's not possible to divide by zero, so b cannot be zero. I didn't raise this issue with the students at this time since we had discussed this earlier in the year. However, you may want to take a detour from fractions and address the issue at this time.

In my experience, the issue of dividing by zero is complicated for children to understand, and there are several ways to help them think about why we can't divide by zero. Also, while the issue of dividing by zero fascinates some students, others are confused by it or simply disinterested. If you decide to bring up this issue with your students, I suggest that you use a light touch.

One way I've found to be successful for explaining why division by zero doesn't make sense is to build on children's understanding of how we use multiplication to check answers to division problems. For example, to check that $12 \div 4 = 3$, students know that they can multiply the quotient by the divisor, $3 \times 4 = 12$. Explore some examples like this with the students, using simple whole number problems.

$$12 \div 3 = 4 \qquad 4 \times 3 = 12$$
$$12 \div 2 = 6 \qquad 6 \times 2 = 12$$
$$12 \div 1 = 12 \qquad 12 \times 1 = 12$$

Then raise the issue of trying to solve $12 \div 0$. Typically, children think that the answer should be zero, but it doesn't check!

$$12 \div 0 = 0 \qquad 0 \times 0 = 0$$

The answer to 0×0 would have to equal 12 for the answer of zero to check. Students then typically then suggest another possible answer—12. But it doesn't check, either!

$$12 \div 0 = 12 \qquad 12 \times 0 = 0$$

Trying other answers reveals to the students that no answer works since zero times any other number gives zero. There is no possible answer to $12 \div 0$, so mathematicians have agreed that it's not possible to divide by zero.

The Lesson

▲▲

To begin the lesson, I said to the students, "Today I'd like you to begin thinking about dividing fractions. When you first started thinking about multiplying fractions, we talked about six statements. Since I think that division and multiplication are connected in various ways, let's review those first." I pointed to the chart and chose a student to read each statement aloud. We didn't discuss the statements. Instead, I introduced the division statements I had prepared.

I said, "All but the last statement I'll introduce are true. Please read this statement to yourself and raise a hand if you can give an example to explain it." I turned to the board and wrote:

> 1. *You can solve a division problem by subtracting.*

The students indicated that they agreed with it. "It's like what we do when we do long division," Sabrina said. But no one had an example to offer. I wrote on the board:

$$12\overline{)276}$$

Together, we did the division by subtracting first ten twelves, then ten more twelves, and finally three twelves. (For information about this algorithm for long division, see the Teaching Arithmetic book *Lessons for Extending Division, Grades 4–5* [Math Solutions Publications, 2003].)

$$
\begin{array}{r}
23 \\
12\overline{)276} \\
120 \quad\big|\ 10 \\
\overline{156} \\
120 \quad\big|\ 10 \\
\overline{36} \\
36 \quad\big|\ 3 \\
\overline{0}
\end{array}
$$

I then illustrated the idea with two other problems, writing one as if it were long division and solving the other just by subtracting:

$$
\begin{array}{r}
7 \\
6\overline{)42} \\
42\ \big|\ 7 \\
\overline{0}
\end{array}
\qquad
\begin{array}{r}
8 \\
-2 \\
\overline{6} \\
-2 \\
\overline{4} \\
-2 \\
\overline{2} \\
-2 \\
\overline{0}
\end{array}
\qquad 8 \div 2 = 4
$$

STATEMENT 2

I then wrote the second statement on the board:

> 2. *To divide two numbers,* a ÷ b, *you can think, "How many* bs *are in* a?"

Josh said, "I don't get the problem. How do you divide *a* and *b*?"

Kayla said, "They can stand for any numbers."

Josh said, "I don't get it."

I erased the *a*s and *b*s in the statement and replaced them with *6* and *3* so that the statement read:

> 2. *To divide two numbers, 6 ÷ 3, you can think, "How many 3s are in 6?"*

"Does this make better sense?" I asked Josh.

"That's good; it's two," Josh responded.

"You're saying that two is the answer?" I asked.

Josh nodded. "Because two goes into six three times."

I said, "I can check that by subtracting the way we did for the first statement. I have to subtract three two times to get to zero, so the answer is two." I wrote this on the board.

$$
\begin{array}{r}
6 \\
-3 \\
\overline{3} \\
-3 \\
\overline{0}
\end{array}
$$

I then asked Josh, "What other numbers could I write in this statement?"

"Wow, there are lots of them," Josh said.

"I agree," I said. "And I wanted a statement that would tell about any numbers. So instead of choosing particular ones, I used the letter *a* to stand for one number and *b* to stand for the other."

"Oh, that's OK," Josh said, now satisfied. I changed the 6 and the 3 in the statement back to *a* and *b*.

"Does this statement hold true for the other division problems on the board?" I asked.

Brendan said, "It works. You did how many twelves in two hundred seventy-six, then how many sixes in forty-two, and then how many twos in eight."

STATEMENT 3

I wrote the third statement on the board:

> 3. You can check a division problem by multiplying.

Hands flew up. Saul said, "To check the first one you did, you have to multiply the number on the top, you know, the answer, by the other number on the side. I can't remember what they're called." I reviewed the correct terminology of *quotient, divisor,* and *dividend,* and wrote these words on the board next to the numbers for the problem of forty-two divided by six.

```
                quotient
   divisor         |       dividend
                   23
              12)276
                 120  10
                 ---
                 156
                 120  10
                 ---
                  36
                  36   3
                 ---
                   0
```

Saul now said, "You multiply the quotient times the divisor, so you do twenty-three times twelve." I wrote on the board:

> 23 × 12

Anita raised her hand to explain the multiplication. She said, "First you do twenty-three times ten, then you do twenty-three times two, and then you add them." I recorded on the board as Anita explained:

> 23 × 10 = 230
> 23 × 2 = 46
> 230 + 46 = 276

"Does the problem check?" I asked.

Helene said, "It checks because you got two hundred seventy-six, and that's what we were dividing into."

"And two hundred seventy-six is called the . . . ?" I prompted.

"The dividend," Helene said.

"The others check, too," Julio added. "Seven times six is forty-two, and four times two is eight."

STATEMENT 4

"Here's the fourth statement," I said. I wrote on the board:

> 4. The division sign (÷) means "into groups of."

Craig said, "It kind of makes sense. If you do eight divided by two, you can think about that as making twos." I drew eight circles on the board and circled groups of two.

"Yeah, like that," Craig said. "You put the eight circles into twos."

"And how many groups of two are there?" I asked.

"Four," several answered in unison.

STATEMENT 5

I wrote the fifth statement on the board:

> 5. The quotient tells "how many groups" there are.

"That's right," Maria said. "When you drew the circles around the other circles, you have four groups. That's how many groups there are, and that's the answer, and the answer is the quotient."

STATEMENT 6

No other students had a comment, so I wrote the next statement on the board:

> 6. You can break the dividend apart to make dividing easier.

No one raised a hand. "Turn and talk with your neighbor about this," I said. Often when students don't have an idea on their own, their thinking is sparked when they have the chance to talk with someone else. The room got noisy for a moment, then quieted down as some students raised their hands. I called on Celia.

"I think I can explain it with the forty-two divided by six problem," she said. "If you didn't know how to do that one, you could do two smaller ones if you break apart the forty-two into thirty and twelve. Then you do thirty divided by six and twelve divided by six." I recorded on the board:

$$42 \div 6$$
$$42 = 30 + 12$$
$$30 \div 6 = 5$$
$$12 \div 6 = 2$$
$$5 + 2 = 7$$
$$42 \div 6 = 7$$

"Why did you decide to break forty-two into thirty plus twelve?" I asked.

Celia said, "Because you can divide six into those numbers."

"That's cool," Brendan commented.

STATEMENT 7

I next wrote the seventh statement on the board:

> 7. Remainders can be represented as whole numbers or fractions.

The room broke out into conversation when students read this statement. Clark had a suggestion for a problem. "It's an easy one," he said. "Nine divided by two. You get four remainder one." I wrote on the board:

$$9 \div 2 = 4 R1$$

Also, I drew nine circles on the board and circled them in twos to illustrate Clark's problem:

"See, the extra one is the remainder," Clark said.

"So you wrote the remainder as a whole number," I said. Clark nodded.

Juanita said, "I know how to write it as a fraction. If you think of it as snacks, it works. You have nine snacks and you share them with two people. They each get four snacks and then they share the extra, so they each get four and a half snacks. So you could say the answer is four and one-half." I wrote on the board:

$$9 \div 2 = 4\tfrac{1}{2}$$

STATEMENT 8

I wrote the eighth statement on the board:

> 8. If you divide a number by itself, the answer is one.

This was easy for the students and many had ideas to give—6 divided by 6, 10 divided by 10, 127 divided by 127, and so on. I recorded each of these in three different ways to reinforce the different representations:

$6 \div 6 = 1$	$\frac{6}{6} = 1$	$6\overline{)6}^{\;1}$
$10 \div 10 = 1$	$\frac{10}{10} = 1$	$10\overline{)10}^{\;1}$
$127 \div 127 = 1$	$\frac{127}{127} = 1$	$127\overline{)127}^{\;1}$

STATEMENT 9

Next I wrote the ninth statement on the board:

> 9. If you divide a number by one, the answer is the number itself.

As with the previous statement, this was easy for the students, and I recorded some of their suggestions on the board as I did for Statement 8:

$6 \div 1 = 6$	$\frac{6}{1} = 6$	$1\overline{)6}^{\;6}$
$10 \div 1 = 10$	$\frac{10}{1} = 10$	$1\overline{)10}^{\;10}$
$127 \div 1 = 127$	$\frac{127}{1} = 127$	$1\overline{)127}^{\;127}$

STATEMENT 10

Finally, I wrote the tenth statement:

> 10. You can reverse the order of the dividend and the divisor, and the quotient stays the same.

There was some discussion about this statement. At first, some students thought that it should be true, but others objected.

Kayla explained, "If you have eight divided by two, then you put eight into two groups, and the answer if four. But if you do two divided by eight, then you have to put two into eight groups. That's not the same. You only started with two, so you can't have four in each group."

"How could I rewrite this statement to make it true?" I asked. "Talk to your neighbor about this."

After a few moments, I called the class back to attention and called on Pierre. He said, "I think you should write something like 'If you switch the order of the dividend and the divisor, you don't get the same quotient." I wrote this on the board and asked for any other ideas.

> If you switch the order of the dividend and the divisor, you don't get the same quotient.

Annie said, "You can't switch the order of the numbers in the problem because you get a different answer." I recorded this on the board:

> You can't switch the order of the numbers in the problem because you get a different answer.

Craig's hand shot up. "What if they're both the same, like six divided by six? Then you could switch them." A buzz broke out in the room. Pierre and Annie edited their statements to include "unless the dividend and divisor are the same number."

With this, I ended the class. Afterward, I copied the statements to a piece of chart paper so that we could have them as a reference for the lessons we'd be experiencing over the next several days.

Questions and Discussion

▲▲

▲ *I notice that you didn't talk about division as sharing. Isn't it easier for students to think about division as sharing?*

There are two models for division. You mention the sharing model, which is also called partitioning. You could think of the problem 8 ÷ 2, for example, as sharing by thinking of dividing eight into two groups; there are four in each group. For the grouping model, you would think about the problem as dividing eight into groups of two; there are four groups. Below are illustrations for each.

8 ÷ 2

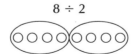

8 shared into 2 groups.
Each group has 4.

8 divided into groups of 2
There are 4 groups.

While both models produce the same answer, when dividing by a fraction, for example, $8 \div \frac{1}{2}$, it doesn't make sense to think of dividing eight "into one-half groups." However, it does make sense to interpret this problem as dividing eight "into groups of one-half." When thinking about division, we choose the model that makes sense in the context of the problem.

In her explanation near the end of class, Kayla used the sharing or partitioning model for division. In the situation, it made sense. However, in the lessons that follow, I rely on the grouping model of division to help students make sense of what they're doing.

CHAPTER EIGHT
INTRODUCING DIVISION OF FRACTIONS

Overview

This lesson builds on what students know about division with whole numbers to develop their understanding of what occurs when we think about dividing fractions. The students use the statements from the lesson in Chapter 7, "Whole Number Division: The Building Block," to help them arrive at answers to several problems, and then they check their answers by multiplying. All of the problems presented in this lesson were carefully chosen so that the students could reason fairly easily and use simple drawings to solve them.

Materials

▲ none

Time

▲ one class period

Teaching Directions

1. Post the list of statements about division from the previous lesson so all students can see it.

2. Write on the board: $3 \div \frac{1}{2}$.

3. Ask students to talk with their neighbors about what the answer might be. Suggest that they refer to the posted list of statements.

4. When you call the class to attention, have several students give the answer and explain their reasoning. Record their thinking on the board.

5. Use this problem to show students how to use the first three statements on the list to find the answer. For example, statement 1 states: You can solve a division problem by subtracting. Demonstrate how to subtract $\frac{1}{2}$ from 3 enough times to reach zero and verify that it took six subtractions and, therefore, the answer to the problem is 6. ("The Lesson" section provides help with how to lead this discussion.) Then review the rest of the statements to see if others are also helpful for solving the problem.

6. Write another problem on the board: $\frac{1}{2} \div \frac{1}{4}$. Repeat Steps 3, 4, and 5.

7. Repeat Steps 3, 4, and 5 for four more problems:

$\frac{3}{4} \div \frac{1}{8}$

$4\frac{1}{2} \div \frac{1}{2}$

$4\frac{1}{2} \div \frac{1}{4}$

$3 \div \frac{3}{4}$

8. Write five problems on the board for students to solve. Ask that they either solve each in two different ways, or solve them in one way and check by multiplying.

1. $5 \div \frac{1}{2}$

2. $3 \div 1\frac{1}{2}$

3. $1 \div \frac{1}{2}$

4. $1 \div \frac{1}{3}$

5. $6 \div \frac{3}{4}$

9. After a few minutes, write two additional problems on the board. The asterisk indicates that these are optional problems for students who finish quickly.

* $12 \div \frac{2}{3}$

** $4\frac{1}{2} \div \frac{3}{4}$

Teaching Notes

The lesson in Chapter 7, "Whole Number Division: The Building Block," is a prerequisite for this lesson. In the previous lesson, students discussed the following ten statements about division:

1. You can solve a division problem by subtracting.
2. To divide two numbers, $a \div b$, you can think, "How many bs are in a?"
3. You can check a division problem by multiplying.
4. The division sign ($\div$) means "into groups of."
5. The quotient tells "how many groups" there are.
6. You can break the dividend apart to make dividing easier.

7. Remainders can be represented as whole numbers or fractions.

8. If you divide a number by itself, the answer is one.

9. If you divide a number by one, the answer is the number itself.

10. If you reverse the order of the dividend and the divisor, you don't get the same quotient unless the dividend and divisor are the same number.

In this second lesson on division, students use those ideas to figure out answers to six problems that involve division of fractions:

$$3 \div \tfrac{1}{2}$$

$$\tfrac{1}{2} \div \tfrac{1}{4}$$

$$\tfrac{3}{4} \div \tfrac{1}{8}$$

$$4\tfrac{1}{2} \div \tfrac{1}{2}$$

$$4\tfrac{1}{2} \div \tfrac{1}{4}$$

$$3 \div \tfrac{3}{4}$$

The problems all have divisors that are smaller than the dividends and all have whole number answers. These two characteristics make solving the problems fairly easy for the students. Also, except for the last problem, the divisors are all unit fractions, which also makes the problems easier for students to solve. Choosing problems carefully in this way provides students with a successful first experience with dividing fractions and helps build their confidence. Subsequent lessons extend this first experience to more complex problems.

At one point in this lesson, Craig said, "When you divide with fractions, the answers get bigger." Craig was delighted by his discovery, and the idea made sense to him because he understood why the answers to the division problems made sense. When you figure out, for example, how many one-fourths are in four and one-half, the answer of eighteen isn't surprising. In this approach to teaching, in which students learn to figure out answers by reasoning instead of by following a rule, they develop understanding that can lead them to discoveries such as the one Craig made and build their overall understanding of the nature of fractions.

The Lesson

▲▲▲

I began the lesson by writing a problem on the board:

$$3 \div \tfrac{1}{2}$$

I said to the students, "Talk with your neighbor about what you think the answer might be to this problem. It may help to refer to the statements we talked about yesterday." I had posted the chart of the statements so that all of the students could see it. Lively conversation broke out. After a minute or so, I asked the students for their attention. I called on Pierre.

"We think the answer is six," he said. There were both nods of agreement and head shakes of disagreement. Pierre explained, "Well, it takes two halves to make a whole, so that's two halves in one whole. And in three there are three wholes, so it takes six halves to make three wholes. That's why we think it's six." I recorded on the board:

2 halves = 1 whole

6 halves = 3 wholes

$$3 \div \tfrac{1}{2} = 6$$

Hassan disagreed. "We think the answer should be one-sixth," he said. "What we did is we took one-half and divided it into three parts. One-half is three-sixths, so one part is one-sixth." I wrote on the board:

$\frac{1}{2}$ *divided into 3 parts*

$\frac{1}{2} = \frac{3}{6}$

Each part is $\frac{1}{6}$.

$3 \div \frac{1}{2} = \frac{1}{6}$

Helene said, "I agree with Pierre. One-half goes into one twice. So one-half goes into three six times. I think the answer is six." I wrote on the board:

$\frac{1}{2}$ *goes into 1 twice.*

$\frac{1}{2}$ *goes into 3 six times.*

$3 \div \frac{1}{2} = 6$

Clark also agreed with Pierre. He explained how he had used his fingers to figure. "I said that each finger was worth one-half, so that means that six of my fingers are worth three." He held up all of the fingers on one hand and the thumb on his other hand. "You can see that there are six one-halves in three," he added. Hassan was now looking confused.

I said, "Let's go down the list of statements and see if they help us think about this problem. The first statement says: 'You can solve a division problem by subtracting.' Watch as I use that idea to solve this problem." I wrote a *3* on the board, and with the students' help, subtracted $\frac{1}{2}$ over and over again until I reached 0. Then I circled each $\frac{1}{2}$ that I subtracted to show that I had subtracted it six times. (See top right.)

"Here's another way I could write it," I said, and I wrote the problem as if it were a long division problem with whole numbers. I realize that this is an unconventional way to represent the problem, but I thought it would relate to what the students were comfortable doing with whole numbers. Again, with their help, I subtracted

two one-halves three times to get the answer of six.

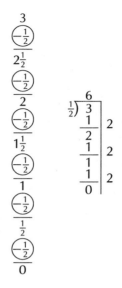

I then said, "Let's look at the second statement: 'To divide two numbers, *a* divided by *b*, you can think, "How many *b*s are in *a*?"' I'll use the numbers from our problem." I reread the statement. "To divide two numbers, three divided by one-half, you can think, 'How many one-halves are in three?'"

Julio said, "Oh, that makes it clear. I got what Hassan got, but I was thinking wrong. It's easy to see how many one-halves are in three if you draw circles. Can I come up and show?" I agreed. Julio came to the board, drew three circles, divided each in half, labeled each half, and said, "See, there are six halves. Six is right."

I read the third statement, "You can check a division problem by multiplying."

Sabrina said, "That proves that six is right. Six times one-half is three." I wrote on the board:

$3 \div \frac{1}{2} = 6$

$6 \times \frac{1}{2} = 3$

"Let's see what happens if we check the answer of one-sixth," I said. I wrote on the board:

$3 \div \frac{1}{2} = \frac{1}{6}$

$\frac{1}{6} \times \frac{1}{2} = \frac{1}{12}$

"I get that I was wrong," Hassan said, "but I don't get why."

I explained, "You figured out that if you divide one-half into three equal parts, each part is worth one-sixth. The problem you solved was one-half divided by three, not three divided by one-half. You got the right answer, but to a different problem." Hassan nodded, but I wasn't sure he fully understood. I knew, however, that we would be talking about many problems and he would have many opportunities to revisit this idea.

Kayla's hand shot up. "I have another way," she said. "It's easy if you double both numbers."

"Which numbers did you double?" I asked, not sure what Kayla meant.

"Can I come up and show?" she asked. I agreed. Kayla wrote:

$3 \div \frac{1}{2} = 6$

$6 \div 1 = 6$

"I doubled both numbers in the problem, so I know that the answer will stay the same," Kayla explained. She was remembering the patterns we had explored with division of whole numbers. But Craig wasn't convinced.

"Hey, can you do that?" he asked.

"Let's try Kayla's idea with other numbers that are easier to think about," I said. I wrote on the board:

$6 \div 2 = 3$

$12 \div 4 = 3$

"I doubled both the dividend and the divisor in the first problem, and the answer stayed the same," I said. "Another way to see it is to write the division

problems as fractions." I wrote on the board:

$6 \div 2 = \frac{6}{2} = 3$

$12 \div 4 = \frac{12}{4} = 3$

$\frac{6}{2} = \frac{12}{4}$

"That's cool," Craig said, seeming satisfied.

ANOTHER PROBLEM

I next wrote on the board:

$\frac{1}{2} \div \frac{1}{4}$

Conversation broke out again. I waited until students looked as if they had reached a conclusion and then brought the class to attention. I said, "Before I hear an answer, who would like to explain what the problem is that we're solving?"

Juanita said, "We have to find out how many one-fourths fit into one-half." Others agreed.

Anita explained first. "I did it by subtracting," she said. "One-half minus one-fourth is one-fourth, then minus one-fourth again is zero. So we took away one-fourth two times. The answer is two." I wrote on the board:

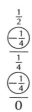

"It checks," Maria added. "Two times one-fourth is one-half." I wrote on the board:

$\frac{1}{2} \div \frac{1}{4} = 2$

$2 \times \frac{1}{4} = \frac{1}{2}$

Brendan said, "I can do it by doubling, like Kayla did. But you have to double twice." He came up and wrote on the board:

$$\tfrac{1}{2} \div \tfrac{1}{4} = 2$$

$$1 \div \tfrac{1}{2}$$

$$2 \div 1 = 2$$

I said, "Before you leave the board, Brendan, I notice that you didn't put an answer for the second problem, one divided by one-half. Do you know how many halves are in one?"

"Two," he said easily and then grinned. "Oh yeah, that one has to be two, too." He recorded the answer.

A THIRD PROBLEM

I then wrote on the board:

$$\tfrac{3}{4} \div \tfrac{1}{8}$$

Again, conversation broke out. The students were pleased with their success so far and were feeling confident. This time, after I brought them back to attention, I said, "Let's all say the answer together in a whisper voice."

I heard two answers: six and six-eighths.

Gloria explained, "Six of the eighths fit into three-fourths, so isn't it six-eighths?"

Sabrina said, "I think it's six. The problem says how many one-eighths are in three-fourths, so the answer is six. And it checks if you multiply." I wrote on the board;

$$\tfrac{3}{4} \div \tfrac{1}{8} = 6$$

$$6 \times \tfrac{1}{8} = \tfrac{1}{8} + \tfrac{1}{8} + \tfrac{1}{8} + \tfrac{1}{8} + \tfrac{1}{8} + \tfrac{1}{8} = \tfrac{6}{8} = \tfrac{3}{4}$$

I've found that the confusion that Gloria expressed generally surfaces in this discussion, and students make this error on and off for a while. With more experience, however, especially when checking problems by multiplying, the confusion gets resolved.

A FOURTH PROBLEM

I wrote on the board:

$$4\tfrac{1}{2} \div \tfrac{1}{2}$$

Celia explained how she solved it. "I used number six," she began, referring to the list of statements. "I did break apart. I made four and a half into four plus one-half. Then I know that there are eight halves in four, and there is one one-half in one-half. So I think the answer is nine." I recorded Celia's thinking:

$$4\tfrac{1}{2} = 4 + \tfrac{1}{2}$$

$$4 \div \tfrac{1}{2} = 8$$

$$\tfrac{1}{2} \div \tfrac{1}{2} = 1$$

$$8 + 1 = 9$$

Saul said, "You can draw a picture. If you draw four and a half circles, and divide the whole circles in half, you see there are nine halves, so nine is right." I drew as Saul explained.

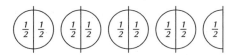

"It checks," Pierre said. "Nine times one-half is four and a half because half of nine is four and a half." I recorded:

$$4\tfrac{1}{2} \div \tfrac{1}{2} = 9$$

$$9 \times \tfrac{1}{2} = 4\tfrac{1}{2}$$

A FIFTH PROBLEM

I then wrote on the board:

$$4\tfrac{1}{2} \div \tfrac{1}{4}$$

The students were excited to solve this one. David explained that you could draw four and a half circles, divide them into fourths, and count them up. "There are eighteen," he said. I drew a picture to show David's idea:

"That answer seems awfully big," Anita said, surprised by the result of eighteen.

"Does it seem wrong?" I asked.

"No, it seems right," she said. "I did break apart. There are sixteen fourths in the four wholes and two more fourths in the extra half, so eighteen has to be right. It just seems too big."

"Hey!" Craig burst out. "When you divide with fractions, the answers get bigger. It's kind of the opposite of multiplying. When we multiply with fractions, the answers get smaller. Now they get bigger. That's really something!"

Juanita explained how it checked. She said, "Eighteen times one-fourth is four and a half. Eighteen times one-fourth is eighteen-fourths. And four goes into eighteen four times with two left over. And two is half of four." I recorded:

$$4\tfrac{1}{2} \div \tfrac{1}{4} = 18$$
$$18 \times \tfrac{1}{4} = \tfrac{18}{4} = 4\tfrac{1}{2}$$

A LAST PROBLEM

Then I presented the last problem before giving them some to try on their own:

$$3 \div \tfrac{3}{4}$$

This was the first problem that didn't have a unit fraction as the divisor, and it confused some of the students. Francis, for example, was convinced that the answer was twelve.

"I disagree," Celia said. "I added how many three-fourths it took to get to three, and it takes four of them. First I did three-fourths plus three-fourths, and that was one and one-half, so I had to do it again because one and one-half plus one and one-half is three." I recorded:

$$\tfrac{3}{4} + \tfrac{3}{4} = 1\tfrac{1}{2}$$
$$\tfrac{3}{4} + \tfrac{3}{4} = 1\tfrac{1}{2}$$
$$1\tfrac{1}{2} + 1\tfrac{1}{2} = 3$$
$$3 \div \tfrac{3}{4} = 4$$

Pierre added, "That checks because four times three-fourths is three-fourths plus three-fourths four times, and that's

twelve-fourths, and that's three." I recorded:

$$4 \times \tfrac{3}{4} = \tfrac{3}{4} + \tfrac{3}{4} + \tfrac{3}{4} + \tfrac{3}{4} = \tfrac{12}{4} = 3$$

Saul checked the answer of four by doubling. I recorded as he explained:

$$3 \div \tfrac{3}{4} = 4$$
$$6 \div 1\tfrac{1}{2} = 4$$
$$12 \div 3 = 4$$

"How do you know that six divided by one and one-half is four?" I asked.

Saul said, "Easy. Two times one and a half is three, so four times one and a half has to be six."

I find that students develop personal preferences for how they think about problems like these, and my goal is to encourage them to use the methods that make sense to them while exposing them to other ideas.

A WRITTEN ASSIGNMENT

I then put five problems on the board for students to solve on paper. "Try these problems," I said, "and be sure to explain how you reasoned so I can see how you're thinking. Either solve the problems in two different ways, or solve them in one way and then check your answer by multiplying."

"Can we work together?" Hassan asked.

"It's fine for you to work together, but you each must write on your own paper," I told them.

"Do we have to explain for all of them?" Annie asked. I nodded.

No one else had a question, so I wrote the problems on the board:

1. $5 \div \tfrac{1}{2}$
2. $3 \div 1\tfrac{1}{2}$
3. $1 \div \tfrac{1}{2}$
4. $1 \div \tfrac{1}{3}$
5. $6 \div \tfrac{3}{4}$

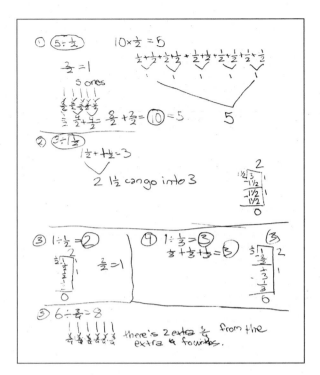

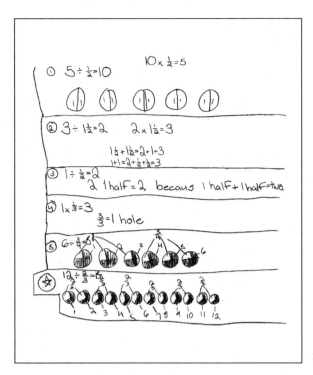

▲▲▲▲▲▲Figure 8–1 *Maggie solved the first five problems correctly. She checked several of them by using the same method she used for long division of whole numbers.*

▲▲▲▲▲▲Figure 8–2 *Sachi solved the five problems and then the two extra problems.*

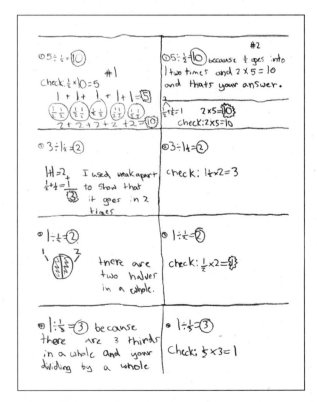

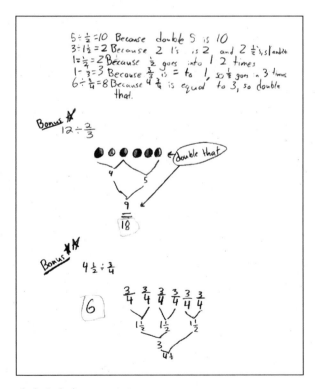

▲▲▲▲▲▲Figure 8–3 *Brendan worked more slowly and only solved the first four problems.*

▲▲▲▲▲▲Figure 8–4 *For the first bonus problem, $12 \div \frac{2}{3}$, Pierre solved $6 \div \frac{2}{3}$ and then doubled the answer.*

I had two additional problems ready for students who finished more quickly than most, and I wrote these on the board after a few minutes so that they would be available for students who were ready for them:

$$* \; 12 \div \tfrac{2}{3}$$
$$** \; 4\tfrac{1}{2} \div \tfrac{3}{4}$$

Figures 8–1 through 8–4 on page 82 show how four students worked on this assignment.

Questions and Discussion

▲▲

▲ *Why did you want the students to work together on the problems? How can you know what they each understand?*

At this point, the students are just beginning to learn about division. Rather than focus on assessing their understanding, my goal is to give them as much support as possible for their learning. I encourage conversation among students so that they can talk about their ideas, clarify their thinking, and hear the ideas of others. There is plenty of time later for assessment.

CHAPTER NINE
DIVISION PATTERNS

Overview

In this lesson, students explore division and multiplication problems that have the same answer and for which the first factor of the multiplication problem is the same as the dividend in the division problem. For example, both of the problems $8 \div 2 = 4$ and $8 \times \frac{1}{2} = 4$ begin with 8 and have the answer of 4. Students examine several sets of problems with this characteristic, look for patterns, and discuss what they notice. The exploration prepares students for understanding the strategy of solving a division problem by changing it to a multiplication problem that results in the same answer.

Materials

▲ none

Time

▲ two class periods, plus time for additional experiences

Teaching Directions

1. Write two problems on the board, side by side:

$8 \div 2 =$ $\qquad$ $8 \times \frac{1}{2} =$

Ask students for the answers and have them explain their reasoning. (Both answers are 4.)

2. Underneath the two problems, write two more:

$8 \div \frac{1}{2} =$ $\qquad$ $8 \times 2 =$

Ask students for the answers and have them explain their reasoning. (Both answers are 16.)

3. Point out that in these pairs of problems, dividing by two and multiplying by one-half resulted in the same answers as did dividing by one-half and multiplying by two. Lead a discussion for students to talk about why this is so.

4. Introduce the division problems shown below, with dividends from eight to one and divisors of two. Have students give the answers. Then ask them to describe the patterns they notice in the list. (**Note:** You can either list the problems one by one and ask for answers or list them all at one time. Both methods are described in the lesson for different sets of problems.)

$8 \div 2 = 4$

$7 \div 2 = 3\frac{1}{2}$

$6 \div 2 = 3$

$5 \div 2 = 2\frac{1}{2}$

$4 \div 2 = 2$

$3 \div 2 = 1\frac{1}{2}$

$2 \div 2 = 1$

$1 \div 2 = \frac{1}{2}$

5. Next to each division problem, write a multiplication problem with the same first number and one-half for the second factor. Have students give the answers.

$8 \div 2 = 4$ $8 \times \frac{1}{2} = 4$

$7 \div 2 = 3\frac{1}{2}$ $7 \times \frac{1}{2} = 3\frac{1}{2}$

$6 \div 2 = 3$ $6 \times \frac{1}{2} = 3$

$5 \div 2 = 2\frac{1}{2}$ $5 \times \frac{1}{2} = 2\frac{1}{2}$

$4 \div 2 = 2$ $4 \times \frac{1}{2} = 2$

$3 \div 2 = 1\frac{1}{2}$ $3 \times \frac{1}{2} = 1\frac{1}{2}$

$2 \div 2 = 1$ $2 \times \frac{1}{2} = 1$

$1 \div 2 = \frac{1}{2}$ $1 \times \frac{1}{2} = \frac{1}{2}$

6. Ask students to look for patterns in the second list and also in the two lists together.

7. Repeat Steps 4, 5, and 6 for a second set of problems:

Set 2

$6 \div 6 = 1$ $6 \times \frac{1}{6} = 1$

$5 \div 5 = 1$ $5 \times \frac{1}{5} = 1$

$4 \div 4 = 1$ $4 \times \frac{1}{4} = 1$

$3 \div 3 = 1$ $3 \times \frac{1}{3} = 1$

$2 \div 2 = 1$ $2 \times \frac{1}{2} = 1$

$1 \div 1 = 1$ $1 \times \frac{1}{1} = 1$ $1 \times 1 = 1$

$\frac{1}{2} \div \frac{1}{2} = 1$ $\frac{1}{2} \times \frac{2}{1} = 1$ $\frac{1}{2} \times 2 = 1$

$\frac{1}{4} \div \frac{1}{4} = 1$ $\frac{1}{4} \times \frac{4}{1} = 1$ $\frac{1}{4} \times 4 = 1$

Note: Read in the vignette about the alternative forms for the last three multiplication problems. Both are correct, and discussing them helps reinforce for students how to write a whole number as a fraction with the numerator of one.

8. On Day 2, repeat Steps 4, 5, and 6 for two more sets of problems:

Set 3

$12 \div 6 = 2$	$12 \times \frac{1}{6} = 2$
$12 \div 4 = 3$	$12 \times \frac{1}{4} = 3$
$12 \div 3 = 4$	$12 \times \frac{1}{3} = 4$
$12 \div 2 = 6$	$12 \times \frac{1}{2} = 6$
$12 \div 1 = 12$	$12 \times \frac{1}{1} = 12$
$12 \div \frac{1}{2} = 24$	$12 \times \frac{2}{1} = 24$
$12 \div \frac{1}{3} = 36$	$12 \times \frac{3}{1} = 36$
$12 \div \frac{1}{4} = 48$	$12 \times \frac{4}{1} = 48$

Note: The last problem in this set was the first problem presented in this lesson with a fraction for an answer. Read in the vignette how I addressed this problem with the students.

Set 4

$2 \div \frac{1}{6} = 12$	$2 \times 6 \ (\text{or } \frac{6}{1}) = 12$
$2 \div \frac{1}{4} = 8$	$2 \times 4 \ (\text{or } \frac{4}{1}) = 8$
$2 \div \frac{1}{3} = 6$	$2 \times 3 \ (\text{or } \frac{3}{1}) = 6$
$2 \div \frac{1}{2} = 4$	$2 \times 2 \ (\text{or } \frac{2}{1}) = 4$
$2 \div 1 = 2$	$2 \times 1 \ (\text{or } \frac{1}{1}) = 2$
$2 \div 2 = 1$	$2 \times \frac{1}{2} = 1$
$2 \div 4 = \frac{1}{2}$	$2 \times \frac{1}{4} = \frac{1}{2}$

9. On subsequent days, introduce other sets of problems. See the "Extensions" section for additional sets of problems.

Teaching Notes

The students in this class had experienced the two previous lessons related to division of fractions, in Chapters 7 and 8. These are valuable prerequisites for this lesson.

In this lesson, students examine sets of division and multiplication problems that were carefully chosen for several purposes. One purpose was to provide the students practice with reasoning to find the answers to division problems with fractions. To that end, I carefully chose the problems for this lesson, as I did for the previous lessons on dividing fractions, so that the answers were whole numbers. (The only exception I made was the problem $2 \div 4$, which I included to give the students a taste of what was to come and to give me some feedback on how they would think about a problem like this.) In this lesson, I wanted to strengthen students' ability to rely on their own reasoning to figure out answers.

A second purpose of the problems is to provide students experience with patterns. The problems in each set are ordered so that students can see and rely on patterns as a way to check on their reasoning. This strengthens students' general understanding of the value of patterns while also giving them support for justifying their thinking.

A third purpose of the problems is to begin to build students' understanding of a specific relationship between division and multiplication that will eventually lead to helping students understand and have available for their use an algorithm for dividing fractions. In the problems presented, each division problem is paired with a multiplication problem with the same answer and the same first number. Investigating these problems prepares students for subsequent lessons in which they will more specifically focus on using this relationship to solve division problems.

The Lesson

▲▲

DAY 1

I began the lesson by writing two problems on the board, side by side:

$$8 \div 2 = \qquad 8 \times \tfrac{1}{2} =$$

"Four," the students said in unison when I pointed to the first problem. I recorded the answer.

$$8 \div 2 = 4 \qquad 8 \times \tfrac{1}{2} =$$

Francis explained, "Two goes into eight four times." I pointed to the second problem and called on Anita.

"It's four, too," she said. "One-half of eight is four." The others agreed and I recorded the answer.

$$8 \div 2 = 4 \qquad 8 \times \tfrac{1}{2} = 4$$

I then wrote two other problems on the board underneath the first two:

$$8 \div 2 = 4 \qquad 8 \times \tfrac{1}{2} = 4$$
$$8 \times \tfrac{1}{2} = \qquad 8 \times 2 =$$

"Talk with your neighbor about the answers to these problems," I said.

Conversation broke out and, after a few moments, more than half of the students had raised their hands. I waited, and a few more hands went up.

"Who would like to explain the answer to this problem?" I asked, pointing to $8 \div \tfrac{1}{2}$. I called on Ally.

Ally held up her paper to show me what she and Carla had done and said, "We got sixteen. We drew eight circles and cut them in half and counted up the halves."

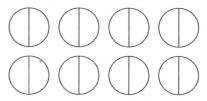

Kara commented, "We did it that way, too. I was surprised that the answer was so big."

Pierre had a different way to explain. He said, "Two halves fit into one whole, so since there are eight wholes, I multiplied two times eight and got sixteen."

Craig shared next. He began, "What I did was. . . ." Then he paused and said, "No, my way is the same as Pierre's way. Well, maybe it's a little different."

"Let's hear what you were thinking," I said.

Craig said, "Like Pierre said, there are two halves in one whole, so there are four halves in two wholes, and eight halves in four wholes, and sixteen halves in eight wholes."

No other students volunteered to share. I recorded the answer on the board, pointed to the other problem, and called on Kayla.

"It's sixteen, too," she said. "Eight twos are sixteen, and two eights are sixteen. Either way works." I recorded the answer.

$$8 \div 2 = 4 \qquad 8 \times \tfrac{1}{2} = 4$$
$$8 \div \tfrac{1}{2} = 16 \qquad 8 \times 2 = 16$$

I then said, "The first two problems have the same answer, and the second two also have the same answer. In the first two problems, when we divided eight by two and then multiplied it by one-half, we got four both times. Why did that happen?"

Celia said, "I think that when you multiply by one-half, you take half of the number, and that's the same as what happens when you divide by two."

Brendan added, "Two is an even number. And dividing by two is like splitting something in half."

Maria said, "Eight times one is eight. But we're multiplying by one-half, and one-half is half of one. The answer is half of eight, and that's the same as eight divided by two."

I then pointed to the second pair of problems and said, "Here, when we divided eight by one-half, we got sixteen, the same answer as when we multiplied eight by two. Why do you think this happened?"

Julio said, "They're kind of the opposites of each other. When you divide by two, the answer gets smaller, and when you multiply by a fraction, the answer gets smaller, too. But when you multiply by two, the answer gets bigger, and the answer gets bigger when you divide by a fraction."

Hassan commented on Julio's idea, "What he said is right, but it's weird."

"What's weird about it?" I asked Hassan.

Hassan said, "Well, it's weird to divide something by one-half and get so much more. I mean, I know it's right, but it's just hard to get used to."

I responded, "So all of these years, whenever you divided, you got an answer that was smaller than what you started with, and now that's changed?" Hassan nodded.

"Mathematics often presents us with surprises," I added.

Introducing a Set of Problems

I extended this introduction with an investigation of a set of eight division problems and eight related multiplication problems. For the division problems, I used dividends from eight to one and the divisor of two for all of them. To begin, I wrote the first problem on the board:

$$8 \div 2 =$$

"Tell me the answer together in a whisper voice," I said.

I heard a whispered chorus, "Four." I then wrote another problem underneath:

$$8 \div 2 = 4$$
$$7 \div 2 =$$

This time I heard several different whispered answers. "Three and a half." "Three." "Fourteen."

"Who would like to explain?" I asked.

Pierre said, "Seven times two is fourteen."

Craig responded, "But the problem says to divide, not to multiply."

"Oops," Pierre said.

"Oh, I get it now," Maggie said, who had thought that the answer was three. "You made the eight one less, so I made the answer one less. But I was wrong. It should be three and a half, not three." Others agreed. I recorded the answer and added another problem to the list:

$$8 \div 2 = 4$$
$$7 \div 2 = 3\tfrac{1}{2}$$
$$6 \div 2 =$$

"Three!" they whispered. I recorded the answer and continued the rest of the division problems, having the students whisper the answer for each:

$$8 \div 2 = 4$$
$$7 \div 2 = 3\tfrac{1}{2}$$

$$6 \div 2 = 3$$
$$5 \div 2 = 2\frac{1}{2}$$
$$4 \div 2 = 2$$
$$3 \div 2 = 1\frac{1}{2}$$
$$2 \div 2 = 1$$
$$1 \div 2 = \frac{1}{2}$$

As I wrote problems, students began to anticipate, calling out the answer before I finished writing the problem. They were following the decreasing pattern of the answers and not thinking about the division. To focus them on the division required for the answers, I pointed to the third-to-last problem, with the answer of $1\frac{1}{2}$, and asked, "Who can explain why one and one-half is the correct answer to three divided by two?"

Damien said, "If you divide three by two, you split it in half. So there's one and a half in each part."

Ally said, "Two goes into three one time, and there's a remainder of one, and that's worth one-half."

"Why is the remainder of one worth one-half?" I asked. Ally couldn't think of a way to explain. I called on Sabrina to help.

"It's easy if you think about cookies," she said. "Divide three cookies for two people and each person gets one cookie and then they split the extra. So they each get one and a half cookies."

"I get it now," Ally said.

"Can you explain Sabrina's idea in your own words?" I asked.

Ally said, "If you divide three cookies up between two people, there's one cookie left over. But they divide that one, too, so they each get one cookie and one-half of a cookie."

I then focused the students on the patterns in the list of problems. "What patterns do you notice in the problems I wrote?" I asked.

Brendan said, "The first numbers go down by one."

I paraphrased Brendan's statement to use the correct terminology. "Yes, you're right. The dividends decrease by one each time." In general, I try to avoid repeating what students say so that students develop the habit of listening to one another. If I repeat their comments, I worry that some students will pay attention only to what I say, not to what their classmates say. However, I paraphrase when I want to model correct terminology, as I did here.

Kayla said, "I'm not sure this is a pattern because they're all the same, but you divided every number by two."

I confirmed, "Yes, that's a pattern. The pattern is that the divisors stay the same."

David said, "The answers go down by one-half."

I pointed to the numbers and paraphrased David's comment. "Yes, the quotients decrease by one-half each time."

Julio added, "The answers are all half of the number you divided." Instead of paraphrasing, I wrote *divisor*, *dividend*, and *quotient* on the board and prompted Julio, "Can you restate your idea using some of these words?" When students don't take my lead and begin using the terminology that I'm modeling, I make my expectation explicit, as I did in this instance with Julio.

Julio restated his idea. "The quotients are all half of the dividends." I nodded my agreement.

Related Multiplication Problems I started a second list of problems next to the first list. Next to each division problem, I wrote a multiplication problem that gave the same answer. The first factor in the multiplication problem was the same as the starting number, the dividend, of the division problem, and the second factor was $\frac{1}{2}$. The first problem I wrote was $8 \times \frac{1}{2}$. Hands went up, as students were eager to give the answer. I called on Juanita.

"It's four," she said. "You can switch them around, and then it's one-half of eight, and that's four." I recorded the answer on the board:

$\frac{1}{2} \times 8 = 4$

Ally suggested another way to solve the problem. "You can add," she said. "If you add one-half eight times, that's eight halves, and that's the same as four wholes."

$\frac{1}{2} + \frac{1}{2} + \frac{1}{2} + \frac{1}{2} + \frac{1}{2} + \frac{1}{2} + \frac{1}{2} + \frac{1}{2} = \frac{8}{2} = 4$

I then wrote another problem underneath:

$$8 \div 2 = 4 \qquad\qquad 8 \times \tfrac{1}{2} = 4$$
$$7 \div 2 = 3\tfrac{1}{2} \qquad\quad 7 \times \tfrac{1}{2} =$$
$$6 \div 2 = 3$$
$$5 \div 2 = 2\tfrac{1}{2}$$
$$4 \div 2 = 2$$
$$3 \div 2 = 1\tfrac{1}{2}$$
$$2 \div 2 = 1$$
$$1 \div 2 = \tfrac{1}{2}$$

As I did with $8 \times \frac{1}{2}$, I had several students explain how they got the answer to $7 \times \frac{1}{2}$ and I recorded their thinking. These problems were easy for the students, but I spent the time talking about these first two to make sure that the students had made the shift from thinking about dividing to thinking about multiplying. I didn't record students' explanations for the answers for the rest of the problems on the list, however, as it didn't seem necessary. The final list looked like this:

$$8 \div 2 = 4 \qquad\qquad 8 \times \tfrac{1}{2} = 4$$
$$7 \div 2 = 3\tfrac{1}{2} \qquad\quad 7 \times \tfrac{1}{2} = 3\tfrac{1}{2}$$
$$6 \div 2 = 3 \qquad\qquad 6 \times \tfrac{1}{2} = 3$$
$$5 \div 2 = 2\tfrac{1}{2} \qquad\quad 5 \times \tfrac{1}{2} = 2\tfrac{1}{2}$$
$$4 \div 2 = 2 \qquad\qquad 4 \times \tfrac{1}{2} = 2$$
$$3 \div 2 = 1\tfrac{1}{2} \qquad\quad 3 \times \tfrac{1}{2} = 1\tfrac{1}{2}$$
$$2 \div 2 = 1 \qquad\qquad 2 \times \tfrac{1}{2} = 1$$
$$1 \div 2 = \tfrac{1}{2} \qquad\qquad 1 \times \tfrac{1}{2} = \tfrac{1}{2}$$

When we completed the list, I said to the students, "Talk to your neighbor about the patterns you notice in the second list of problems. Then look at the two lists together and see what patterns you notice." Conversations broke out as

the students looked at the lists and shared ideas. After a few moments, I called them to attention and asked what they noticed.

"The answers go down, like the other answers," Clark said.

"Which list are you talking about?" I asked, pushing for clarity.

"The second list," Clark said and then amended his idea. "Well, it's the same in both lists. The answers go in a pattern, down one-half each time."

"The first numbers in the problems on both lists are the same," Maggie added.

"The answers across are the same," Kara said.

"Which answers are you referring to?" I asked, again for clarification.

"If you go across from one problem to the one next to it, they have the same answer all the way down," Kara explained.

"We noticed something that was different," Eddie said. "The first problems you did division and the second you did multiplication."

Julio said, "This is a pattern that Kayla said before, but now it works for both lists. The second number in the problem is the same all the way down the lists."

"What number did we divide by in the first list?" I asked.

"Two," the students responded.

"And what number did we multiply by in the second list?" I asked.

"One-half," they responded.

"Why were the answers the same?" I asked.

Celia said, "It's like we talked about before. Dividing something by two is the same as multiplying it by one-half. Both times you get half of the number."

A Second Set of Problems

I introduced a new set of problems. This time, I listed the entire sequence of division problems. As with the first set, the dividends were different, but each of these problems had the same divisor and dividend:

$6 \div 6 =$

$5 \div 5 =$

$4 \div 4 =$

$3 \div 3 =$

$2 \div 2 =$

$1 \div 1 =$

$\frac{1}{2} \div \frac{1}{2} =$

"They're all one," Craig said. Others agreed. I recorded the answers.

$6 \div 6 = 1$

$5 \div 5 = 1$

$4 \div 4 = 1$

$3 \div 3 = 1$

$2 \div 2 = 1$

$1 \div 1 = 1$

$\frac{1}{2} \div \frac{1}{2} = 1$

"Who can explain why all of the answers are one?" I asked. Hands shot up. Several students explained.

"Whenever you divide something by itself, the answer is one," Juanita said.

Brendan added, "If you think about how many sixes there are in six, then you know that it's one. And you can do the same for the rest of the problems."

Sabrina said, "They check. If you multiply the one times one of the other numbers, you get the other number."

"But what about one-half divided by one-half?" I asked. "Are you sure the answer to this fraction problem should be one?"

Celia said, "It's the same. You ask how many times one-half fits into one-half, and it's one."

Pierre said, "I don't think that's right. I think the answer should be one-fourth, because half of a half is a fourth."

Julio said, "I disagree with Pierre. That's what you get when you multiply. Then you get one-fourth, but this is division." I wrote on the board separate from the list:

$\frac{1}{2} \times \frac{1}{2} = \frac{1}{4}$

$\frac{1}{2} \div \frac{1}{2} = ?$

"Oh yeah, you're right," Pierre said. "I was thinking about times."

Sabrina said, "The answer has to be one. It checks. One times one-half is one-half. If the answer was one-fourth, it doesn't check. One-fourth times one-half doesn't give you one-half." Sabrina was consistent in her use of multiplication to check a division problem. She was comfortable with this idea and used it regularly.

"So how much is one-fourth divided by one-fourth?" I asked Pierre, quizzing him with a new problem.

"It's one," he said. I added this problem to the list.

Related Multiplication Problems I then began a second list next to the first list. As with the first set of problems, I wrote multiplication problems that began with the same first number and that had the same answer. I began:

$6 \div 6 = 1 \qquad 6 \times \frac{1}{6} = 1$

$5 \div 5 = 1$

$4 \div 4 = 1$

$3 \div 3 = 1$

$2 \div 2 = 1$

$1 \div 1 = 1$

$\frac{1}{2} \div \frac{1}{2} = 1$

$\frac{1}{4} \div \frac{1}{4} = 1$

"Who can explain why six times one-sixth equals one?" I asked.

Maria said, "One-sixth is one-sixth of a whole. So six times one-sixth is six-sixths, and that equals one whole." I wrote on the board:

$\frac{1}{6} = \frac{1}{6}$ of 1 whole

$6 \times \frac{1}{6} = \frac{6}{6} = 1$ whole

Craig said, "You have one-sixth six times. You can add them and you get six-sixths. And that's the same as one." I wrote on the board:

$\frac{1}{6} + \frac{1}{6} + \frac{1}{6} + \frac{1}{6} + \frac{1}{6} + \frac{1}{6} = \frac{6}{6} = 1$

Ally said, "You can show it with a circle. If you divide it into six parts, each part is one-sixth, and all six parts make the whole circle."

I drew on the board:

Francis said, "You can show it with six circles, too. Divide them all into six parts. Then if you take one-sixth of each and put them together, you'll make a whole circle." I drew Francis's idea on the board:

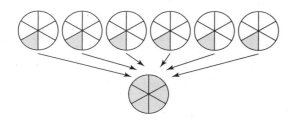

No one had another idea. To reinforce the strategy of drawing rectangles, I drew a 1-by-6 rectangle on the board, divided the short side into sixths, shaded five of them to show they were weren't part of the problem, and labeled the dimensions of the rectangle that represented the problem.

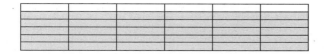

I explained, "Each unshaded piece is one-sixth of a square, and I could arrange them to make one whole."

I then refocused the class on the problems. "Who knows what I should write for the next problem in the list?" The pattern seemed obvious to the students and, following their suggestions, I listed each problem, asked the students for the

answer, and recorded it. I stopped after I wrote $2 \times \frac{1}{2} = 1$.

$6 \div 6 = 1$	$6 \times \frac{1}{6} = 1$
$5 \div 5 = 1$	$5 \times \frac{1}{5} = 1$
$4 \div 4 = 1$	$4 \times \frac{1}{4} = 1$
$3 \div 3 = 1$	$3 \times \frac{1}{3} = 1$
$2 \div 2 = 1$	$2 \times \frac{1}{2} = 1$
$1 \div 1 = 1$	
$\frac{1}{2} \div \frac{1}{2} = 1$	
$\frac{1}{4} \div \frac{1}{4} = 1$	

"How did you know to write one-sixth, then one-fifth, then one-fourth, then one-third, and then one-half?" I asked, pointing to the second factor in each problem.

Julio said, "You just make the number the denominator and put a one on top." Others nodded. No one offered another way to describe the pattern.

"What should I write for the next problem?" I asked.

Kara said, "One times one over one equals one." I added $1 \times \frac{1}{1} = 1$ to the list. The others nodded their agreement.

I said, "What if I just wrote one times one equals one? Would that be OK?" I wrote $1 \times 1 = 1$ next to $1 \times \frac{1}{1} = 1$.

$6 \div 6 = 1$	$6 \times \frac{1}{6} = 1$	
$5 \div 5 = 1$	$5 \times \frac{1}{5} = 1$	
$4 \div 4 = 1$	$4 \times \frac{1}{4} = 1$	
$3 \div 3 = 1$	$3 \times \frac{1}{3} = 1$	
$2 \div 2 = 1$	$2 \times \frac{1}{2} = 1$	
$1 \div 1 = 1$	$1 \times \frac{1}{1} = 1$	$1 \times 1 = 1$
$\frac{1}{2} \div \frac{1}{2} = 1$		
$\frac{1}{4} \div \frac{1}{4} = 1$		

Brendan said, "It's not really right, but in a way it's right. I mean, one times one *is* one, but it doesn't follow the pattern that Julio said."

"So you think that Kara's way fits the pattern better?" I asked. Brendan nodded.

"What should I write for the next problem?" I asked. "What ideas do you have?"

Annie said, "You write 'one-half times,' and then you write a one on top and one-half on the bottom." I wrote $\frac{1}{2} \times \dfrac{1}{\frac{1}{2}}$ on the board as Annie suggested, not in the list, but to the side

"That fraction is really strange looking!" Pierre said.

"Is it right?" Annie wanted to know.

"Can you make sense of it?" I asked, pointing to the fraction $\dfrac{1}{\frac{1}{2}}$.

"Well, not really," she said. "But I followed Julio's idea and it worked for the others. Is it wrong?"

"No, it's not mathematically wrong. This fraction is called a complex fraction because it has a fraction for the denominator. A complex fraction is a fraction that has a fraction for the denominator, the numerator, or both. You'll learn more about complex fractions when you're in high school. But for our pattern, we should use something that we can explain." The students were stuck.

I referred back to the list of problems. I said, "Julio made a good observation, but let's think about the fractions one-sixth, one-fifth, one-fourth, and so on, in another way. The idea is to write multiplication problems that give the same answers as the division problems, so all of the answers are one. The fractions you used so far did that, and they also are fractions that make sense to you. Now we need to know what to multiply by one-half and then one-fourth to get one." On the list, I started the last two problems, writing a blank line for the missing factor in each.

$6 \div 6 = 1 \qquad 6 \times \frac{1}{6} = 1$
$5 \div 5 = 1 \qquad 5 \times \frac{1}{5} = 1$
$4 \div 4 = 1 \qquad 4 \times \frac{1}{4} = 1$
$3 \div 3 = 1 \qquad 3 \times \frac{1}{3} = 1$
$2 \div 2 = 1 \qquad 2 \times \frac{1}{2} = 1$
$1 \div 1 = 1 \qquad 1 \times \frac{1}{1} = 1 \qquad 1 \times 1 = 1$

$\frac{1}{2} \div \frac{1}{2} = 1 \qquad \frac{1}{2} \times \underline{} = 1$
$\frac{1}{4} \div \frac{1}{4} = 1 \qquad \frac{1}{4} \times \underline{} = 1$

"Talk with your neighbor about what numbers I could write in these last two problems so that they are correct," I said. After a moment, hands went up, including Annie's. I called on her, interested in what she was now thinking.

Annie said, "When you look at it that way, then you should write two in the first one and four in the last one." Others agreed and I erased the blanks and recorded her suggestions:

$6 \div 6 = 1 \qquad 6 \times \frac{1}{6} = 1$
$5 \div 5 = 1 \qquad 5 \times \frac{1}{5} = 1$
$4 \div 4 = 1 \qquad 4 \times \frac{1}{4} = 1$
$3 \div 3 = 1 \qquad 3 \times \frac{1}{3} = 1$
$2 \div 2 = 1 \qquad 2 \times \frac{1}{2} = 1$
$1 \div 1 = 1 \qquad 1 \times \frac{1}{1} = 1 \qquad 1 \times 1 = 1$
$\frac{1}{2} \div \frac{1}{2} = 1 \qquad \frac{1}{2} \times 2 = 1$
$\frac{1}{4} \div \frac{1}{4} = 1 \qquad \frac{1}{4} \times 4 = 1$

"They're right now," David said.

I said, "But in all of the other problems, we were able to write a fraction for the second factor, and that's what Annie was suggesting with the complex fraction."

Sabrina said, "But one over one is the same as one whole. You can write just one if you want to."

"We can," I agreed. "But what about if we leave the one over one so it's a fraction like the others before it? Can you think about how to write the two and the four in the last two problems as fractions?" It was obvious how to do this for some students but not for others. I called on David.

He said, "Two is the same as two wholes, so you could write two over one. And the same for four, you could write four over one." I wrote to the side of the lists:

$\frac{2}{1} = 2$

$\frac{4}{1} = 4$

"Hey, then Julio's pattern works!" Craig said.

I said, "Talk with your neighbor about how you could explain to someone else why the fraction two over one is equal to two and why four over one is equal to four." Conversation broke out, and after a moment, I had several students explain. This idea wasn't difficult for the students to understand, but it was an idea that didn't naturally occur to some of them, so the discussion was useful.

I then replaced the 2 and 4 in the last two problems with $\frac{2}{1}$ and $\frac{4}{1}$ and wrote the problems with the whole number factors beside them. "All of these are mathematically correct," I said.

$$6 \div 6 = 1 \qquad 6 \times \tfrac{1}{6} = 1$$
$$5 \div 5 = 1 \qquad 5 \times \tfrac{1}{5} = 1$$
$$4 \div 4 = 1 \qquad 4 \times \tfrac{1}{4} = 1$$
$$3 \div 3 = 1 \qquad 3 \times \tfrac{1}{3} = 1$$
$$2 \div 2 = 1 \qquad 2 \times \tfrac{1}{2} = 1$$
$$1 \div 1 = 1 \qquad 1 \times \tfrac{1}{1} = 1 \qquad 1 \times 1 = 1$$
$$\tfrac{1}{2} \div \tfrac{1}{2} = 1 \qquad \tfrac{1}{2} \times \tfrac{2}{1} = 1 \qquad \tfrac{1}{2} \times 2 = 1$$
$$\tfrac{1}{4} \div \tfrac{1}{4} = 1 \qquad \tfrac{1}{4} \times \tfrac{4}{1} = 1 \qquad \tfrac{1}{4} \times 4 = 1$$

In this class, no student made the connection that the second factors in the multiplication problems were the reciprocals of the corresponding divisors if you first converted the whole numbers to fractions—6 to $\frac{6}{1}$, 5 to $\frac{5}{1}$, and so on. I didn't push for this generalization. At this time, I wanted to keep the emphasis on having the students reason to arrive at answers. In other classes, however, students have sometimes come up with this observation. When they do, I acknowledge their idea but don't dwell on it.

A little time was remaining in the period, but I thought that the students had done enough thinking about patterns for now and I planned to return to them the next day. For the rest of the class, the students solved several multiplication problems with fractions, each in at least two

ways. I've found that regular practice with a few problems helps students cement their skills. As the students worked, I circulated and gave individual help as needed.

DAY 2

I began the next day's lesson by introducing a third set of problems, this time using the same dividend for all of the problems, twelve, and varying the divisors. I listed the division problems and had students give answers and explain their reasoning. Then I wrote the multiplication problems with the same first number and the same answer. After students had given the answers and explained their reasoning, I led a discussion about the patterns they noticed. All of the division problems I chose had whole number answers, avoiding the problem of remainders. The completed lists looked like this:

$$12 \div 6 = 2 \qquad 12 \times \tfrac{1}{6} = 2$$
$$12 \div 4 = 3 \qquad 12 \times \tfrac{1}{4} = 3$$
$$12 \div 3 = 4 \qquad 12 \times \tfrac{1}{3} = 4$$
$$12 \div 2 = 6 \qquad 12 \times \tfrac{1}{2} = 6$$
$$12 \div 1 = 12 \qquad 12 \times \tfrac{1}{1} = 12$$
$$12 \div \tfrac{1}{2} = 24 \qquad 12 \times \tfrac{2}{1} = 24$$
$$12 \div \tfrac{1}{3} = 36 \qquad 12 \times \tfrac{3}{1} = 36$$
$$12 \div \tfrac{1}{4} = 48 \qquad 12 \times \tfrac{4}{1} = 48$$

Several of the problems required discussion for the students to agree on the answers. For example, Helene thought that the answer to $12 \div \tfrac{1}{2}$ should be 6, thinking of the problem as a multiplication problem instead of as a division problem.

Several students explained why they didn't agree. David said, "I don't think you can have six be the answer. It was the answer already." David was referring to $12 \div 2 = 6$.

Sabrina said, "It won't check. Six times one-half is three, not twelve."

Julio said, "One-half goes into twelve twenty-four times. It's twenty-four, not six." Helene then seemed convinced.

After we resolved the answers, I gave the students time to talk with their neighbors about the patterns they noticed. Then I led a class discussion for them to share their discoveries.

Juanita said, "This is kind of what we noticed before. Dividing by two is the same as multiplying by one-half, and dividing by three is the same as multiplying by one-third, and dividing by four is the same as multiplying by one-fourth."

Ally added, "They work backwards, too. Dividing by one-half is the same as multiplying by two, and dividing by one-third is the same as multiplying by three, like that."

Clark said, "When you have a whole number, you can make it into a fraction by putting it over a one. It's the same thing." This was a new discovery for Clark.

Kara said, "The answers all get bigger. They go up from two to forty-eight."

Maria said, "The numbers you divide by. . . ." Maria paused as she searched for the correct word and then said, "Oh, I mean the divisors. The divisors get smaller while the answers get bigger."

Another Set of Problems

I repeated the same experience for another set of problems, again with the same dividend for all of them. The finished lists looked like this:

$2 \div \frac{1}{6} = 12$ $2 \times 6 \ (or \ \frac{1}{6}) = 12$

$2 \div \frac{1}{4} = 8$ $2 \times 4 \ (or \ \frac{4}{1}) = 8$

$2 \div \frac{1}{3} = 6$ $2 \times 3 \ (or \ \frac{3}{1}) = 6$

$2 \div \frac{1}{2} = 4$ $2 \times 2 \ (or \ \frac{2}{1}) = 4$

$2 \div 1 = 2$ $2 \times 1 \ (or \ \frac{1}{1}) = 2$

$2 \div 2 = 1$ $2 \times \frac{1}{2} = 1$

$2 \div 4 = \frac{1}{2}$ $2 \times \frac{1}{4} = \frac{1}{2}$

The last problem in this set was the first problem I included that had a fraction for an answer. The students were perplexed.

"Would anyone like to take a chance and suggest an answer?" I asked. "Even if it's not right, we'll all learn something."

Kayla said, "OK, I'll take a chance. I think it has to be smaller than one because of the pattern. I guess one-half." I wrote $2 \div 4 = \frac{1}{2}$.

"Does this make sense?" I asked. "Talk with your neighbor." Conversation broke out. After a moment, I asked for their attention.

"It checks," Craig said. "One-half times four is two."

"I see how it checks," Maria said, "but I don't see why it makes sense."

"I think I can explain," Anita said. "You say, 'How many fours fit in two?' but the answer is you can't fit it in because it's too big. But half of it fits in, so that's why it's one-half." Maria nodded, but I wasn't sure that she was totally convinced. I didn't worry, however, as I knew that I would be providing the class with more experiences with problems like these.

After the discussion, I used the rest of the class time to give students additional practice with multiplying fractions, as I had done the day before.

EXTENSIONS

Over the next several days, present additional sets of problems and have students look for patterns. With more experience, students become more able to understand the relationships that can exist between division and multiplication problems. For example:

Dividends vary, same divisors

$6 \div \frac{1}{2} = 12$ $6 \times 2 = 12$

$5 \div \frac{1}{2} = 10$ $5 \times 2 = 10$

$4 \div \frac{1}{2} = 8$ $4 \times 2 = 8$

$3 \div \frac{1}{2} = 6$ $3 \times 2 = 6$

$2 \div \frac{1}{2} = 4$ $2 \times 2 = 4$

$1 \div \frac{1}{2} = 2$ $1 \times 2 = 2$

$\frac{1}{2} \div \frac{1}{2} = 1$ $\frac{1}{2} \times 2 = 1$

All dividends 1, divisors all fractions

$1 \div \frac{1}{2} = 2$	$1 \times 2 = 2$	$1 \div \frac{1}{6} = 6$	$1 \times 6 = 6$
$1 \div \frac{1}{3} = 3$	$1 \times 3 = 3$	$1 \div \frac{1}{8} = 8$	$1 \times 8 = 8$
$1 \div \frac{1}{4} = 4$	$1 \times 4 = 4$	$1 \div \frac{1}{12} = 12$	$1 \times 12 = 12$
$1 \div \frac{1}{5} = 5$	$1 \times 5 = 5$	$1 \div \frac{1}{16} = 16$	$1 \times 16 = 16$

Questions and Discussion

▲▲▲

▲ *I'm interested in a few choices you made in the first discussion. One was asking Craig to say his idea even though he thought it was the same as Pierre's. And another was asking Ally to say Sabrina's idea in her own words. Can you explain?*

Explaining is a way for students to clarify, cement, and/or extend their thinking, which supports their learning. It's also a way for the rest of the students to hear ideas expressed in a variety of ways. And it's a way for me to assess what students understand. Because of this, I try to give as many students as possible the chance to voice their ideas. Although Craig thought his idea was similar to Pierre's, I knew he would benefit from explaining his idea, others would hear the same or a similar idea expressed differently, and I would get insights into how Craig was thinking. And having Ally state Sabrina's idea let me know if she understood while it helped her cement the idea for herself and gave the rest of the class the chance to hear the idea again.

▲ *Several times, you pushed students to use the terminology of* **dividend, divisor,** *and* **quotient.** *Is it necessary for them to learn this terminology?*

It's important for students to hear correct mathematical terminology and be encouraged to use it, and I prefer to do this in the context of an activity or exploration, not as an isolated vocabulary lesson. A good opportunity occurred when students were describing the patterns they saw. Also, I find that writing the words on the board, or keeping an ongoing vocabulary list on which I write terminology as it comes up, helps students become familiar with words and expressions that are new to them.

▲ *In the first list of the second set, after writing $1 \div 1$, you wrote $\frac{1}{2} \div \frac{1}{2}$ and then $\frac{1}{4} \div \frac{1}{4}$. Why did you skip $\frac{1}{3} \div \frac{1}{3}$?*

I had no reason for skipping $\frac{1}{3} \div \frac{1}{3}$, and it would be fine to include it. As a matter of fact, it would be a good idea. I think that halves and fourths are typically easier for students, so including thirds would have been a wise choice for this pattern to stretch their thinking.

CHAPTER TEN
THE QUOTIENT STAYS THE SAME

Overview

This lesson continues instruction on dividing fractions. Students solve division problems and then write multiplication problems to check the answers. Then, for each division problem, they write a multiplication problem using the same first number from the division problem and that has the same answer. This requires them to figure out the missing factor. The students notice that dividing by a fraction is the same as multiplying by the "flip" of the fraction. The lesson helps prepare students for the generalization required for the standard invert-and-multiply procedure.

Materials

▲ *The Quotient Stays the Same* worksheet, 1 per student (see Blackline Masters)

Time

▲ two class periods, plus time for additional experiences

Teaching Directions

1. Write on the board:

The Quotient Stays the Same

÷ *Problem*   *Check*   × *Problem*

$4 \div \frac{1}{6} =$

2. Ask students to discuss the answer to the problem with a neighbor. Then lead a class discussion and have several students explain the answer of twenty-four. Record the answer.

3. Ask: "Who can explain how to check the answer to a division problem by multiplying?" If necessary, give a whole number example to help students remember that the product of the quotient and the divisor should be the dividend. Then ask a student for a multiplication problem to check that $4 \div \frac{1}{6} = 24$. Record $24 \times \frac{1}{6}$ and have students explain why the answer is 4. Record.

The Quotient Stays the Same

$\div$ Problem	Check	$\times$ Problem
$4 \div \frac{1}{6} = 24$	$24 \times \frac{1}{6} = 4$	

4. In the third column, write: $4 \times \underline{} = 24$. Explain: "The multiplication problem starts with the same first number as the division problem and has the same answer." Ask for the missing factor and record.

The Quotient Stays the Same

$\div$ Problem	Check	$\times$ Problem
$4 \div \frac{1}{6} = 24$	$24 \times \frac{1}{6} = 4$	$4 \times \underline{6} = 24$

5. In the first column, write the problem $4 \div \frac{1}{4} =$. Repeat Steps 2, 3, and 4 for this problem. Then do the same for two additional problems—$4 \div \frac{1}{3}$ and $4 \div \frac{1}{2}$.

The Quotient Stays the Same

$\div$ Problem	Check	$\times$ Problem
$4 \div \frac{1}{6} = 24$	$24 \times \frac{1}{6} = 4$	$4 \times \underline{6} = 24$
$4 \div \frac{1}{4} = 16$	$16 \times \frac{1}{4} = 4$	$4 \times \underline{4} = 16$
$4 \div \frac{1}{3} = 12$	$12 \times \frac{1}{3} = 4$	$4 \times \underline{3} = 12$
$4 \div \frac{1}{2} = 8$	$8 \times \frac{1}{2} = 4$	$4 \times \underline{2} = 8$

6. Discuss the chart so far. Point out that each matching multiplication problem in the third column starts with the same first number as the division problem and has the same answer. Ask the students to discuss what they notice about how the second number changes. Point out that if they represent the second factors in the multiplication problems as fractions—$\frac{6}{1}, \frac{4}{1}, \frac{3}{1}$, and $\frac{2}{1}$—they are flips of the divisors in the division problems—$\frac{1}{6}, \frac{1}{4}, \frac{1}{3}$, and $\frac{1}{2}$.

7. Repeat Steps 2, 3, and 4 for three more problems—$4 \div \frac{2}{3}, 6 \div \frac{3}{4}$, and $6 \div \frac{3}{8}$. The completed chart should look like this:

The Quotient Stays the Same

$\div$ Problem	Check	$\times$ Problem
$4 \div \frac{1}{6} = 24$	$24 \times \frac{1}{6} = 4$	$4 \times \underline{6} = 24$
$4 \div \frac{1}{4} = 16$	$16 \times \frac{1}{4} = 4$	$4 \times \underline{4} = 16$
$4 \div \frac{1}{3} = 12$	$12 \times \frac{1}{3} = 4$	$4 \times \underline{3} = 12$
$4 \div \frac{1}{2} = 8$	$8 \times \frac{1}{2} = 4$	$4 \times \underline{2} = 8$
$4 \div \frac{2}{3} = 6$	$6 \times \frac{2}{3} = 4$	$4 \times 1\frac{1}{2} = 6$
$6 \div \frac{3}{4} = 8$	$8 \times \frac{3}{4} = 6$	$6 \times 1\frac{1}{3} = 8$
$6 \div \frac{3}{8} = 16$	$16 \times \frac{3}{8} = 6$	$6 \times 2\frac{2}{3} = 16$

8. On Day 2, review the chart from the day before and then distribute *The Quotient Stays the Same* worksheets. Ask students to figure out the answer to each division problem, check it with a multiplication problem, and then write another multiplication problem with the same first number as the division problem and the same answer. It's fine for students to work together, but each student should complete his or her own worksheet. Circulate and provide assistance as needed.

The Quotient Stays the Same		
÷ **Problem**	**Check**	× **Problem**
$2 \div \frac{1}{6} =$		$2 \times$
$2 \div \frac{1}{4} =$		$2 \times$
$2 \div \frac{1}{3} =$		$2 \times$
$2 \div \frac{1}{2} =$		$2 \times$
$2 \div 1 =$		$2 \times$
$2 \div 2 =$		$2 \times$
$2 \div 4 =$		$2 \times$
$2 \div \frac{2}{3} =$		
$3 \div \frac{3}{4} =$		
$3 \div \frac{3}{8} =$		
$3 \div 1\frac{1}{2} =$		

Teaching Notes

The students in this class had experienced the three previous lessons related to division of fractions, in Chapters 7, 8, and 9. These are valuable prerequisites for this lesson.

This chapter specifically builds on the previous lesson, in which students explored patterns in sets of division and multiplication problems. This lesson, however, focuses on helping students understand that when they divide by a fraction, they get the same answer if they multiply by the flip of the fraction; for example, $4 \div \frac{1}{3} = 12$ and $4 \times 3 = 12$, and since 3 can also be represented as $\frac{3}{1}$, $\frac{1}{3}$ and $\frac{3}{1}$ are flips of each other. The correct mathematical term for the flip of a fraction is *reciprocal* or *multiplicative inverse*. The product of a number and its reciprocal, for example, $\frac{1}{3} \times 3$, is always 1. (Try this for a few other examples: $\frac{1}{2} \times \frac{2}{1} = 1$; $\frac{3}{4} \times \frac{4}{3} = \frac{12}{12}$ or 1; and so on.) The only number that doesn't have a reciprocal is the number 0, because you can't multiply 0 times any other number and get an answer of 1. Reciprocals are the key to why the standard procedure of inverting and multiplying works for solving division problems with fractions.

While I encourage students to notice that you get the same answer to a division problem when you multiply by the flip of the fraction, I don't point out the relationship that a fraction times its flip always produces a product of one. In this lesson, I keep the focus on having students find answers by reasoning and looking for patterns. It's best to talk about the relationship between a number and its flip, and then introduce the correct mathematical terminology of *reciprocal* and *multiplicative inverse* later when the students have a firm base of understanding.

The Lesson

▲▲▲

DAY 1

To begin the lesson, I wrote on the board:

The Quotient Stays the Same

÷ *Problem*   *Check*   × *Problem*

$4 \div \frac{1}{6} =$

I said to the students, "Please think quietly and figure out the answer to this problem. That's four divided by one-sixth, or you can think about how many one-sixths fit into four." As the students sat, I drew four circles on the board, divided them each into sixths, and shaded a one-sixth section on the first circle. I did this as an assist to students who needed help and also to give all of them time to think.

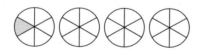

I then turned and said to the class, "Talk with your neighbor about what you think the answer is." The room got noisy. After a moment, most of the students had raised their hands. I called the class to attention and called on Anita.

"It's twenty-four," she said.

"Can you explain how you figured?" I asked.

Anita said, "I know that there are six sixths in one whole, so in four wholes, there will be twenty-four sixths because four times six is twenty-four." I recorded

on the board:

$\frac{6}{6} = 1$

$6 \times 4 = 24$

Brendan had another way to explain. "You can just count them up," he said, pointing to the circles I had drawn on the board. "There are six in each circle, so that's twenty-four, like Anita said."

I recorded the answer on the board and then said, "Who can explain how to check the answer to a division problem by multiplying?"

Maria explained, "You multiply the answer by what you divided by and then you see if you get the starting number."

I began to paraphrase Maria's explanation using the correct terminology, "So you multiply the quotient by the divisor—"

Maria interrupted me and said, "Oh yeah. You multiply the quotient by the divisor and you should get the dividend."

"Yes, that's how we check. So who can tell the problem I should write in the next column?" I asked, pointing to where I had written *Check* on the board.

Ally said, "Twenty-four times one-sixth." I added this to what I had already recorded on the board:

The Quotient Stays the Same

÷ *Problem*   *Check*   × *Problem*

$4 \div \frac{1}{6} = 24$ $24 \times \frac{1}{6} =$

"Does this check?" I asked. "How much is twenty-four times one-sixth? Talk to your neighbor about this." After a moment, I asked for the students' attention and called on Juanita.

Juanita said, "It's four. If you add one-sixth twenty-four times, you have twenty-four–sixths, and that's four." I wrote on the board:

$24 \times \frac{1}{6} = \frac{24}{6} = 4$

"So it checks," Sabrina added.

"How do you know it checks?" I asked.

Sabrina said, "Because the answer is four, and that's the number we divided into . . . I mean, that's the dividend. The fours match, so our answer is right." I completed the problem on the board and then wrote a problem in the third column:

The Quotient Stays the Same

÷ Problem	Check	× Problem
$4 \div \frac{1}{6} = 24$	$24 \times \frac{1}{6} = 4$	$4 \times \_\_ = 24$

I explained, "Now comes the part that relates to the title on the board—*The Quotient Stays the Same*. In the third column, I wrote a multiplication problem that started with four, the same first number as in the division problem. And the answer to this multiplication problem has to be the same as the answer we got for the division problem, the quotient of twenty-four. What's the missing factor? Four times what number gives twenty-four?" The answer seemed obvious to the students.

"Let's say the factor together in a whisper voice," I said.

"Six," they said. I recorded the factor and then wrote another problem in the first column.

The Quotient Stays the Same

÷ Problem	Check	× Problem
$4 \div \frac{1}{6} = 24$	$24 \times \frac{1}{6} = 4$	$4 \times \underline{6} = 24$
$4 \div \frac{1}{4} =$		

Hands flew up, but I asked the students to think about the problem for a moment while I redrew the circles to show fourths instead of sixths. Again, this gave those who didn't think as quickly some time to consider the problem.

Practically every student had a hand raised. I called on Clark. "It's sixteen," he said. "You can see it from your drawing. There are sixteen one-fourths in the four circles." I recorded the answer.

Celia then explained how to check the answer. "You write sixteen times one-fourth, and that's four. It's easy because one-fourth of sixteen is four." I recorded the check problem and then wrote the corresponding problem in the third column. The students easily identified the missing factor of four:

The Quotient Stays the Same

÷ Problem	Check	× Problem
$4 \div \frac{1}{6} = 24$	$24 \times \frac{1}{6} = 4$	$4 \times \underline{6} = 24$
$4 \div \frac{1}{4} = 16$	$16 \times \frac{1}{4} = 4$	$4 \times \underline{4} = 16$

I again explained the purpose of the problems in the third column. "Remember, we're trying to write a multiplication problem that has the same answer as the division problem and the same first number. Then we figure out the missing number." I wrote the next problem on the board:

The Quotient Stays the Same

÷ Problem	Check	× Problem
$4 \div \frac{1}{6} = 24$	$24 \times \frac{1}{6} = 4$	$4 \times \underline{6} = 24$
$4 \div \frac{1}{4} = 16$	$16 \times \frac{1}{4} = 4$	$4 \times \underline{4} = 16$
$4 \div \frac{1}{3} =$		

I repeated the procedure I had used before, asking the students to think quietly while I drew four circles on the board, divided each into thirds, and shaded in one of the thirds on the first circle. Then I had the students check their answers with their neighbors. Each time a student gave an answer, I also asked for an explanation and then checked to see if someone had a different way to explain. For the third column, I now had students talk with their neighbors about what the corresponding multiplication problem would be and then called on a volunteer to write it on the chart. Then we discussed the missing factor. After a few more problems, the chart looked like this:

The Quotient Stays the Same

÷ Problem	Check	× Problem
$4 \div \frac{1}{6} = 24$	$24 \times \frac{1}{6} = 4$	$4 \times \underline{6} = 24$
$4 \div \frac{1}{4} = 16$	$16 \times \frac{1}{4} = 4$	$4 \times \underline{4} = 16$
$4 \div \frac{1}{3} = 12$	$12 \times \frac{1}{3} = 4$	$4 \times \underline{3} = 12$
$4 \div \frac{1}{2} = 8$	$8 \times \frac{1}{2} = 4$	$4 \times \underline{2} = 8$

Looking for Patterns

I then directed the students' attention to the division and multiplication problems. I said, "Each matching multiplication problem starts with the same number as the division problem and, as the title says, the answer stays the same. But the division changes to multiplication, and the second number changes. What do you notice about this?"

The students had begun to think about this relationship when we looked for patterns in other sets of problems (see Chapter 9), and most of them were interested in sharing their ideas.

"The division problems have fractions and the multiplication problems don't," Sabrina said.

"I see something else," Kayla said. "The denominator of the fractions in the division problems is the whole number in the multiplication problems."

"It's like you throw away the one," Craig said.

No other student had an idea, so I said, "Here's another idea. How can we write the whole number factors from the multiplication problems as fractions?"

"I don't get what you mean," Damien said.

I explained, "Well, in the first multiplication problem, you figured that the missing factor was six. And six is the same as six wholes. How could I write six wholes as a fraction?"

Damien said, "Oh, I get it. You mean like a six over a one?" I nodded.

"Oh, look!" Kara said. "That's like the one-sixth upside down."

"It's flipped," Hassan added.

"What's flipped?" I asked Hassan.

"The one-sixth fraction. You flip it and switch the top and bottom numbers," he said.

"Does the same pattern hold for all of the problems?" I then asked. "Are the missing factors in the multiplication problems the flip of the divisors in the division problems?" Now all of the students saw the pattern and I recorded on the board:

Divisor	Flipped Fraction
$\frac{1}{6}$	$\frac{6}{1} = 6$
$\frac{1}{4}$	$\frac{4}{1} = 4$
$\frac{1}{3}$	$\frac{3}{1} = 3$
$\frac{1}{2}$	$\frac{2}{1} = 2$

A New Problem—$4 \div \frac{2}{3}$

"Here's another problem," I said, writing a new problem on the board.

The Quotient Stays the Same

÷ Problem	Check	× Problem
$4 \div \frac{1}{6} = 24$	$24 \times \frac{1}{6} = 4$	$4 \times \underline{6} = 24$
$4 \div \frac{1}{4} = 16$	$16 \times \frac{1}{4} = 4$	$4 \times \underline{4} = 16$
$4 \div \frac{1}{3} = 12$	$12 \times \frac{1}{3} = 4$	$4 \times \underline{3} = 12$
$4 \div \frac{1}{2} = 8$	$8 \times \frac{1}{2} = 4$	$4 \times \underline{2} = 8$
$4 \div \frac{2}{3} =$		

As I did before, I asked the students to think on their own as I drew on the board four circles, divided each into thirds, and shaded in two-thirds on the first circle.

Then I asked the students to check their ideas with their neighbors and raise their hands if they were willing to report. I was pleased to see Eddie's hand up. He was a quiet boy who rarely volunteered, and I called on him.

"It's six," he said. "I counted up the one-thirds and there are twelve of them. So that means that there are only six two-thirds." I wrote on the board:

$4 \div \frac{1}{3} = 12$

$4 \div \frac{2}{3} = 6$

"You can color in the two-thirds and see that there are six of them," Helene said. "Can I come up and show?" I agreed. Helene came up and shaded in two-thirds of each of the other circles.

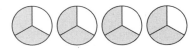

Then she explained, "So this shows four two-thirds, but there still are the extra spaces. And you can put these two together to make another two-thirds." Helene pointed to the unshaded thirds in the first two circles and drew a line to link them. "And you can do the same for the other one-thirds. So that shows six two-thirds."

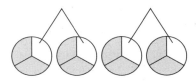

I recorded the answer, and then David came up and recorded the multiplication problem to check it:

The Quotient Stays the Same

÷ Problem	Check	× Problem
$4 \div \frac{1}{6} = 24$	$24 \times \frac{1}{6} = 4$	$4 \times \underline{6} = 24$
$4 \div \frac{1}{4} = 16$	$16 \times \frac{1}{4} = 4$	$4 \times \underline{4} = 16$
$4 \div \frac{1}{3} = 12$	$12 \times \frac{1}{3} = 4$	$4 \times \underline{3} = 12$
$4 \div \frac{1}{2} = 8$	$8 \times \frac{1}{2} = 4$	$4 \times \underline{2} = 8$
$4 \div \frac{2}{3} = 6$	$6 \times \frac{2}{3} = 4$	

David explained, "I added two-thirds and two-thirds and two-thirds, and that makes two complete circles, so you double that and you get all four circles."

Julio had another way to explain. He said, "Six times two-thirds is twelve-thirds, and twelve-thirds is the same as four."

Kayla explained, "One-third of six is two, so two-thirds is twice as much, and that's four."

"What problem should we write in the third column?" I then asked. Sachi came up, wrote $4 \times \underline{} = 6$, and then sat down.

"That's a weird problem," Brendan said.

"Let's try to think about it together," I said. "What if we tried two? What is four times two?"

"It's eight. That's too big," Francis said. I recorded on the board:

$4 \times 2 = 8$ *Too big*

4×1

"Well, let's go down to one," I suggested.

"Too small," several students said.

"Does it have to be a fraction?" Anita asked.

"Maybe it's one-half," Sabrina said. I recorded this suggestion.

$4 \times 2 = 8$ *Too big*

$4 \times 1 = 4$ *Too small*

$4 \times \frac{1}{2}$

"It's way too small—that's only two. Half of four is two," Julio said. I recorded:

$4 \times 2 = 8$ *Too big*

$4 \times 1 = 4$ *Too small*

$4 \times \frac{1}{2} = 2$ *Too small*

Maggie said, "I've got it. At least, I think so. It has to be in between one and two, so maybe it's one and a half. Oh, it works. Four times one is four and four times one-half is two." I wrote on the board, completing Maggie's idea.

$4 \times 1\frac{1}{2}$

$4 \times 1 = 4$

$4 \times \frac{1}{2} = 2$

$4 + 2 = 6$

Brendan said, "That's right. One and one-half two times is three, and three plus three is six. So Maggie is right." I wrote the answer on the chart:

The Quotient Stays the Same

÷ Problem	Check	× Problem
$4 \div \frac{1}{6} = 24$	$24 \times \frac{1}{6} = 4$	$4 \times \underline{6} = 24$
$4 \div \frac{1}{4} = 16$	$16 \times \frac{1}{4} = 4$	$4 \times \underline{4} = 16$
$4 \div \frac{1}{3} = 12$	$12 \times \frac{1}{3} = 4$	$4 \times \underline{3} = 12$
$4 \div \frac{1}{2} = 8$	$8 \times \frac{1}{2} = 4$	$4 \times \underline{2} = 8$
$4 \div \frac{2}{3} = 6$	$6 \times \frac{2}{3} = 4$	$4 \times \underline{1\frac{1}{2}} = 6$

I then said to the class, "We get the same answer by doing the problem four divided by two-thirds and the problem four times one and one-half. Both answers are six. Is dividing by two-thirds the same as multiplying by one and one-half?"

"It seems so," Julio responded. "But I don't see why."

Another Problem—$6 \div \frac{3}{4}$

I said, "Well, let's try another problem and see what we can figure out." I added another problem to the chart.

The Quotient Stays the Same

÷ Problem	Check	× Problem
$4 \div \frac{1}{6} = 24$	$24 \times \frac{1}{6} = 4$	$4 \times \underline{6} = 24$
$4 \div \frac{1}{4} = 16$	$16 \times \frac{1}{4} = 4$	$4 \times \underline{4} = 16$
$4 \div \frac{1}{3} = 12$	$12 \times \frac{1}{3} = 4$	$4 \times \underline{3} = 12$
$4 \div \frac{1}{2} = 8$	$8 \times \frac{1}{2} = 4$	$4 \times \underline{2} = 8$
$4 \div \frac{2}{3} = 6$	$6 \times \frac{2}{3} = 4$	$4 \times \underline{1\frac{1}{2}} = 6$
$6 \div \frac{3}{4} =$		

I followed the same procedure, and the students figured out the answer of eight and were able to check it. Drawing the circles seemed to help show that there were eight three-fourths in six circles.

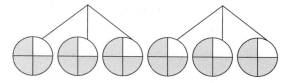

The Quotient Stays the Same

÷ Problem	Check	× Problem
$4 \div \frac{1}{6} = 24$	$24 \times \frac{1}{6} = 4$	$4 \times \underline{6} = 24$
$4 \div \frac{1}{4} = 16$	$16 \times \frac{1}{4} = 4$	$4 \times \underline{4} = 16$
$4 \div \frac{1}{3} = 12$	$12 \times \frac{1}{3} = 4$	$4 \times \underline{3} = 12$
$4 \div \frac{1}{2} = 8$	$8 \times \frac{1}{2} = 4$	$4 \times \underline{2} = 8$
$4 \div \frac{2}{3} = 6$	$6 \times \frac{2}{3} = 4$	$4 \times \underline{1\frac{1}{2}} = 6$
$6 \div \frac{3}{4} = 8$	$8 \times \frac{3}{4} = 6$	$6 \times \underline{} = 8$

Figuring out the missing factor in the corresponding problem was hard for most of the students. We did it by trial and error:

$6 \times 2 = 12$	*Too big*
$6 \times 1 = 6$	*Too small*
$6 \times 1\frac{1}{2} = 9$	*Too big*
$6 \times 1\frac{1}{3} = 8$	

Kayla explained, "It's six times one and one-third. Six times one is six, and one-third of six is two more, so it's eight." I recorded:

$6 \times 1\frac{1}{3}$

$6 \times 1 = 6$

$6 \times \frac{1}{3} = 2$

$6 + 2 = 8$

I recorded this answer on the chart and said to the students, "So it seems that dividing six by three-fourths gave the same answer as multiplying six by one and one-third." I then directed the students to the list I had started of flipped fractions and added the fractions that were divisors in the last two problems—$\frac{2}{3}$ and $\frac{3}{4}$—and the same fractions flipped.

Divisor	Flipped Fraction
$\frac{1}{6}$	$\frac{6}{1} = 6$
$\frac{1}{4}$	$\frac{4}{1} = 4$
$\frac{1}{3}$	$\frac{3}{1} = 3$
$\frac{1}{2}$	$\frac{2}{1} = 2$
$\frac{2}{3}$	$\frac{3}{2}$
$\frac{3}{4}$	$\frac{4}{3}$

Celia got very excited. "Look, the flip still works. All you have to do is change those fractions to mixed numbers." She came up and recorded:

Divisor	Flipped Fraction
$\frac{1}{6}$	$\frac{6}{1} = 6$
$\frac{1}{4}$	$\frac{4}{1} = 4$
$\frac{1}{3}$	$\frac{3}{1} = 3$
$\frac{1}{2}$	$\frac{2}{1} = 2$
$\frac{2}{3}$	$\frac{3}{2} = 1\frac{1}{2}$
$\frac{3}{4}$	$\frac{4}{3} = 1\frac{1}{3}$

Others then saw what Celia had noticed and many had comments to make. "One and one-half is another way to show three-halves."

"Four-thirds is the same as one and one-third."

I was interested in helping students make the generalization that dividing by a fraction produces the same answer as multiplying by its flip, but I knew that it was too soon for many of the students to draw this conclusion or understand the idea. So we did one more problem together, and with this, I ended the class.

The Quotient Stays the Same

÷ Problem	Check	× Problem
$4 \div \frac{1}{6} = 24$	$24 \times \frac{1}{6} = 4$	$4 \times \underline{6} = 24$
$4 \div \frac{1}{4} = 16$	$16 \times \frac{1}{4} = 4$	$4 \times \underline{4} = 16$
$4 \div \frac{1}{3} = 12$	$12 \times \frac{1}{3} = 4$	$4 \times \underline{3} = 12$
$4 \div \frac{1}{2} = 8$	$8 \times \frac{1}{2} = 4$	$4 \times \underline{2} = 8$
$4 \div \frac{2}{3} = 6$	$6 \times \frac{2}{3} = 4$	$4 \times 1\frac{1}{2} = 6$
$6 \div \frac{3}{4} = 8$	$8 \times \frac{3}{4} = 6$	$6 \times 1\frac{1}{3} = 8$
$6 \div \frac{3}{8} = 16$	$16 \times \frac{3}{8} = 6$	$6 \times 2\frac{2}{3} = 16$

I left the chart on the board as a reference for the next day's lesson.

DAY 2

My plan for this day was to have the students work on an assignment so that I could circulate, see how students were thinking, and offer help where needed. To begin class, I reviewed the chart we had completed. Then I showed the students the worksheet I had prepared.

The Quotient Stays the Same		
÷ Problem	Check	× Problem
$2 \div \frac{1}{6} =$		$2 \times$
$2 \div \frac{1}{4} =$		$2 \times$
$2 \div \frac{1}{3} =$		$2 \times$
$2 \div \frac{1}{2} =$		$2 \times$
$2 \div 1 =$		$2 \times$
$2 \div 2 =$		$2 \times$
$2 \div 4 =$		$2 \times$
$2 \div \frac{2}{3} =$		
$3 \div \frac{3}{4} =$		
$3 \div \frac{3}{8} =$		
$3 \div 1\frac{1}{2} =$		

"These problems are similar to the ones we worked on together yesterday," I explained. "For each problem that I wrote on the worksheet, find the answer and write a multiplication problem to check your answer. Then write a multiplication problem in the third column that starts with the same number as the division problem and has the same answer, just as we did yesterday. There are seven problems with two as the dividend, and then four others that are kind of a mix."

Josh had a question. "Do we do the check and the multiplication problem for the last four problems, too?"

"Yes," I responded.

Anita asked, "Should we show our work?"

I replied, "If you make any sketches or write down any numbers, I'd like to see them. That helps me understand how you were thinking about the problems."

"Can we do that on a separate paper?" Hassan asked.

"Yes," I answered.

"Do we have to explain the answers if we do them in our heads?" Maria asked.

"No," I replied.

"Can we work together?" Sabrina asked.

"Yes, that's fine," I replied. "But you have to do your own paper, and you have to understand all that you write on it."

No one else had a question. I distributed the worksheets and the students began to work.

Observing the Students

The first set of problems was fairly easy for the students to solve, especially since the information from the previous day was posted for their reference. As typically occurs when students get started on an assignment, there was a flurry of questions, most of which were calls for confirmation. For example, Annie called me over and asked, about the first problem ($2 \div \frac{1}{6}$), "Is my answer right?" She had written the correct answer of 12.

"Tell me what the problem is asking," I said.

"It's two divided by one-sixth," Annie said.

"Can you tell what you're supposed to be finding out?" I asked.

"How many one-sixths go into two," Annie said and then added, "Oh, I'm right. That's easy."

"How would you check that you're right?" I asked.

"I could draw a picture," Annie said. She took another piece of paper, drew two circles, and divided them both into sixths. "I'm right. See, there are six one-sixth pieces in the two circles."

"So now you have to write a multiplication problem to check the answer," I said.

"OK," Annie replied and continued working. For the second problem, she also drew a sketch. But then she didn't make any

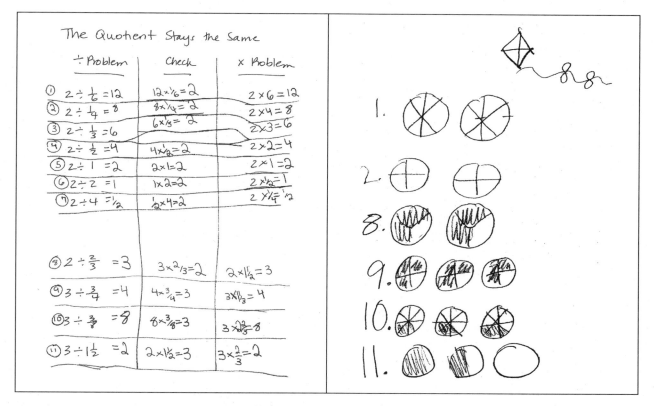

▲▲▲▲▲▲**Figure 10–1** *Annie made sketches for the first two problems and then didn't need to make any more until the last four problems.*

drawings until she reached the eighth problem. When I asked her later why she had stopped drawing, she said, "They were easy and I didn't need to." (See Figure 10–1.)

The problem $2 \div 4$ posed a problem for many of the students. I had purposely put this challenge on the worksheet to see what students would do. A common error was to write $2 \div 4 = 2$. But then when students wrote the problem to check their work, $2 \times 4 = 8$, they realized that they had made an error. For some, this was enough for them to revisit the problem. When David made this discovery, he then figured that the correct answer had to be $\frac{1}{2}$. He said to me, "I know that one-half times four is two, so it has to be right. And then it makes sense for the multiplication problem, because if you flip four, you get one-fourth." David was also relying on the flip pattern we had discussed.

Maria, however, wasn't satisfied with reasoning the way David did. "I see why the answer should be one-half, but it doesn't make sense. You can't fit four into two."

Maria's partner, Ally, said, "I think it makes sense. You can't fit all of four into two, but you can fit half of four into two. That's why it's one-half." This seemed to satisfy Maria. I could see from looking at their papers later whether students had first thought that the answer was two and then erased it to make the correction.

Hassan also struggled with the same problem, but he justified his answer in a different way. "First I thought it was two," he said, "but then I looked at the other answers. They were all getting smaller, so I knew that two wasn't right."

Celia said, "It couldn't be right because it was already the answer to two divided by one."

This reason didn't make sense to Hassan. "Lots of times you get the same answer to different problems," he said.

Celia persisted, "But you can't divide two by different numbers and get the same answer." Hassan shrugged, not able to understand Celia's thinking.

Gloria used a method she had figured out for three of the last four problems. For the problem $2 \div \frac{2}{3}$, for example, she figured the correct answer of 3 and wrote: $2 \times 3 = 6$ and $\frac{1}{2}$ of $6 = 3$.

I asked her, "When you wrote 'two times three equals six,' which two in the problem did you use?"

"The whole number two," she answered quickly. "See, my method works for all of them." She had also followed the same procedure for the next two problems. (See Figure 10–2.) Gloria's method is the same as

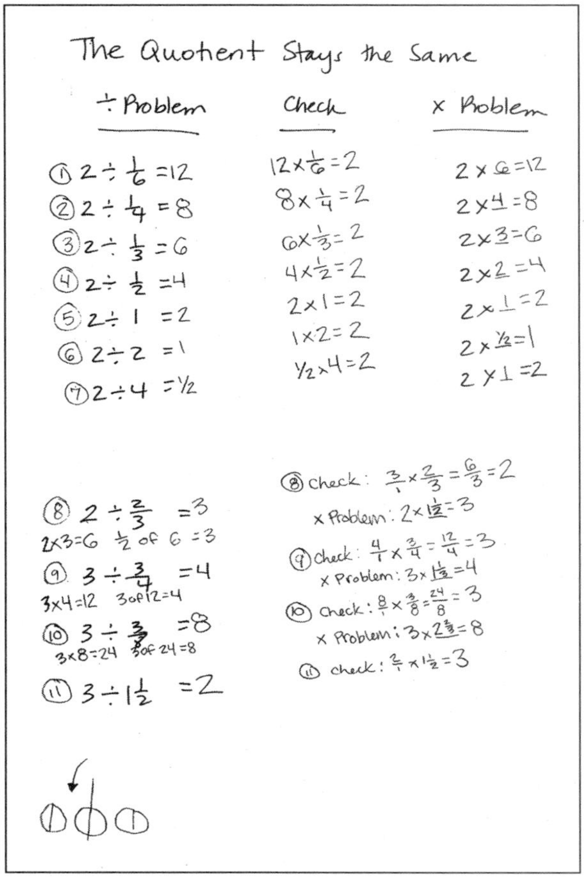

▲▲▲▲▲▲Figure 10–2 *Gloria showed the method she figured out for solving three of the last four problems, a version of the standard invert-and-multiply method. For the last problem, however, she made a sketch.*

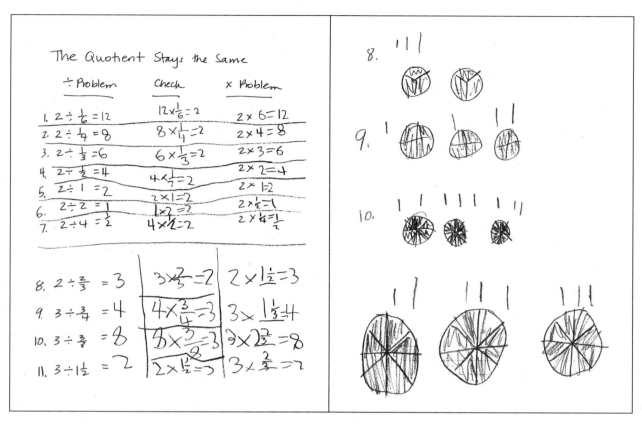

The Quotient Stays the Same

÷ Problem	Check	× Problem
1. $2 \div \frac{1}{6} = 12$	$12 \times \frac{1}{6} = 2$	$2 \times 6 = 12$
2. $2 \div \frac{1}{4} = 8$	$8 \times \frac{1}{4} = 2$	$2 \times 4 = 8$
3. $2 \div \frac{1}{3} = 6$	$6 \times \frac{1}{3} = 2$	$2 \times 3 = 6$
4. $2 \div \frac{1}{2} = 4$	$4 \times \frac{1}{2} = 2$	$2 \times 2 = 4$
5. $2 \div 1 = 2$	$2 \times 1 = 2$	$2 \times 1 = 2$
6. $2 \div 2 = 1$	$1 \times 2 = 2$	$2 \times \frac{1}{2} = 1$
7. $2 \div 4 = \frac{1}{2}$	$4 \times \frac{1}{2} = 2$	$2 \times \frac{1}{4} = \frac{1}{2}$

8. $2 \div \frac{2}{3} = 3$	$3 \times \frac{2}{3} = 2$	$2 \times 1\frac{1}{2} = 3$	
9. $3 \div \frac{3}{4} = 4$	$4 \times \frac{3}{4} = 3$	$3 \times 1\frac{1}{3} = 4$	
10. $3 \div \frac{3}{8} = 8$	$8 \times \frac{3}{8} = 3$	$3 \times 2\frac{2}{3} = 8$	
11. $3 \div 1\frac{1}{2} = 2$	$2 \times 1\frac{1}{2} = 3$	$3 \times \frac{2}{3} = 2$	

▲▲▲▲▲▲**Figure 10–3** *Brendan made sketches for the last four problems, using tally marks to keep track of how many times the divisor went into the dividend.*

the traditional method of inverting and multiplying, except that she didn't invert. If she had, the problem would have been changed to $2 \times \frac{3}{2}$, which can also be written as $\frac{2}{1} \times \frac{3}{2}$. This new problem can be solved by multiplying the numerators, 2×3, then multiplying the denominators, 1×2, and finally dividing 6 by 2. For the last problem, however, because the divisor was a mixed number, Gloria's method fell apart for her, and she solved it by making a sketch.

The assignment was accessible to the students and appropriate for them. In a brief class discussion at the end of class, Juanita said, "I liked doing it. It gave me a lot of practice that will help me remember what to do."

Pierre said, "I liked the harder ones at the end."

Kara said, "At first I thought it was really, really hard. But it wasn't."

Figures 10–3 and 10–4 show two more students' work on this assignment.

EXTENSIONS

Provide students experiences with a few similar problems on each of the next several days. Be sure to choose problems for which the answers are whole numbers, for example:

$3 \div \frac{1}{3}$

$1\frac{1}{2} \div \frac{1}{8}$

$9 \div 1\frac{1}{2}$

$1 \div \frac{1}{12}$

$2\frac{1}{2} \div \frac{1}{4}$

$2\frac{1}{4} \div \frac{3}{4}$

$8 \div \frac{2}{3}$

$3 \div \frac{3}{8}$

$1 \div \frac{1}{6}$

$2\frac{1}{4} \div \frac{1}{8}$

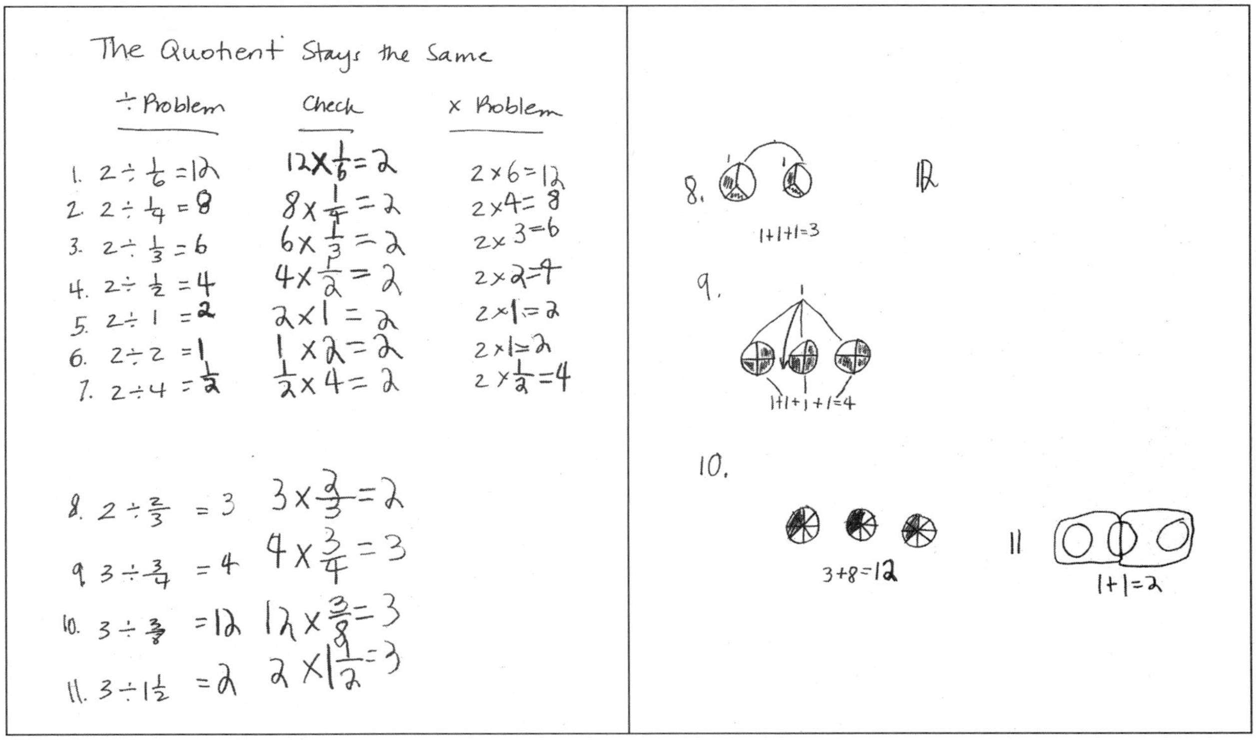

The Quotient Stays the Same

÷ Problem	Check	x Problem
1. $2 \div \frac{1}{6} = 12$	$12 \times \frac{1}{6} = 2$	$2 \times 6 = 12$
2. $2 \div \frac{1}{4} = 8$	$8 \times \frac{1}{4} = 2$	$2 \times 4 = 8$
3. $2 \div \frac{1}{3} = 6$	$6 \times \frac{1}{3} = 2$	$2 \times 3 = 6$
4. $2 \div \frac{1}{2} = 4$	$4 \times \frac{1}{2} = 2$	$2 \times 2 = 4$
5. $2 \div 1 = 2$	$2 \times 1 = 2$	$2 \times 1 = 2$
6. $2 \div 2 = 1$	$1 \times 2 = 2$	$2 \times 1 = 2$
7. $2 \div 4 = \frac{1}{2}$	$\frac{1}{2} \times 4 = 2$	$2 \times \frac{1}{2} = 4$

8. $2 \div \frac{2}{3} = 3$ $3 \times \frac{2}{3} = 2$

9. $3 \div \frac{3}{4} = 4$ $4 \times \frac{3}{4} = 3$

10. $3 \div \frac{3}{8} = 12$ $12 \times \frac{3}{8} = 3$

11. $3 \div 1\frac{1}{2} = 2$ $2 \times 1\frac{1}{2} = 3$

8. $1+1+1 = 3$

9. $1+1+1+1 = 4$

10. $3+8 = 12$

11. $1+1 = 2$

▲▲▲▲▲▲Figure 10–4 *As he typically did, Paul worked slowly on the assignment and didn't have time to write the multiplication problems for the last four problems. Also, his answer for Problem 10 was incorrect.*

Questions and Discussion

▲▲

▲ *What do you do when a student learns the invert-and-multiply method from a parent? Doesn't this undermine trying to build their understanding?*

This happens fairly regularly in classes, especially when a student asks for help at home on a homework assignment. When students offer a method that a parent showed them, I always acknowledge the contribution, and I never tell a student that "we don't do it that way." Rather, I prefer to tell them that my goal is for them to have a toolbox of strategies for solving any problem and that their parent's method is a good addition to their toolbox. I also tell them that I learned the same method and that I will be helping them understand why it works. When the time is appropriate, I do so.

▲ *How do you know when students are ready to learn the standard algorithm? And how do you deal with some students being ready before others?*

I feel that students are ready when they can solve problems by reasoning, ideally in more than one way. Of course, not all students develop the same proficiency at the same time. Some students will always need more time. So the decision about when to add more onto what they're learning is part of the art of teaching. My goal is to keep the students who learn more quickly challenged while giving others the chance to have the practice they need. I

The Quotient Stays the Same   109

sometimes do this by giving class assignments for which I list eight to ten problems on the board in order from easiest to most complex and tell the students to solve any five of them. This allows students to choose problems that match their own level. Some will solve all of them, some will solve the first five, some will solve a mix. The choices they make help me assess how they perceive their own comfort levels.

CHAPTER ELEVEN
DIVISION WITH REMAINDERS

Overview

Dividing fractions when the divisor is larger than the dividend or when the divisor doesn't go into the dividend an even number of times poses difficulties for students. Examples of such problems include $\frac{2}{3} \div \frac{1}{2}$ and $\frac{1}{2} \div \frac{2}{3}$. When students do long division with whole numbers, they express the remainder either as a whole number or as a fraction of the divisor. However, deciding how to handle the remainders with the extra complication of fractions presents a challenge. This lesson suggests a way to help students face this challenge by relying on reasoning.

Materials

▲ fraction kit pieces, as discussed and shown in the "Teaching Notes" section

Time

▲ one class period

Teaching Directions

1. Write on the board: $1 \div \frac{1}{2} =$.

2. Ask students to talk with a neighbor about the problem. Then discuss with the class why the answer of two makes sense. (One-half fits into one two times.)

3. Show how to check the answer by multiplying:

$1 \div \frac{1}{2} = 2$ $\qquad$ $2 \times \frac{1}{2} = 1$

4. Model the problem with fraction kit pieces or a sketch, as shown:

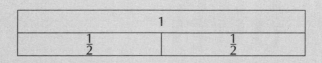

5. Underneath the problem, write another:

$1 \div \frac{1}{2} = 2$ $2 \times \frac{1}{2} = 1$

$\frac{1}{2} \div \frac{1}{2} =$

6. Repeat Steps 2 through 4.

7. Now repeat Steps 2 through 4 for two more problems:

$1 \div \frac{1}{2} = 2$ $2 \times \frac{1}{2} = 1$

$\frac{1}{2} \div \frac{1}{2} = 1$ $1 \times \frac{1}{2} = \frac{1}{2}$

$\frac{1}{4} \div \frac{1}{2} = \frac{1}{2}$ $\frac{1}{2} \times \frac{1}{2} = \frac{1}{4}$

$\frac{3}{4} \div \frac{1}{2} = 1\frac{1}{2}$ $1\frac{1}{2} \times \frac{1}{2} = \frac{3}{4}$

8. Present one more problem, $\frac{2}{3} \div \frac{1}{2}$, writing it underneath the others. This problem typically is more difficult for students. Discuss several ways to solve it. (See the "Teaching Notes" section for elaboration about this.) Present the traditional invert-and-multiply method as one strategy that students can use.

9. Give the students five problems to solve, marking the last one with an asterisk to indicate that it's optional for students who work quickly. Ask the students to solve the problems, check them by multiplying, and then choose one problem and write an explanation about how they solved it.

     1. $\frac{1}{2} \div \frac{1}{4}$

     2. $\frac{1}{8} \div \frac{1}{4}$

     3. $\frac{3}{8} \div \frac{1}{4}$

     4. $\frac{5}{8} \div \frac{1}{4}$

     * $\frac{1}{3} \div \frac{1}{4}$

10. As students work, circulate and help as needed. Also, write two more optional problems on the board:

     * * $\frac{2}{3} \div \frac{1}{4}$

     * * * $\frac{5}{8} \div \frac{1}{2}$

Teaching Notes

Up until this lesson, practically all of the problems I had chosen for the students had whole number answers. I was purposely skirting the issue of what happens when you divide fractions and have a remainder. For example, to solve $1 \div \frac{1}{2}$, students ask, "How many halves fit in one whole?" They conclude fairly easily that the answer is 2 because two halves make one whole. To solve $\frac{1}{2} \div \frac{1}{2}$, students ask,

"How many halves fit in one-half?" Again, they conclude fairly easily that the answer is 1. Solving $\frac{1}{4} \div \frac{1}{2}$ seems more difficult at first glance, but students generally agree that one-half of a half fits into one-fourth and, therefore, the answer is $\frac{1}{2}$. Similarly, they can reason that the answer to $\frac{3}{4} \div \frac{1}{2}$ is $1\frac{1}{2}$, because one-half goes into three-fourths one and a half times. We can check all of these answers by multiplying:

$$1 \div \tfrac{1}{2} = 2 \qquad\qquad 2 \times \tfrac{1}{2} = 1$$
$$\tfrac{1}{2} \div \tfrac{1}{2} = 1 \qquad\qquad 1 \times \tfrac{1}{2} = \tfrac{1}{2}$$
$$\tfrac{1}{4} \div \tfrac{1}{2} = \tfrac{1}{2} \qquad\qquad \tfrac{1}{2} \times \tfrac{1}{2} = \tfrac{1}{4}$$
$$\tfrac{3}{4} \div \tfrac{1}{2} = 1\tfrac{1}{2} \qquad\qquad 1\tfrac{1}{2} \times \tfrac{1}{2} = \tfrac{3}{4}$$

However, it's more difficult to reason about other problems. For example, think about $\frac{2}{3} \div \frac{1}{2}$. We can ask, "How many one-halves fit into two-thirds?" And we can reason that one one-half fits. But then what do we do with the extra amount in the two-thirds that is left over? How much is that? How do we represent the answer?

Applying what I learned in school about inverting and multiplying, I can find the answer by changing the problem to $\frac{2}{3} \times \frac{2}{1}$, which gives the answer of $\frac{4}{3}$ or $1\frac{1}{3}$. However, the goal of this lesson is to help students make sense of problems like these instead of following a rule or algorithm. Once they have a foundation of understanding, then a rule is an appropriate convenience that makes computing more efficient. To build the foundation, students must have time and experience to think and reason about problems like these.

But why does the answer of one and one-third make sense? First think about what the answer means. One interpretation is: One-half fits into two-thirds one and one-third times. Another way to state this is: One-half fits into two-thirds one time, and there is an amount left over in the two-thirds that is equal to one-third of one-half. A picture can help.

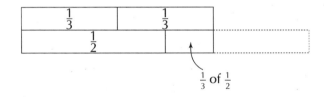

Another way to make sense of the answer is to place the problem in a context so that we can connect the numbers to a concrete reality and, therefore, verify the answer. The context of cutting ribbon works well. For example, suppose we have a length of ribbon and we want to know how many pieces of a particular length we can cut. If we have a length of ribbon that is 1 yard, then we can cut two $\frac{1}{2}$-yard pieces, so $1 \div \frac{1}{2} = 2$. If we have $\frac{1}{2}$ of a yard of ribbon, however, then we already have one $\frac{1}{2}$-yard piece and there's nothing left over, so $\frac{1}{2} \div \frac{1}{2} = 1$. If we have a length that's only $\frac{1}{4}$ of a yard of ribbon, then we don't have enough even for one $\frac{1}{2}$-yard piece; all we have is enough for one-half of a $\frac{1}{2}$-yard piece, so $\frac{1}{4} \div \frac{1}{2} = \frac{1}{2}$. If we have a length of ribbon that's $\frac{3}{4}$ of a yard, we can cut one $\frac{1}{2}$-yard piece, and then we have enough left for half of a $\frac{1}{2}$-yard piece, so $\frac{3}{4} \div \frac{1}{2} = 1\frac{1}{2}$.

Does this context work for $\frac{2}{3} \div \frac{1}{2}$? Yes. The problem restated in the context is: If we have a length of ribbon that's $\frac{2}{3}$ of a yard, how many pieces can we cut that are each $\frac{1}{2}$ yard long? We can cut one piece that is $\frac{1}{2}$-yard long. But then we're left with another small bit of ribbon, and this bit is one-third of a $\frac{1}{2}$-yard piece. We have one and one-third pieces, so $\frac{2}{3} \div \frac{1}{2} = 1\frac{1}{3}$.

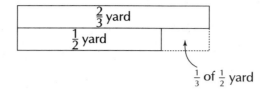

While the ribbon context is useful for helping some students understand, concrete materials are more helpful for others. The fraction kit pieces introduced in the Teaching Arithmetic book *Lessons for Introducing Fractions, Grades 4–5,* and described in the booklet, *The Fraction Kit Guide,* accompanying this book, work well. The pieces include a whole, halves, thirds, fourths, sixths, eighths, twelfths, and sixteenths, as shown:

1															
$\frac{1}{2}$								$\frac{1}{2}$							
$\frac{1}{3}$					$\frac{1}{3}$					$\frac{1}{3}$					
$\frac{1}{4}$				$\frac{1}{4}$				$\frac{1}{4}$				$\frac{1}{4}$			
$\frac{1}{6}$			$\frac{1}{6}$			$\frac{1}{6}$		$\frac{1}{6}$			$\frac{1}{6}$			$\frac{1}{6}$	
$\frac{1}{8}$		$\frac{1}{8}$		$\frac{1}{8}$		$\frac{1}{8}$		$\frac{1}{8}$		$\frac{1}{8}$		$\frac{1}{8}$		$\frac{1}{8}$	
$\frac{1}{12}$	$\frac{1}{12}$	$\frac{1}{12}$	$\frac{1}{12}$	$\frac{1}{12}$	$\frac{1}{12}$	$\frac{1}{12}$	$\frac{1}{12}$	$\frac{1}{12}$	$\frac{1}{12}$	$\frac{1}{12}$	$\frac{1}{12}$				
$\frac{1}{16}$	$\frac{1}{16}$	$\frac{1}{16}$	$\frac{1}{16}$	$\frac{1}{16}$	$\frac{1}{16}$	$\frac{1}{16}$	$\frac{1}{16}$	$\frac{1}{16}$	$\frac{1}{16}$	$\frac{1}{16}$	$\frac{1}{16}$	$\frac{1}{16}$	$\frac{1}{16}$	$\frac{1}{16}$	$\frac{1}{16}$

There are other ways to reason. Celia, a fifth grader, pointed out that if you double both numbers in a division problem, the answer stays the same. For the problem $6 \div 2$, for example, doubling the dividend and divisor produces $12 \div 4$, and both problems have the same quotient of 3. It may help to see this relationship if we represent the division problems as fractions—$\frac{6}{2}$ and $\frac{12}{4}$; both are equal to 3 and, therefore, are equivalent. Celia's suggestion of doubling can be used to solve these problems:

$$1 \div \tfrac{1}{2} = 2 \div 1 = 2$$
$$\tfrac{1}{2} \div \tfrac{1}{2} = 1 \div 1 = 1$$
$$\tfrac{1}{4} \div \tfrac{1}{2} = \tfrac{1}{2} \div 1 = \tfrac{1}{2}$$
$$\tfrac{3}{4} \div \tfrac{1}{2} = 1\tfrac{1}{2} \div 1 = 1\tfrac{1}{2}$$
$$\tfrac{2}{3} \div \tfrac{1}{2} = 1\tfrac{1}{3} \div 1 = 1\tfrac{1}{3}$$

Celia's suggestion was useful for these specific problems because the divisor in each problem is one-half. Doubling one-half gives a divisor of one, and any number divided by one is equal to itself. Doubling is not useful for all problems, but it was a wonderful contribution to our class discussion for this particular set of problems.

Also, as we explored in two previous lessons, we can change a division problem to a multiplication problem that will produce the same answer, but we have to change the divisor to its "flip." This is a way to explain the invert-and-multiply method.

$$1 \div \tfrac{1}{2} = 1 \times 2 = 2$$
$$\tfrac{1}{2} \div \tfrac{1}{2} = \tfrac{1}{2} \times 2 = 1$$
$$\tfrac{1}{4} \div \tfrac{1}{2} = \tfrac{1}{4} \times 2 = \tfrac{2}{4} = \tfrac{1}{2}$$
$$\tfrac{3}{4} \div \tfrac{1}{2} = \tfrac{3}{4} \times 2 = \tfrac{6}{4} = 1\tfrac{1}{2}$$
$$\tfrac{2}{3} \div \tfrac{1}{2} = \tfrac{2}{3} \times 2 = \tfrac{4}{3} = 1\tfrac{1}{3}$$

Another way is to think about division as repeated subtraction. In this class, the students were comfortable using repeated subtraction for division problems with whole numbers. For example, see below for how Juanita, a student from this same class, solved $676 \div 18$ by first subtracting ten 18s, then twenty more 18s, then six 18s, and finally one 18. (For information about this method for long division, see the Teaching Arithmetic book *Lessons for Extending Division, Grades 4–5* [Math Solutions Publications, 2003].)

$$
\begin{array}{r}
37 \ \text{R}10 \\
18)\overline{676} \\
-180 \quad | \ 10 \\
\hline
496 \\
-360 \quad | \ 20 \\
\hline
136 \\
-108 \quad | \ 6 \\
\hline
28 \\
-18 \quad | \ 1 \\
\hline
10 \quad |
\end{array}
$$

One student used this representation to solve $\tfrac{2}{3} \div \tfrac{1}{2}$.

$$
\begin{array}{r}
1 \ \text{R}\tfrac{1}{6} \\
\tfrac{1}{2})\overline{\tfrac{2}{3}} \\
-\tfrac{1}{2} \\
\hline
\tfrac{1}{6}
\end{array}
$$

While representing the remainder in this way, as we do for whole number division, is mathematically correct (yes, there is a one-sixth piece of ribbon left over), it certainly is unconventional. But what part of the divisor, one-half, is the leftover, one-sixth?

In this class, many children reasoned that after you take $\tfrac{1}{2}$ from $\tfrac{2}{3}$, you have a $\tfrac{1}{6}$ piece left, so the answer should be $1\tfrac{1}{6}$. It's true that the remaining piece is $\tfrac{1}{6}$, so you could think of the answer as $1 \ \text{R}\tfrac{1}{6}$. This would be analogous to dividing $7 \div 2$ and getting an answer of $3 \ \text{R}1$, with the remainder telling what was still left to be divided. But we can also express the remainder as a part of another group; for $7 \div 2$, the leftover is part of a group of 2, or $\tfrac{1}{2}$. So the answer can also be $3\tfrac{1}{2}$. If we were dividing a bunch of 7 bananas into groups of 2, then $3 \ \text{R}1$ makes sense—we have 3 groups with 2 in each and 1 leftover banana. But we can also consider that leftover banana as $\tfrac{1}{2}$ of another group, so $3\tfrac{1}{2}$ also makes sense as the answer.

Back to $\tfrac{2}{3} \div \tfrac{1}{2}$: What do we do with the extra one-sixth piece? It's one-third of the divisor, because one-sixth is one-third of one-half. And when we're dividing fractions, we don't express the remainder as the amount left over, as we do with whole number remainders. Rather, we express them as a fractional part of the divisor.

Feeling a bit mathematically dizzy?

At this point, you may be wondering why I just don't teach the invert-and-multiply method and be done with it—it seems like an easier pedagogical route and it efficiently produces the correct answer for all problems. These two things are true, I admit. But if I teach the algorithm without developing a rationale for why it's a logical procedure, then I risk giving students the message that when the going gets rough in mathematics, which it often does, we just need a trick to get us through. I don't want to teach tricks. Rather, I want to develop a foundation of understanding and then build skills on that foundation. Also, when students make an error using a method they don't understand, they don't have a way to evaluate whether their answer makes sense.

The vignette that follows describes what occurred when I taught this lesson to a class of fifth graders. After you read the lesson, try solving some problems on your own, dropping the crutch of the invert-and-multiply method and instead reasoning to get answers. Then you can check your results with the tried-and-true method you know.

The Lesson

▲▲

I began class by writing a division problem on the board:

$1 \div \frac{1}{2} =$

"How many times does one-half go into one?" I asked. "Talk with your neighbor about this." After a moment, I asked for their attention and called on Kara.

She said, "It's two because one-half fits into one two times." I recorded on the board:

$1 \div \frac{1}{2} = 2$

"Who can check this answer using multiplication?" I asked.

Brendan said, "It checks because two times one-half is one." I wrote the multiplication problem next to the division problem:

$1 \div \frac{1}{2} = 2 \qquad 2 \times \frac{1}{2} = 1$

"Here's another way to show why the answer is one," I said. I took the whole piece from the fraction kit and put the two one-half pieces underneath. "You can see

that two one-half pieces fit into one whole," I explained.

1	
$\frac{1}{2}$	$\frac{1}{2}$

I then wrote another division problem underneath the first one and again asked the students to talk with their neighbors:

$1 \div \frac{1}{2} = 2 \qquad 2 \times \frac{1}{2} = 1$

$\frac{1}{2} \div \frac{1}{2} =$

This problem was easy for the students. Pierre gave the answer of one, explaining, "One-half goes into one-half one time." Craig told how to check it by multiplying. I modeled the problem with two one-half pieces from the fraction kit.

$\frac{1}{2}$
$\frac{1}{2}$

I recorded on the board and wrote a third problem:

$1 \div \frac{1}{2} = 2$ $\qquad$ $2 \times \frac{1}{2} = 1$

$\frac{1}{2} \div \frac{1}{2} = 1$ $\qquad$ $1 \times \frac{1}{2} = \frac{1}{2}$

$\frac{1}{4} \div \frac{1}{2} =$

"How many one-half pieces fit into one-fourth?" I asked as I put out a one-fourth piece and a one-half piece from the fraction kit to help the students.

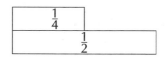

After they had a chance to talk with their neighbors, Sabrina reported. She said, "I think it has to be one-half. The fraction pieces show it. Only half of the half fits into the one-fourth piece."

Hassan said, "It checks, too, because one-half times one-half is one-fourth." I recorded the answer and the check on the board and wrote another problem:

$1 \div \frac{1}{2} = 2$ $\qquad$ $2 \times \frac{1}{2} = 1$

$\frac{1}{2} \div \frac{1}{2} = 1$ $\qquad$ $1 \times \frac{1}{2} = \frac{1}{2}$

$\frac{1}{4} \div \frac{1}{2} = \frac{1}{2}$ $\qquad$ $\frac{1}{2} \times \frac{1}{2} = \frac{1}{4}$

$\frac{3}{4} \div \frac{1}{2} =$

As I arranged fraction pieces, I said, "For this problem, you have to figure out how many one-half pieces fit into three-fourths. Talk with your neighbor."

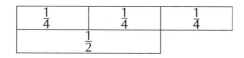

After I called the class to attention, Francis gave the answer. He said, "One-half goes into three-fourths once, and since one-fourth is one-half of one-half, you have half of a piece more. So you have a whole piece and a half piece."

"It checks," David confirmed. "One and a half times one-half is three-fourths because half of one and one-half is three-

fourths." I recorded the answer and drew a sketch to explain.

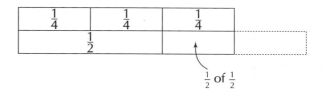

$\frac{1}{2}$ of $\frac{1}{2}$

Then I wrote another problem:

$1 \div \frac{1}{2} = 2$ $\qquad$ $2 \times \frac{1}{2} = 1$

$\frac{1}{2} \div \frac{1}{2} = 1$ $\qquad$ $1 \times \frac{1}{2} = \frac{1}{2}$

$\frac{1}{4} \div \frac{1}{2} = \frac{1}{2}$ $\qquad$ $\frac{1}{2} \times \frac{1}{2} = \frac{1}{4}$

$\frac{3}{4} \div \frac{1}{2} = 1\frac{1}{2}$ $\qquad$ $1\frac{1}{2} \times \frac{1}{2} = \frac{3}{4}$

$\frac{2}{3} \div \frac{1}{2} =$

I set out fraction pieces and said, "The answer is more than one because two-thirds is larger than one-half. Talk about this problem with your neighbor."

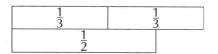

This was the first problem that caused some disagreement. Kayla reported first. She said, "I think the answer is one and one-sixth because you can see that one-half fits into two-thirds one time, and then there's one-sixth left over." Kayla was referring to the spa.ce from the end of the one-half piece to the end of the second one-third piece. I wrote $1\frac{1}{6}$ on the board.

Sachi had a different idea. "I think it's one and one-eighth," she said. "I think there's only room at the end of the one-half piece for one-eighth." I wrote $1\frac{1}{8}$ on the board.

"Why did you think there was one-sixth extra?" I asked Kayla.

She said, "One-third is the same as two-sixths, so two-thirds is four-sixths. And one-half is three-sixths, so there's one-sixth left."

"Oh, that's right," Sachi said. "You can erase my idea." I did so.

Pierre said, "I think it's one and one-third. The extra space there is the same as one-third of a one-half piece. You can fit in one-third more of one-half." I wrote $1\frac{1}{3}$ on the board.

Kayla objected, "But that space is worth one-sixth."

Pierre was adamant. "Look," he said. "One-third is two-sixths, right?" Kayla nodded. "And there are three-sixths in one-half, right?" Kayla nodded again. "So two-sixths plus one-sixth makes one-half, and one-sixth is one-half of one-third." I recorded on the board:

$$\frac{1}{3} = \frac{2}{6}$$

$$\frac{3}{6} = \frac{1}{2}$$

$$\frac{2}{6} + \frac{1}{6} = \frac{1}{2}$$

$$\frac{1}{6} = \frac{1}{2} \text{ of } \frac{1}{3}$$

While everything that Pierre said made sense to Kayla and others, there were still disagreement and confusion about the answer.

Conversation broke out among students, and I let it go for a bit. The students were animated and intent on defending their ideas. I knew that Pierre was correct, but I didn't want to tell this to the class. Telling students answers doesn't necessarily help build understanding. Rather, I wanted the students to have the chance to think about the problem for themselves.

(**Note:** You can verify the answer with the invert-and-multiply method: $\frac{2}{3} \div \frac{1}{2} = \frac{2}{3} \times \frac{2}{1} = \frac{4}{3} = 1\frac{1}{3}$. The answer of $1\frac{1}{3}$ also checks—$1\frac{1}{3} \times \frac{1}{2} = \frac{2}{3}$—because $1\frac{1}{3}$ is the same as $\frac{4}{3}$, and $\frac{1}{2}$ of $\frac{4}{3}$ is $\frac{2}{3}$.)

I finally called the class back to attention. Craig defended Kayla's idea that the answer should be one and one-sixth. But Pierre countered again and said, "The one in the answer is really a one-half piece, not a whole piece, and the one-sixth extra is one-third of a one-half piece."

Anita then said, "One-sixth is one-third of a half, so I think that they are the same. It depends how you look at it."

Kayla now said, "I think that Pierre is right." About half a dozen other students also sided with Pierre, while about a dozen students thought that one and one-sixth made sense. The rest weren't sure what to think. It was interesting to me that no one thought to check the answer, and I decided to wait a bit before making that suggestion. Right now, I attempted to relate the problem to what the students knew about division of whole numbers. I wrote the problem in a rather unorthodox way, as if the problem were a long division problem.

$$\frac{1}{2} \overline{\smash{)}\ \frac{2}{3}}$$

Some students giggled, and when I had everyone's attention, I talked through solving the problem as if it were a long division problem. I said, "I know that one one-half fits into two-thirds, and that uses up one-half because one times one-half is one-half. Then I subtract to see how much is left. Two-thirds minus one-half is the same as four-sixths minus three-sixths, which is one-sixth. So there is a remainder of one-sixth." I recorded as I explained.

$$\frac{1}{2} \overline{\smash{)}\ \frac{2}{3}}^{\ 1\ R\frac{1}{6}} \\ \underline{-\frac{1}{2}} \\ \frac{1}{6}$$

A cheer went up from the students supporting the one and one-sixth answer. But then I said, "We're trying to figure out how many times one-half goes into two-thirds, or how many halves there are in two-thirds. I think that the answer is one with an extra piece. I could say that the extra piece is one-sixth, but I can also say that the extra piece is one-third of the half. We're dividing by one-half, and the remainder is one-third of what we're dividing by."

There was complete silence in the room as I drew a sketch on the board.

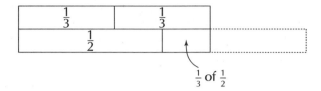

$\frac{1}{3}$ of $\frac{1}{2}$

A PROOF FROM CELIA

Celia then said, "I think I have a way to prove that the right answer is one and one-third. Just double both numbers in the problem, and then it's one and one-third divided by one, and that's one and one-third." I recorded Celia's idea:

$\frac{2}{3} \div \frac{1}{2}$

$1\frac{1}{3} \div 1 = 1\frac{1}{3}$

"Hey, does doubling like that work?" Craig asked.

"Let's try doubling with a whole number problem," I said. I wrote on the board:

$6 \div 2 = 3$

$12 \div 4 = 3$

Julio said, "If you write the division like a fraction, six over two, then you can multiply the six and the two both by two and the new fraction is worth the same." I wrote:

$\frac{6}{2} = \frac{12}{4}$

"Is one and one-third really right?" Annie asked.

CHECKING BY MULTIPLYING

"Well, we can always check a division problem by multiplying," I suggested.

"Oh yeah," Annie said. I wrote on the board:

$\frac{2}{3} \div \frac{1}{2} = ??$ $?? \times \frac{1}{2} = \frac{2}{3}$

I explained, "Whatever the answer to the division problem is, where the question marks are, you have to be able to multiply that by one-half and get two-thirds. One-half times what number gives two-thirds? One-half of what equals two-thirds?"

"Four-thirds," Hassan offered.

"That's the same as one and one-third," Maggie said.

Brendan came to life. "I get it. You're putting one-half into two-thirds, and then one-third of another half to finish it out."

I then offered another context for the problem. "Here's another way to think about it," I said. "Suppose we had two-thirds of a yard of ribbon and we want to cut pieces that are one-half yard long. How many one-half-yard pieces could we cut?" I drew a sketch on the board.

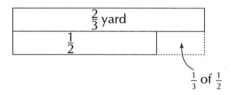

$\frac{1}{3}$ of $\frac{1}{2}$

"You get one piece and a dinky little bit left over," Francis said.

"You're right," I said. "And that dinky little bit is one-third of a half-yard piece."

SUGGESTING A SHORTCUT

I said to the class, "We've been talking about lots of different ways to think about dividing two-thirds by one-half. When mathematicians see the same kind of problem over and over again, they try to find some procedure that works for all of them that's easy to use and that gives the right answer. For a problem like this, one way that mathematicians solve it is by changing the division problem to a multiplication problem by flipping the divisor."

Pierre's hand shot up. "I know how to do the flip thing," he said. "Can I come up and try?" I agreed. Pierre came up and wrote:

$\frac{2}{3} \div \frac{1}{2}$

$\frac{2}{3} \times \frac{2}{1}$

$\frac{2}{3} \times 2 = \frac{2}{3} + \frac{2}{3} = \frac{4}{3} = 1\frac{1}{3}$

"I think that's what my mother showed me," Julio said. "But I get mixed up."

"It's easy to get mixed up when problems are complicated," I said. "That's why it's a good idea to have more than one way to do a problem so that you have a check."

A CLASS ASSIGNMENT

I then wrote five problems on the board for the students to work on. I numbered the first four and put an asterisk next to the fifth problem.

1. $\frac{1}{2} \div \frac{1}{4}$

2. $\frac{1}{8} \div \frac{1}{4}$

3. $\frac{3}{8} \div \frac{1}{4}$

4. $\frac{5}{8} \div \frac{1}{4}$

* $\frac{1}{3} \div \frac{1}{4}$

I said, "This last one is an extra one that you don't have to do. What you need to do is solve the first four problems, and then check your answers by multiplying. Finally, choose one of the problems and write an explanation of how you solved it."

"Can we work together?" Eddie asked.

"Yes," I said, "but you each should do your own paper."

"Can we do them any way we want?" Annie asked.

"Yes, you can figure them out in any way that makes sense to you."

"But we only have to explain one of them?" Anita asked to check.

"That's right," I said.

The classroom was noisy but felt productive as students worked together on the problems. Sometimes students would bring an answer to me to verify and sometimes students would call me over for help. I reminded several students who had solved all five problems to choose one and explain how they reasoned.

As always, some students finished more quickly than others. To deal with this situation, I had two extra problems planned and wrote them on the board when they were needed. I find that putting asterisks next to them is a motivating challenge for the quicker learners.

* * $\frac{2}{3} \div \frac{1}{4}$

* * * $\frac{5}{8} \div \frac{1}{2}$

Of the twenty-five students present, eight of them chose to write an explanation for the fifth problem—$\frac{1}{3} \div \frac{1}{4}$. These students were comfortable solving all of the problems and liked the challenge of explaining the one I perceived to be the most difficult. (See Figures 11–1 and 11–2.) Seven students explained $\frac{3}{8} \div \frac{1}{4}$ (see Figure 11–3), and one student chose $\frac{1}{2} \div \frac{1}{4}$. By giving students the choice of a problem to explain, I got a sense of their comfort level with these problems.

Two students, Brendan and Craig, each wrote two explanations, first for an easier problem and then for the last problem (see Figure 11–4 for Brendan's explanations).

① $\frac{1}{2} \div \frac{1}{4} = 2$

② $\frac{1}{8} \div \frac{1}{4} = \frac{1}{2}$

③ $\frac{3}{8} \div \frac{1}{4} = 1\frac{1}{2}$

④ $\frac{5}{8} \div \frac{1}{4} = 2\frac{1}{2}$

★ $\frac{1}{3} \div \frac{1}{4} = 1\frac{1}{3}$

$1\frac{1}{3} \times \frac{1}{4} = \frac{2}{6} = \frac{1}{3}$

I knew $\frac{1}{4}$ goes into $\frac{1}{3}$ at least 1 time. I didn't know what fraction of $\frac{1}{4}$ also goes into $\frac{1}{3}$ so I guess $1\frac{1}{3}$. Then I checked it by multiplying $1\frac{1}{3} \times \frac{1}{4}$ and I got $\frac{2}{6}$ which is equal to $\frac{1}{3}$.

I found out that $\frac{1}{3}$ is $\frac{1}{3}$ greater than $\frac{1}{4}$. $\frac{1}{12}$ is $\frac{1}{3}$ of $\frac{1}{4}$ because $\frac{1}{12}$ goes into $\frac{1}{4}$ 3 times and it goes into $\frac{1}{3}$ 4 times which means it goes into $\frac{1}{3}$ 1 more time than it goes into $\frac{1}{4}$ and since $\frac{1}{12}$ goes into $\frac{1}{4}$ 3 times $\frac{1}{12}$ is $\frac{1}{3}$ of $\frac{1}{4}$.

▲▲▲▲▲▲**Figure 11–1** *Kayla wrote a lengthy explanation for why $\frac{1}{3} \div \frac{1}{4} = 1\frac{1}{3}$.*

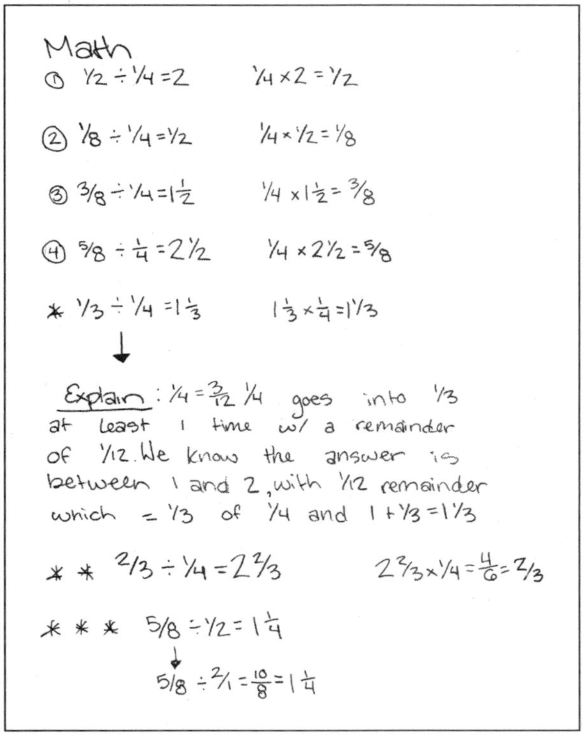
Math
① 1/2 ÷ 1/4 = 2   1/4 × 2 = 1/2
② 1/8 ÷ 1/4 = 1/2   1/4 × 1/2 = 1/8
③ 3/8 ÷ 1/4 = 1 1/2   1/4 × 1 1/2 = 3/8
④ 5/8 ÷ 1/4 = 2 1/2   1/4 × 2 1/2 = 5/8
* 1/3 ÷ 1/4 = 1 1/3   1 1/3 × 1/4 = 1/3
Explain: 1/4 = 3/12 1/4 goes into 1/3 at least 1 time w/ a remainder of 1/12. We know the answer is between 1 and 2, with 1/12 remainder which = 1/3 of 1/4 and 1 + 1/3 = 1 1/3
** 2/3 ÷ 1/4 = 2 2/3   2 2/3 × 1/4 = 4/6 = 2/3
*** 5/8 ÷ 1/2 = 1 1/4
5/8 ÷ 2/1 = 10/8 = 1 1/4

Figure 11–2 *Gloria solved all of the problems correctly, including the two extra problems.*

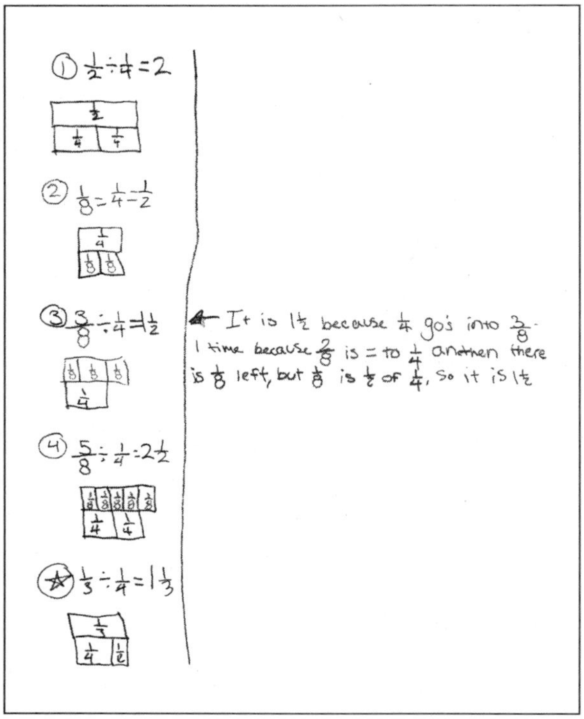
① 1/2 ÷ 1/4 = 2
② 1/8 ÷ 1/4 = 1/2
③ 3/8 ÷ 1/4 = 1 1/2
It is 1 1/2 because 1/4 go's into 3/8 1 time because 2/8 is = to 1/4 and then there is 1/8 left, but 1/8 is 1/2 of 1/4, so it is 1 1/2
④ 5/8 ÷ 1/4 = 2 1/2
★ 1/3 ÷ 1/4 = 1 1/3

Figure 11–3 *Ally drew pictures to figure out the answers and then explained her answer for $\frac{3}{8} \div \frac{1}{4}$.*

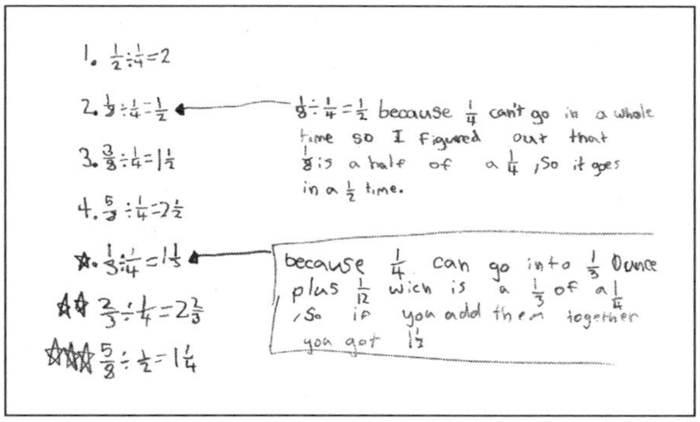
1. 1/2 ÷ 1/4 = 2
2. 1/8 ÷ 1/4 = 1/2
1/8 ÷ 1/4 = 1/2 because 1/4 can't go in a whole time so I figured out that 1/8 is a half of a 1/4, so it goes in a 1/2 time.
3. 3/8 ÷ 1/4 = 1 1/2
4. 5/8 ÷ 1/4 = 2 1/2
★. 1/3 ÷ 1/4 = 1 1/3
because 1/4 can go into 1/3 once plus 1/12 wich is a 1/3 of a 1/4, so if you add them together you got 1 1/3
★★ 2/3 ÷ 1/4 = 2 2/3
★★★ 5/8 ÷ 1/2 = 1 1/4

Figure 11–4 *Brendan wrote explanations for two of the problems.*

"The first one was too easy," Craig told me. Two students didn't write explanations but made drawings to show how they figured; Kara drew fraction pieces and Paul drew circles. Both of these students struggled with the problems. Five students didn't complete explanations. Eddie and Clark were having difficulty and I spent most of the time working with them to solve the problems, and there was no time left for them to try to write. Sachi and Maria worked carefully on the problems, solving problems to check each and also changing each to a multiplication problem by flipping the divisor as another check, and ran out of time (see Figure 11–5). Helene worked slowly and, by her

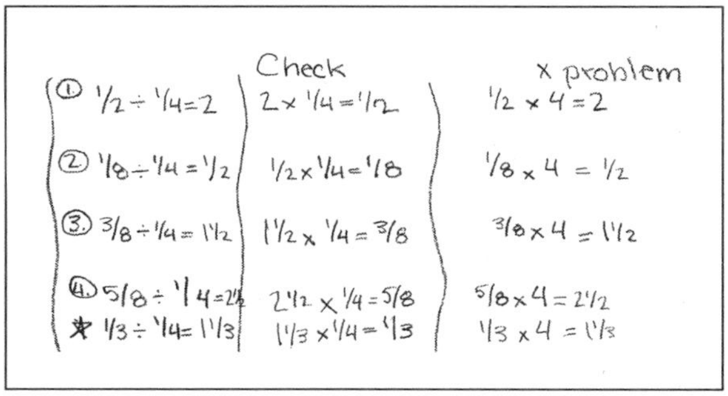
Check
x problem
① 1/2 ÷ 1/4 = 2   2 × 1/4 = 1/2   1/2 × 4 = 2
② 1/8 ÷ 1/4 = 1/2   1/2 × 1/4 = 1/8   1/8 × 4 = 1/2
③ 3/8 ÷ 1/4 = 1 1/2   1 1/2 × 1/4 = 3/8   3/8 × 4 = 1 1/2
④ 5/8 ÷ 1/4 = 2 1/2   2 1/2 × 1/4 = 5/8   5/8 × 4 = 2 1/2
★ 1/3 ÷ 1/4 = 1 1/3   1 1/3 × 1/4 = 1/3   1/3 × 4 = 1 1/3

Figure 11–5 *After solving a problem, Maria checked it by multiplying and then, as another check, changed each problem to a multiplication problem by flipping the divisor.*

choice, by herself, seeking help when she was stuck. Ten students completed one or both of the last two challenge problems, and David and Francis went on to pose another for themselves and solve it— $1\frac{1}{8} \div 1\frac{1}{10}$.

Questions and Discussion

▲▲

▲ *Why did you ask the students to explain their thinking for just one of the problems? Would it be appropriate to have them explain for all of the problems, or do you think it's better to give them more problems for practice?*

Any of these options makes sense, depending on the class and the situation. On this day, I didn't think that most of the students would have time to solve the problems and write more than one explanation, and I didn't want to give an assignment that would be frustrating for them. Also, I thought that an explanation for one problem was sufficient for helping me assess their progress on problems like these. To gain additional information, I circulated and talked with students about their thinking as they worked on problems.

▲ *What about the students who aren't "getting it" with these more difficult problems?*

This invariably happens. Some students learn more slowly and some lack a firm enough foundation either in division with whole numbers or with understanding the ideas about fractions that we've learned so far. The challenge is to find ways to keep the students who learn more easily productively involved while attending to the needs of others. One technique I have is to write additional problems on the board for students who finish early, as I did with the two- and three-asterisk problems. Also, I keep track of the students' work on practice and homework assignments so that I know who needs more help. Then I make time during class to sit and work with those students. There is no one way to deal with this teaching challenge, and I find that the more complex the mathematics is, the more pronounced the spread is in the class. Students who are struggling need extra help, and I have to find the time to provide it to them.

CHAPTER TWELVE
TOOL KIT FOR DIVIDING FRACTIONS

Overview

In this lesson, the class compiles a list of strategies for dividing fractions. The goal of this lesson is create a tool kit for solving division problems that offers students a collection of strategies to use that rely on different ways to reason. While the standard invert-and-multiply algorithm is included on the list, it is presented as just one of the strategies that students can use to divide fractions and mixed numbers. Students then practice, using the tool kit as a reference for solving problems in two different ways.

Materials

▲ 1 sheet of chart paper

Time

▲ two class periods, plus time for solving additional problems

Teaching Directions

1. Write on the board: $2 \div \frac{1}{6}$. Read the problem aloud and then ask the students to talk with a neighbor about how many one-sixths fit into two.

2. Ask the students to say the answer together. Record: $2 \div \frac{1}{6} = 12$. Then have a student explain why the answer of 12 makes sense. Record his or her thinking on the board.

3. Explain and illustrate how to solve the problem by thinking about ribbon: "How many one-sixth-yard pieces of ribbon can you cut from a two-yard piece?"

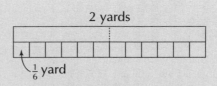

2 yards

$\frac{1}{6}$ yard

4. Ask a student to change the problem to a multiplication problem by flipping the divisor. Record next to the original problem. (**Note:** If a student suggests "two times six over one," you may wish to record the two ways as shown.)

$2 \div \frac{1}{6} = 12$ $\qquad$ $2 \times 6 = 12$ $\qquad$ $(2 \times \frac{6}{1} = 12)$

5. Write another problem on the board underneath the first one: $2 \div \frac{1}{4}$. Repeat Steps 1 through 4 for this problem, asking the class to say the answer together, asking a student to explain the answer, recording his or her thinking, making a ribbon illustration, and finally asking a student to give the corresponding multiplication problem as another way to find the answer.

6. Repeat Step 5 for five additional problems. After the first two or three times, stop recording the multiplication problem in two ways.

$2 \div \frac{1}{6} = 12$ $\qquad$ $2 \times 6 = 12$ $\qquad$ $(2 \times \frac{6}{1} = 12)$

$2 \div \frac{1}{4} = 8$ $\qquad$ $2 \times 4 = 8$ $\qquad$ $(2 \times \frac{4}{1} = 8)$

$2 \div \frac{1}{2} = 4$ $\qquad$ $2 \times 2 = 4$

$2 \div 1 = 2$ $\qquad$ $2 \times 1 = 2$

$2 \div 2 = 1$ $\qquad$ $2 \times \frac{1}{2} = 1$

$2 \div 4 = \frac{1}{2}$ $\qquad$ $2 \times \frac{1}{4} = \frac{1}{2}$

$2 \div 6 = \frac{1}{3}$ $\qquad$ $2 \times \frac{1}{6} = \frac{2}{6}$

7. Post a sheet of chart paper and title it *Tool Kit for Dividing Fractions*. Tell the students that you'll list the different ways they can solve division problems.

8. Write a problem on the board: $1\frac{1}{8} \div \frac{1}{4}$. Give students a few moments to solve the problem. Then ask for solutions. Record their thinking and list each method presented on the chart paper. The strategies on the list below emerged from the class described. See the "Teaching Notes" and "The Lesson" sections for more information about these strategies. The list from your class will most likely differ, and you may want to introduce some of the methods below that do not come up with your students.

Tool Kit for Dividing Fractions

Break apart.
How many fit?
Flip and ×.
Change both to fractions, then flip and ×.
Change fractions to same denominator.
Use fraction kit.

Change to improper fractions and ÷ numerators and denominators.
Double (and keep doubling) to ÷ by 1.
Draw a picture.
Think about ribbon.
Check by ×.

9. On Day 2, begin class by writing a problem on the board: $1\frac{3}{4} \div \frac{3}{4}$. Give students time to solve it and then have students present the answer and identify the tools they used. Record their thinking on the board. Ask for other methods as well and record. If a student comes up with a method that isn't on the list, add it to the chart.

10. Give the students three problems to solve and ask them to solve them each in two different ways and to indicate on their papers the tools they used.

1. $2\frac{3}{8} \div \frac{1}{4}$
2. $3\frac{1}{4} \div \frac{3}{4}$
3. $2 \div 3$

Teaching Notes

This two-day lesson is appropriate after students have experienced the previous lessons in this book. Students should be comfortable with multiplying fractions so that they can use multiplication as a check for dividing and also for the standard invert-and-multiply method. Also, students should be comfortable using several strategies to solve problems that involve division of fractions.

On the first day of the lesson, the students solve a series of problems that reinforce their previous learning about how to change a division problem to a multiplication problem that gives the same answer—the basis for the invert-and-multiply algorithm. The pattern the students explore is more evident when considered for problems with whole numbers. For the problem $6 \div 2$, for example, we know that the answer is 3. The question students answer for a division problem like this is: What could we multiply by six to get the same answer of three? Students know that one-half of six is three and, therefore, $6 \times \frac{1}{2} = 3$. When changing a division problem to a multiplication problem that gives the same answer, the divisor of two changes to the factor of one-half. Using mathematical terminology, if the product of two factors is one—for example, $2 \times \frac{1}{2} = 1$—then one-half is called the reciprocal or multiplicative inverse of two. The students in this class described these numbers as "flips," and I used their language to describe the pattern they discovered. I chose not to introduce the standard terminology of *reciprocal* and *multiplicative inverse*. It seemed to me that the formal language would separate the experience from the students' own discoveries and was something that they could learn at a later time.

A strategy that many students found helpful was to break apart the dividend and think of the problem as two problems. In this class, this came to be known as the break-apart method. For the same reason as above, I didn't introduce the mathematical terminology of the *distributive property* but instead used the students' wording. For the problem $1\frac{1}{2} \div \frac{1}{8}$, for example, it's possible to break apart the dividend by thinking of it as $1 + \frac{1}{2}$ and solving first $1 \div \frac{1}{8}$ and then $\frac{1}{2} \div \frac{1}{8}$. Students then think, "One-eighth goes into one eight times; one-eighth goes into one-half four times; eight plus four gives the answer of twelve."

In all classes that I taught, I noticed most students developed personal preferences for particular strategies that made sense to them and they used them, as much as possible. In this class, for example, Saul relied on doubling, Kara chose to make drawings, David preferred to flip and multiply, Francis liked the ribbon context, and Gloria liked the break-apart method. One of my goals is to help students strengthen their preferred strategies and also expand their personal repertoires to include other strategies as well. Therefore, I ask students to solve problems in at least two different ways to encourage them to practice other strategies.

This culminating lesson in the book doesn't imply the end of instructional time needed for multiplication or division of fractions. It's important to provide students regular practice and additional opportunities to discuss their thinking. And it's also important to continue to keep the emphasis on thinking and reasoning to solve problems.

The Lesson

▲▲

DAY 1

I began class by writing on the board: $2 \div \frac{1}{6}$. I asked the students, "How much is two divided by one-sixth? Talk with your neighbor about how many one-sixths fit into two." After a moment, I asked the students to say the answer together. I recorded:

$2 \div \frac{1}{6} = 12$

Sachi explained, "It's twelve because there are six sixths in one whole, so in two wholes there's twelve, because six plus six is twelve." There seemed to be general understanding of Sachi's explanation.

"It helps me to think about ribbon," I said. I drew on the board:

2 yards

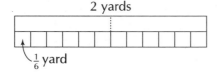

$\frac{1}{6}$ yard

I then explained, "I can think about the problem by first thinking about a two-yard piece of ribbon. Then I ask, 'How many one-sixth-yard pieces can I cut from the

two-yard piece?' I can see that I'll get twelve."

"It's like thinking of the fraction pieces," Craig said, connecting my ribbon example to the fraction kits.

"How can we change the division problem into a multiplication problem?" I asked, referring to the idea we had previously discussed. (See Chapters 10 and 11.)

David answered, "You flip the one-sixth and you get two times six over one, and that's the same as two times six, so it checks." I wrote David's idea on the board and also wrote another problem:

$2 \div \frac{1}{6} = 12 \qquad 2 \times 6 = 12 \qquad (2 \times \frac{6}{1} = 12)$
$2 \div \frac{1}{4} =$

Again, I asked the students to answer together. Then Saul explained why the answer was eight using reasoning similar to what Sachi had used for the first problem. He said, "The one-fourth goes into one four times, so it goes into two eight times." I revised my ribbon illustration for the first problem to match this problem.

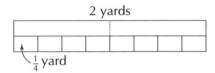

2 yards

$\frac{1}{4}$ yard

"Who can tell me how to change the problem to a multiplication problem by flipping?" I asked. Maria explained as David had for the first problem. I recorded and wrote a new problem:

$2 \div \frac{1}{6} = 12$ $2 \times 6 = 12$ $(2 \times \frac{6}{1} = 12)$

$2 \div \frac{1}{4} = 8$ $2 \times 4 = 8$ $(2 \times \frac{4}{1} = 8)$

$2 \div \frac{1}{2} =$

When I turned back to the students, most of them gave the answer of four and Brendan gave the corresponding multiplication problem. I also revised my ribbon illustration.

2 yards

$\frac{1}{2}$ yard

I repeated this procedure of writing a problem, asking the class to say the answer together, asking for an explanation, revising my ribbon illustration, and then asking a student to give the corresponding multiplication problem as another way to find the answer. Also, I stopped writing the third representation that I had put in parentheses for the next problems.

$2 \div \frac{1}{6} = 12$ $2 \times 6 = 12$ $(2 \times \frac{6}{1} = 12)$

$2 \div \frac{1}{4} = 8$ $2 \times 4 = 8$ $(2 \times \frac{4}{1} = 8)$

$2 \div \frac{1}{2} = 4$ $2 \times 2 = 4$

$2 \div 1 = 2$ $2 \times 1 = 2$

$2 \div 2 = 1$

For $2 \div 2$, Anita explained, "It's one because two goes into two one time."

But then when I asked Annie to write the corresponding multiplication problem for $2 \div 2$, she got confused. "How do I flip two?" she asked. Other hands went up, and I suggested to Annie that she call on someone to help her. She asked Celia.

"All you have to do is think about two as a fraction," Celia said. "Just make it two over one, and it's still two. Then you can flip it to one-half. So the multiplication problem is two times one-half." Annie nodded.

Julio added, "And that's one because half of two is one." I recorded and added another problem:

$2 \div \frac{1}{6} = 12$ $2 \times 6 = 12$ $(2 \times \frac{6}{1} = 12)$

$2 \div \frac{1}{4} = 8$ $2 \times 4 = 8$ $(2 \times \frac{4}{1} = 8)$

$2 \div \frac{1}{2} = 4$ $2 \times 2 = 4$

$2 \div 1 = 2$ $2 \times 1 = 2$

$2 \div 2 = 1$ $2 \times \frac{1}{2} = 1$

$2 \div 4 =$

When I turned back to the class, I noticed that some students weren't certain about the answer to this problem and there was only a smattering of responses.

I asked Kayla to explain. "The answer is one-half," she said, "because half of four fits into two." There was some agreement, but others were still silent. I revised my ribbon illustration (see below).

"Does my ribbon drawing help?" I asked.

Kara said, "It gives the same answer as Kayla. You can't cut the two yards. You only have half of what you need." This seemed to help some of the students.

I turned to Annie and asked, "Can you change this problem into a multiplication problem by flipping?" I wanted to see if Celia's explanation had helped Annie.

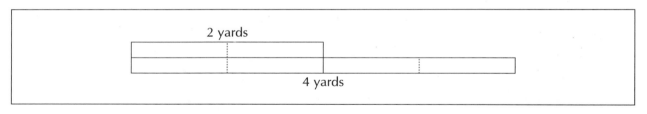

2 yards

4 yards

Annie said, "I think so. Four is the same as four over one, so you flip it to one-fourth."

"So what should I write?" I asked.

"Two times one-fourth," Annie answered. I recorded:

$2 \div \frac{1}{6} = 12$ $2 \times 6 = 12$ $(2 \times \frac{6}{1} = 12)$

$2 \div \frac{1}{4} = 8$ $2 \times 4 = 8$ $(2 \times \frac{4}{1} = 8)$

$2 \div \frac{1}{2} = 4$ $2 \times 2 = 4$

$2 \div 1 = 2$ $2 \times 1 = 2$

$2 \div 2 = 1$ $2 \times \frac{1}{2} = 1$

$2 \div 4 = \frac{1}{2}$ $2 \times \frac{1}{4} = \frac{1}{2}$

I asked the class, "Is that right? Is two times one-fourth really one-half?"

Sabrina answered, "You can show it with circles. Can I do it?" I agreed, and Sabrina came to the board, drew two circles, and divided each into fourths. She shaded one-fourth of each circle and explained, "See, one-fourth of one circle is one-fourth, so one-fourth of two circles is two-fourths, and that's the same as one-half."

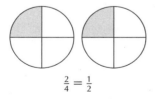

$\frac{2}{4} = \frac{1}{2}$

Helene said, "You can add. Two times one-fourth is one-fourth two times, and one-fourth plus one-fourth is one-half." I wrote on the board:

$2 \times \frac{1}{4} = \frac{1}{4} + \frac{1}{4} = \frac{1}{2}$

"So do you think that two divided by four really is one-half?" I asked, pointing to the division problem.

Hassan answered, "Yeah, because you can't fit all of four into two, just half of four into two. The ribbon shows how it works."

I turned to the board and wrote one last problem—$2 \div 6$. I also adjusted my ribbon illustration (see below).

Julio explained first. He said, "I think the answer is one-third because one-third of six is two, so that's all that will fit into two."

Anita then gave the corresponding multiplication sentence. She said, "You flip the six to one-sixth and then you can write two times one-sixth, and that's two-sixths." I recorded:

$2 \div \frac{1}{6} = 12$ $2 \times 6 = 12$ $(2 \times \frac{6}{1} = 12)$

$2 \div \frac{1}{4} = 8$ $2 \times 4 = 8$ $(2 \times \frac{4}{1} = 8)$

$2 \div \frac{1}{2} = 4$ $2 \times 2 = 4$

$2 \div 1 = 2$ $2 \times 1 = 2$

$2 \div 2 = 1$ $2 \times \frac{1}{2} = 1$

$2 \div 4 = \frac{1}{2}$ $2 \times \frac{1}{4} = \frac{1}{2}$

$2 \div 6 = \frac{1}{3}$ $2 \times \frac{1}{6} = \frac{2}{6}$

I said, "The answer I wrote to the division problem is one-third." I pointed to $2 \div 6 = \frac{1}{3}$ and continued, "But the answer to the multiplication problem, after Anita flipped the six to one-sixth, is two-sixths. What's going on here?"

"They're both the same," Maria said. "One-third and two-sixths are the same."

Pierre jumped up and said, "I just realized something. Two-sixths is the same as one-third, and two-fourths is the same as one-half, and two-halves is the same as one." I didn't understand what Pierre was referring to, so he came up to the board to explain his idea. He pointed to the last division problem and said, "This answer

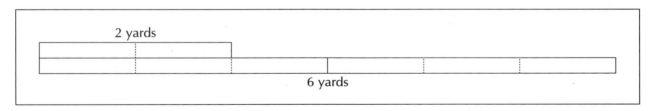

2 yards

6 yards

128   **Lessons for Multiplying and Dividing Fractions**

could be two-sixths, and that's two over six." He pointed to the dividend and divisor of the problem. "And it works here, too," he said, pointing to $2 \div 4 = \frac{1}{2}$. "The answer could be two-fourths, and that's two over four. And it works for two divided by two." Pierre was pleased with his discovery.

"Can you really do that?" Craig wanted to know.

"You'll have to test it with other problems. Remember, if you're not sure about an idea, be sure to check it in other ways," I responded.

Developing a Tool Kit for Dividing Fractions

I then posted a sheet of chart paper and titled it *Tool Kit for Dividing Fractions*. I explained to the students what we were going to do. "I'm going to write a new problem on the board. For this problem, I want to see how many different ways you can think of to solve it. Then, for each way you suggest, we'll describe the method and record it on the chart paper." I wrote the problem on the board:

$$1\tfrac{1}{8} \div \tfrac{1}{4}$$

"First talk with your neighbor about how to solve the problem and what the answer is," I said. Conversation broke out. After a few moments, when the room was quieter and a few hands were up, I interrupted them and asked for their attention. I called on Juanita to explain first.

Juanita said, "Well, one-fourth goes into one whole four times. And then it goes into one-eighth only half of a time. So we think the answer is one and one-half."

"You mean *four* and one-half," Juanita's partner, Sabrina, corrected.

"Oh yeah," Juanita said, "It's four and one-half." I recorded on the board:

$$1 \div \tfrac{1}{4} = 4$$
$$\tfrac{1}{8} \div \tfrac{1}{4} = \tfrac{1}{2}$$
$$4 + \tfrac{1}{2} = 4\tfrac{1}{2}.$$

"How many of you agree with Juanita's answer?" I asked. Most hands went up.

"Did anyone do it the same way?" I asked. Some hands remained up.

"What can I write on the chart to describe what Juanita did?" I asked.

Julio said, "I think she did break apart."

"What did Juanita break apart?" I asked.

"She broke apart the one and one-eighth into one and then one-eighth," Julio said. I looked at Juanita and she nodded. On the chart paper, I wrote *Break apart*.

"Who solved the problem in a different way?" I asked. I called on Craig.

He said, "I thought about how many times one-fourth fit into one and one-eighth. It fits into one whole four times, and half of it fits into one-eighth." I wrote on the board:

$\tfrac{1}{4}$ *fits into 1 whole 4 times.*

$\tfrac{1}{2}$ *of* $\tfrac{1}{4}$ *fits into* $\tfrac{1}{8}$.

$4 + \tfrac{1}{2} = 4\tfrac{1}{2}$

"How would you describe what you did?" I asked.

Craig said, "I'm not sure. I kind of did break apart, too, but it's different, too."

I said, "How about calling your way 'how many fit?'?" Craig agreed and I wrote the description on the chart paper.

"Who used another way?" I asked. I called on David.

He said, "You can change it to a multiplication problem. It would be one and one-eighth times four. Then you do four times one and four times one-eighth, and you get four and four-eighths, and that's the same as four and one-half." I recorded on the board:

$$1\tfrac{1}{8} \div \tfrac{1}{4} = 1\tfrac{1}{8} \times 4$$
$$1 \times 4 = 4$$
$$\tfrac{1}{8} \times 4 = \tfrac{4}{8}$$
$$4 + \tfrac{4}{8} = 4\tfrac{4}{8} = 4\tfrac{1}{2}$$

"That's kind of break apart, too," Annie noticed.

"Yes, the break-apart method is really useful," I said. I wrote on the chart paper:

Tool Kit for Dividing Fractions

Break apart.

How many fit?

Flip and ×.

"Who has another way to explain?" I asked again.

Julio said, "I did flip and multiply, but first I made them both fractions. I made one and one-eighth into nine-eighths. Then I flipped the one-fourth to four over one. And then I multiplied the tops and bottoms."

"Come up and write the problem first and then show us what you did," I said. Julio came up and recorded what he had done on his paper:

$1\frac{1}{8} \div \frac{1}{4}$

$\frac{9}{8} \div \frac{1}{4}$

$\frac{9}{8} \times \frac{4}{1}$

$\frac{36}{8}$

$4\frac{4}{8} \text{ or } 4\frac{1}{2}$

Julio explained, "After I multiplied, I divided eight into thirty-six and that's how I got four and four-eighths, and that's four and one-half." I wrote on the chart paper:

Tool Kit for Dividing Fractions

Break apart.

How many fit?

Flip and ×.

Change both to fractions, then flip and ×.

Kayla offered another idea. She said, "I did what Julio did, but I made both of the fractions have the same denominator. I changed one-fourth to two-eighths. Then I knew that two-eighths plus two-eighths is four-eighths, and four-eighths and four-eighths is eight-eighths, so four two-eighths make a whole. And one-eighth is half of two-eighths, so the answer is four and one-half." I recorded on the board as Kayla explained:

$1\frac{1}{8} \div \frac{1}{4}$

$\frac{9}{8} \div \frac{2}{8}$

$\frac{2}{8} + \frac{2}{8} + \frac{2}{8} + \frac{2}{8} = \frac{8}{8}$

$\frac{1}{8} \text{ is } \frac{1}{2} \text{ of } \frac{2}{8}$

$4 + \frac{1}{2} = 4\frac{1}{2}$

Kayla's method was hard for others to follow. I didn't dwell on it longer but thanked Kayla and added to the tool kit: *Change fractions to same denominator.*

Helene explained next. "You can use the fraction kit," she said. She came up and placed the whole strip and one of the one-eighth strips end-to-end. Then she showed how a one-fourth piece fit four and a half times, moving it along and counting.

I added to the chart: *Use fraction kit.* Then I called on Celia.

"I've been thinking about something that I'm not sure about," she said. "If I change the fractions the way Julio did, to nine-eighths divided by one-fourth, can't we just divide the numerators and the denominators instead of flipping and multiplying?" I recorded on the board:

$\frac{9}{8} \div \frac{1}{4} = \frac{9 \div 1}{8 \div 4}$

$\frac{9}{2} = 4\frac{1}{2}$

"Your idea works, too," I said, writing on the chart paper: *Change to improper fractions and ÷ numerators and denominators.*

The students were excited about the different ways and were trying to think of other ways as well. Saul next said, "You could double both numbers, but that only gives you two and two-eighths divided by two-fourths. But if you double both again, then it's easy because you have four and four-eighths divided by four-fourths, and that's one, and it's easy to divide anything by one. It's four and four-eighths, and that's the same as four and one-half." I wrote on the board:

$$1\tfrac{1}{8} \div \tfrac{1}{4}$$
$$2\tfrac{2}{8} \div \tfrac{2}{4}$$
$$4\tfrac{4}{8} \div \tfrac{4}{4} = 4\tfrac{4}{8} \div 1 = 4\tfrac{4}{8}$$
$$4\tfrac{4}{8} = 4\tfrac{1}{2}$$

I added Saul's idea to the growing list on the chart paper: *Double (and keep doubling) to ÷ by 1.*

No one had another idea to offer. However, there were a few more methods I wanted to have on the list. I knew that Clark and Eddie typically solved problems by drawing circles, and I asked them how they would use their method to do this.

"That's how we did it," Clark said. "Can you draw for me?" I agreed and did so as Clark directed, "Draw two circles and divide them into fourths. There are four-fourths in the first circle. Then you have to show just one-eighth on the other circle, so mark off three of the fourths, and divide the other one in half, and that will show one-eighth. And that's one-half of the fourth." To help clarify Clark's idea, I wrote *How many fourths?* underneath the circles.

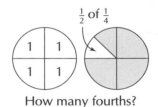

How many fourths?

I wrote on the chart paper: *Draw a picture.* Then, underneath, I wrote: *Think about ribbon.* I drew on the board:

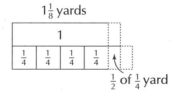

"It kind of looks like what Helene did with the fraction pieces," Sabrina commented.

"Yes, it's kind of the same, but the idea of ribbon can come in handy when the problem involves fractions that we don't have in our fraction kit," I said. Than I asked, "Any other ideas for our chart?"

I waited a moment to see if anyone would respond. The class was quiet, but I continued to wait to be sure that there were no other ideas floating around. Then David raised a hand. "What about putting on the list to check by multiplying, you know, by multiplying the answer by what we divide by?" I wrote on the board:

$$1\tfrac{1}{8} \div \tfrac{1}{4} = 4\tfrac{1}{2}$$
$$4\tfrac{1}{2} \times \tfrac{1}{4}$$

"Like this?" I asked David.

David nodded and said, "It checks. Four times one-fourth is one, and one-half of one-fourth is one-eighth, and one and one-eighth is the number we started with." I recorded:

$$4 \times \tfrac{1}{4} = 1$$
$$\tfrac{1}{2} \times \tfrac{1}{4} = \tfrac{1}{8}$$
$$1 + \tfrac{1}{8} = 1\tfrac{1}{8}$$

I added David's idea to the chart paper:

Tool Kit for Dividing Fractions

Break apart.

How many fit?

Flip and ×.

Change both to fractions, then flip and ×.

Change fractions to same denominator.

Use fraction kit.

Change to improper fractions and ÷ numerators and denominators.

Double (and keep doubling) to ÷ by 1.

Draw a picture.

Think about ribbon.

Check by ×.

"Tomorrow you'll have a chance to use these tools to solve some other problems. In the meantime, if you think of anything else to add to the list, please let me know," I said to end the class.

DAY 2

Using the Tool Kit

I began class by focusing the students on the chart and reading the list aloud. Then I wrote a problem on the board:

$$1\frac{3}{4} \div \frac{3}{4}$$

I said to the students, "Try solving this problem. You can work with your neighbor, but you should each record on your own paper. After you solve the problem, look over the list and see which tool you used. You may use just one of the tools, or two or more together. Or you may use a method that we don't have on our list yet, and you can tell us about it when we discuss the problem. Also, if you can, try solving the problem in more than one way so that you have a check on what you've done."

From past experience with this problem, I thought that students would be able to reason that there were two three-fourths in one and three-fourths—one in the whole and one in the three-fourths—but I thought that the remaining one-fourth could pose difficulty. I knew that some of the students might be confused about whether the answer was two and one-fourth or two and one-third and would need more time to realize that the remaining one-fourth was one-third of the divisor, three-fourths.

As the students worked, I circulated. I spent most of the time with Damien, who generally lacked confidence in math. Francis, who sat next to Damien, was absent, so Damien didn't have any support. "I don't know how to start," he said.

"Let's read over the tools on the list," I suggested. "Decide which one you'd like to try, and I'll help you."

Damien looked at the list and decided on drawing a picture. "Can I draw on the board?" he asked.

"I'd rather you do it on paper," I said. "That way we'll have a record of what you do."

Damien drew two circles, divided them both into fourths, and crossed out one-fourth in the second circle. Then he brightened. "Oh, I know," he said. "I can see how many three-fourths there are." He carefully outlined three-fourths in the first circle and then the three-fourths in the second circle.

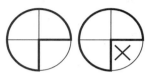

"So it goes in two times?" he asked me.

"Why do you think that?" I said.

"Because here's a three-fourths and here's a three-fourths," Damien said, pointing to what he had outlined on each circle. "But then there is this piece left," he added, pointing to the extra one-fourth in the first circle.

"Those extra pieces can be tricky to think about," I told him. "You're dividing by three-fourths, so you have to ask about the extra piece, 'How much of three-fourths is it?'"

"It's one-fourth, isn't it?" Damien said.

I tried to explain another way. "The piece is one-fourth of a whole circle, but you're trying to find out how many times three-fourths can fit into the one-fourth. It can't fit in at all because it's too big." Damien nodded. "As a matter of fact, that extra piece is one-third of a three-fourths piece, so one-third of three-fourths goes into it."

Damien was lost. He was fixated on the one-fourth piece as one-fourth of the whole circle and wasn't able yet to think of it as a part of the three-fourths. I knew that I'd have to find more time to work with Damien individually, but for now I said, "Let's hear about ways others have thought about the problem. Then we'll talk later. You've done most of the problem and it's just the leftover piece that you have to think more about." Damien nodded and I called the class to attention.

A Class Discussion About $1\frac{3}{4} \div \frac{3}{4}$

I initiated the discussion by telling the students, "I'd like to hear all the different ways you solved the problem, and I'd like you to listen carefully to each other's explanations. When you tell us how you solved the problem, please also tell us which of the tools you think you used."

Anita went first. She said, "I think it's two and one-third because three-fourths goes into three-fourths one time, and three-fourths goes into one whole one time but there's one-third of three-fourths left." I recorded:

$\frac{3}{4}$ goes into $\frac{3}{4}$ one time.

$\frac{3}{4}$ goes into 1 one time.

There is $\frac{1}{3}$ of $\frac{3}{4}$ left because $\frac{1}{4}$ is $\frac{1}{3}$ of $\frac{3}{4}$.

"And which tool did you use?" I asked.

"I think I used two of them—break apart and how many fit?" Anita said.

Craig reported next. "I did double, double," he said. "When I doubled once I got two and six-fourths divided by six-fourths. Then I changed the two and six-fourths to three and a half and the six-fourths to one and a half. I doubled again and got seven divided by three. Then it was easy. I got the same as Anita, two and one-third." I recorded:

$1\frac{3}{4} \div \frac{3}{4}$

$2\frac{6}{4} \div \frac{6}{4}$ Double

$3\frac{1}{2} \div 1\frac{1}{2}$

$7 \div 3$ Double again

$2\frac{1}{3}$

I asked Craig about one part of his explanation. "How did you change two and six-fourths to three and one-half?"

Craig answered easily. "Well, six-fourths is the same as one and two-fourths, and that's one and a half. So two and one and a half makes three and a half."

Next Celia said, "I tried my idea from before. I changed the one and three-fourths into a fraction, and that was seven-fourths. Then I divided the numerators—seven and three—and then the denominators—four divided by four. I got two and one-third over one, and that's the same answer as two and one-third." I recorded:

$1\frac{3}{4} \div \frac{3}{4}$

$\frac{7}{4} \div \frac{3}{4} = \frac{7 \div 3}{4 \div 4}$

$\frac{2\frac{1}{3}}{1} = 2\frac{1}{3}$

When I finished recording, I said, "So Celia used her method of changing to improper fractions and dividing the numerators and denominators." I pointed to this tool on the list.

Celia had something to add. "I think that my method won't work all of the time," she said. "I think it only works if the denominators are the same so that you get a one on the bottom of the answer."

"That will be something to explore with other problems," I said. "But remember, if one tool isn't useful for a particular problem, then you should try another." I knew that if the denominators weren't the same, you could wind up with a fraction as the denominator of the answer, and this would be problematic.

Maria changed both numbers to fractions and then used the flip-and-multiply method. She explained, "I made it into seven-fourths divided by three-fourths. Then I flipped the three-fourths to four-thirds. Then I multiplied across the tops and bottoms, and I got twenty-eight–twelfths. Then I divided twelve into twenty-eight and I got two and four-twelfths, and that's the same as two and one-third." I recorded:

$\frac{7}{4} \div \frac{3}{4}$

$\frac{7}{4} \times \frac{4}{3} = \frac{28}{12}$

$\frac{28}{12} = 2\frac{4}{12} = 2\frac{1}{3}$

Kayla had another way. "I think I used how many fit?" she said, "but I did it a funny way."

"Let's hear," I said.

"I changed the problem like Maria did to seven-fourths divided by three-fourths. Then I thought about how many three-fourths were in seven-fourths, and I knew that three-fourths plus three-fourths is six-fourths. Then there was one-fourth left, and that's one-third of the three-fourths. So it's two and one-third." I recorded Kayla's thinking:

$$\frac{7}{4} \div \frac{3}{4}$$

$$\frac{3}{4} + \frac{3}{4} = \frac{6}{4}$$

$\frac{1}{4}$ is left, which is $\frac{1}{3}$ of $\frac{3}{4}$

$$2 + \frac{1}{3} = 2\frac{1}{3}$$

Julio had a comment about Celia's idea. "If you change seven-fourths and three-fourths to eighths, Celia's way works." I recorded as Julio gave the details of his idea:

$$\frac{7}{4} \div \frac{3}{4}$$

$$\frac{14}{8} \div \frac{6}{8} = \frac{14 \div 6}{8 \div 8}$$

$$\frac{2\frac{2}{6}}{1} = 2\frac{1}{3}$$

No one had another idea to share. Next I planned to give the students three problems to solve on their own, so I wanted to model the other tools for this same problem to have examples of them on the board for the students' reference. I made a presentation using ribbon. First I drew an illustration on the board:

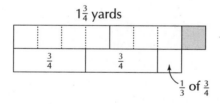

I explained, "Another way to think about this problem is to think about ribbon. The problem is this: I have a length of ribbon that is one and three-fourths yards. To draw that, I drew two yards of ribbon, divided each yard into fourths, and shaded in the extra fourth that's not part of the problem. Now I have to figure out how many pieces I can cut that are each three-fourths of a yard long. I can cut two of

them, and then I have this extra piece left over. I can see that the extra piece is one-third of three-fourths, so I agree with the other answers."

Then I gave an explanation of how to draw a picture. "Here's what Damien drew on his paper to show the problem," I said and then drew on the board:

"You can see the two three-fourths that fit into the one and three-fourths," I said, pointing to the outlined sections. "And the extra piece is one-third of three-fourths," I added, labeling it.

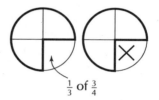

A Class Assignment

I explained to the students what they were to do next. "I'm going to write three problems on the board. Your assignment is to solve each of them in two different ways. For each solution, write on your paper the tool you used. You can work together, but you each must do your own paper. It's OK for your partner to help you, but be sure that you can explain the ideas, too."

"Can we use the same way for all of the problems?" Craig asked.

"You have to use two different ways for each problem," I said, "so you could use the same method for different problems. But be mathematically courageous and try using some tools that you're not too sure about. If you get stuck, I can come and help."

"I don't have a partner," Damien said, reminding me that Francis was absent.

"You can work with us," Brendan said.

"Who can explain what you are to do after I write the problems on the board?" I asked.

Gloria said, "We have to solve three problems and we have to do them in two different ways. Oh, and we should try different tools from the list."

Kayla added, "And we should write down the way we use each time."

I wrote the problems on the board and the students got to work:

1. $2\frac{3}{8} \div \frac{1}{4}$
2. $3\frac{1}{4} \div \frac{3}{4}$
3. $2 \div 3$

Of the twenty-four students present, seventeen were able to complete the assignment correctly. (see Figure 12–1 through 12–4.) Three students' papers were incomplete, but what they did was

correct. (see Figure 12–5.) The papers from four students showed that they needed extra help and more time with problems like these.

EXTENSIONS

On subsequent days, present a problem as was done in this class and follow the procedure of having students present solutions and identify the tools they used. Following are sample problems:

$2\frac{1}{2} \div \frac{1}{3}$

$3\frac{1}{8} \div \frac{1}{2}$

$1\frac{5}{8} \div \frac{1}{4}$

$4 \div \frac{2}{3}$

$5\frac{1}{2} \div \frac{3}{4}$

$\frac{2}{3} \div \frac{3}{4}$

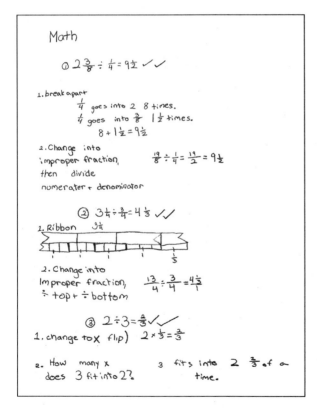

▲▲▲▲▲▲Figure 12–1 *For the first two problems, Celia divided the numerators and denominators, but that strategy didn't help her solve the third probem.*

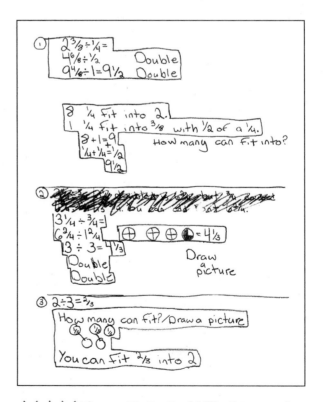

▲▲▲▲▲▲Figure 12–2 *Sachi liked to use the doubling strategy but could use others when it didn't help her solve a problem, as in the last problem.*

Tool Kit for Dividing Fractions 135

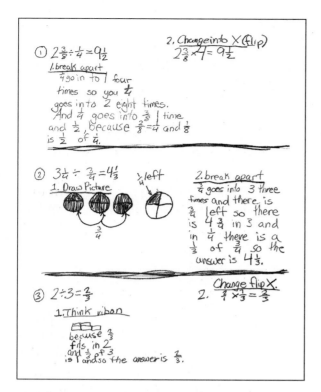

▲▲▲▲▲▲Figure 12–3 *Maggie's paper showed that she was able to use different strategies to solve the problems.*

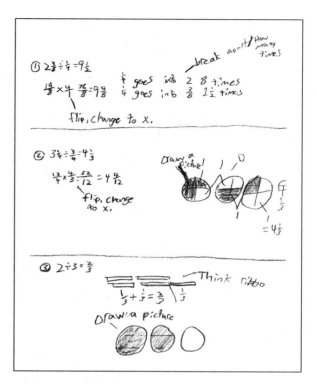

▲▲▲▲▲▲Figure 12–4 *David represented two answers for the first two problems ($9\frac{1}{2}$ and $9\frac{4}{8}$ for the first problem and $4\frac{1}{3}$ and $4\frac{4}{12}$ for the second) but was satisfied that they were the same.*

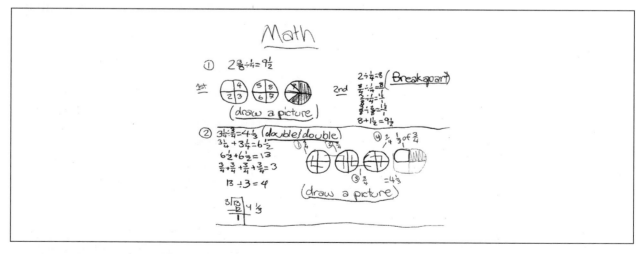

▲▲▲▲▲▲Figure 12–5 *Sabrina worked slowly and was only able to complete two of the problems. However, she did them correctly.*

Questions and Discussion

▲▲

▲ *What do you do for the students who aren't catching on? It seems that there is quite a spread in the students' abilities.*

Yes, the spread is evident, and this occurs in most classes. I have no easy answer, but I know that I have to make time to work with individual students who are having difficulty. And I work to find at least one way that makes sense to them. For example, when I was helping Damien, I took his lead about wanting to try drawing a picture and worked from that approach. I find that students typically have personal preferences for specific methods and I try to start with a student's interest and strength and help him or her develop the understanding and skills that he or she lacks.

▲ *I see that you've included on the tool kit the standard invert-and-multiply method. Do you expect all students to be able to at least use this method?*

My goal is computational fluency, which means that students should be able to solve problems accurately and efficiently. I also want students to develop mathematical flexibility and sufficient number sense so that the specific method they choose to use for a problem makes sense for the numbers at hand. For example, consider the problem $7\frac{1}{2} \div 1\frac{1}{4}$. To use the invert-and-multiply method, you'd most likely change the mixed numbers to improper fractions—$\frac{15}{2} \div \frac{5}{4}$—then write a multiplication problem—$\frac{15}{2} \times \frac{4}{5}$. Then there are several ways you might do the multiplication. However, it's just as efficient to think about how many times $1\frac{1}{4}$ fits into $7\frac{1}{2}$ by thinking: Two $1\frac{1}{4}$s make $2\frac{1}{2}$, $2\frac{1}{2}$ goes into $7\frac{1}{2}$ three times, so $1\frac{1}{4}$ goes into $7\frac{1}{2}$ six times. While the second method isn't an algorithm that works for every problem, it is a method that relies on understanding and reasoning. I'd like the students to have invert-and-multiply in their tool kit of strategies, but I don't want to sacrifice an emphasis on thinking and making sense that the other tools foster.

ASSESSMENTS

Overview

This section suggests nine assessments that are useful for tracking students' progress as they study multiplication and division of fractions. *Halfway Between* assesses students' ability to compare fractions and explain if one-fifth is exactly halfway between one-fourth and one-sixth. *Multiplying with Rectangles, Multiplying with and without Rectangles (Version 1),* and *Multiplying with and without Rectangles (Version 2)* assess students' ability to relate multiplication to rectangles and use rectangles to find answers to problems. *Explain Your Reasoning* and *Two Ways* provide two different formats for assessing students' ability to compute and explain their reasoning. *Problems with $\frac{3}{4}$ and $\frac{1}{4}$* and *Five Problems* ask students to add, subtract, multiply, and divide using the same two fractions each time. *An Experiment with Mice* presents students with a problem-solving situation to solve.

Teaching Notes

In the lessons presented in this book, students work together, collaborate on solving problems, and talk with one another about their ideas. All of this interaction fosters students' learning and helps them develop understanding and skills about fractions. However, it's also important for students to have opportunities to think on their own and practice what they've learned. Students' individual work is key for assessing their learning progress and informing your classroom instruction.

The assessments in this section differ from the assignments I was given when studying about fractions. My experience as an elementary student mainly involved doing computations and solving word problems, with the measure of my success being the number of correct answers. While correct answers are important to the assessments in this section, equal emphasis is put on how students think. Therefore, students are asked to write about their ideas and describe how they reason.

As with the lessons, I've tried all of the assessments with several classes and I've chosen student work to serve as examples of how students have responded. Some papers show acceptable or exemplary work; other papers reveal students' confusion or partial understanding. All of their papers are useful for me both for planning further instruction for the entire class and also for providing help as needed to individual students. At times, I use specific responses from students for whole-class discussions.

You'll notice that this section doesn't follow the format of the lessons presented. No teaching directions, vignettes, or question-and-answer reflections are included. Instead, for each assessment, I've included the prompt that I gave to the students, some comments about my experience with the assignment, and samples of student work. Also, I've noted when assessments are appropriate to be given more than once.

Halfway Between

PROMPT

Conjecture: $\frac{1}{5}$ is halfway between $\frac{1}{4}$ and $\frac{1}{6}$ because 5 is exactly in between 4 and 6. Is this true or false? Explain your reasoning.

In the Teaching Arithmetic book *Lessons for Extending Fractions, Grade 5*, a two-part assessment first asks students if $\frac{1}{4}$ is in between $\frac{1}{3}$ and $\frac{1}{2}$ and then asks them to name a fraction that is *exactly* halfway between $\frac{1}{3}$ and $\frac{1}{2}$. This is a similar but more difficult assessment because it asks students to think about fourths, fifths, and sixths, fractions for which a common denominator for the three of them is not as accessible to students, especially if they lack strong number sense about whole numbers. In this class, only three students converted the fractions to sixtieths. (See Craig's paper in Figure 2.) More commonly, students converted $\frac{1}{6}$ and $\frac{1}{5}$ to thirtieths and $\frac{1}{4}$ and $\frac{1}{5}$ to twentieths. (See Kayla's paper in Figure 1.) Using a clock face as a model to compare the fractions was helpful to some students. (See Maria's paper in Figure 3.) Six of the students incorrectly thought that $\frac{1}{5}$ was exactly halfway between, giving me important information about the extra help they needed. (See Maggie's paper in Figure 4.)

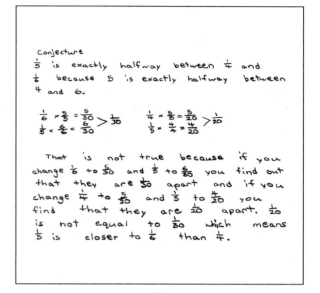

▲▲▲▲▲▲**Figure 1** *To explain why the conjecture was false, Kayla converted $\frac{1}{6}$ and $\frac{1}{5}$ to thirtieths, and $\frac{1}{4}$ and $\frac{1}{5}$ to twentieths.*

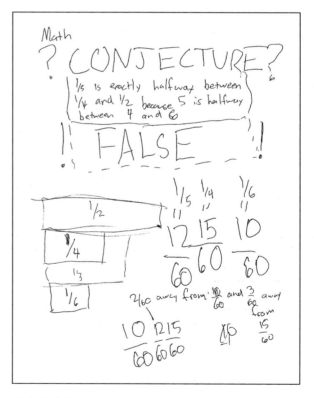

▲▲▲▲▲▲**Figure 2** *Craig converted $\frac{1}{6}$, $\frac{1}{5}$, and $\frac{1}{4}$ to sixtieths and concluded that $\frac{12}{60}$ was $\frac{2}{60}$ from $\frac{10}{60}$ ($\frac{1}{6}$) and $\frac{3}{60}$ from $\frac{15}{60}$ ($\frac{1}{4}$).*

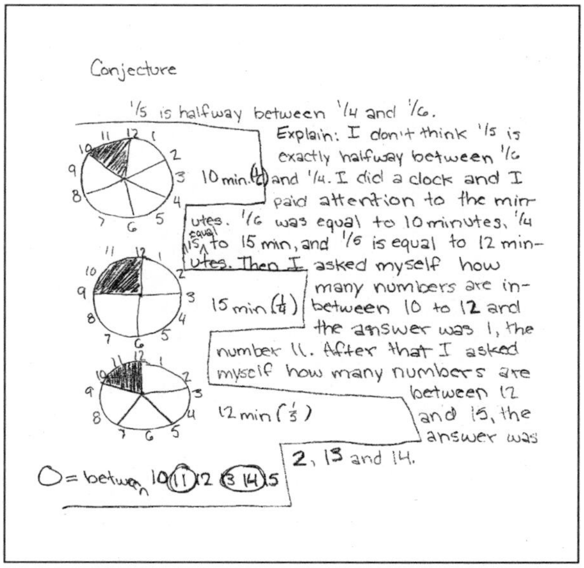
Conjecture
1/5 is halfway between 1/4 and 1/6.
Explain: I don't think 1/5 is exactly halfway between 1/6 and 1/4. I did a clock and I paid attention to the minutes. 1/6 was equal to 10 minutes, 1/4 equal to 15 min, and 1/5 is equal to 12 minutes. Then I asked myself how many numbers are in-between 10 to 12 and the answer was 1, the number 11. After that I asked myself how many numbers are between 12 and 15, the answer was 2, 13 and 14.
10 min. (1/6)
15 min (1/4)
12 min (1/5)
○ = between 10 11 12 13 14 15

Figure 3 *Maria used clock faces to explain why $\frac{1}{5}$ is not exactly halfway between $\frac{1}{4}$ and $\frac{1}{6}$.*

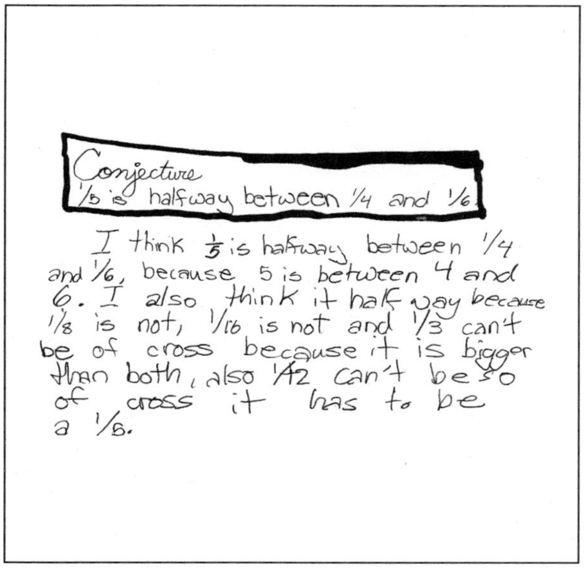
Conjecture
1/5 is halfway between 1/4 and 1/6
I think 1/5 is halfway between 1/4 and 1/6, because 5 is between 4 and 6. I also think it half way because 1/8 is not, 1/16 is not and 1/3 can't be of cross because it is bigger than both, also 1/12 can't be so of cross it has to be a 1/5.

Figure 4 *Maggie gave an incorrect argument for why she believed that $\frac{1}{5}$ was exactly halfway between $\frac{1}{4}$ and $\frac{1}{6}$.*

Multiplying with Rectangles

PROMPT

For each problem, show how you can find the answer by dividing the square.

Provide each student with a copy of *Multiplying with Rectangles*. (See Blackline Masters.) This assessment gives students twelve multiplication problems to solve, each with fractions smaller than one. The assessment is appropriate after the students have experienced the lesson in Chapter 4, "Drawing Rectangles," which focuses on using rectangles to find answers to multiplication problems. Confining the factors to fractions smaller than one allows students to use just one square for each problem. I've given this assessment in two different versions. In one version, the students solved the problems only by dividing the squares. (See Althea's and Sandra's papers, Figures 5 and 6.) In another version, I also asked students to explain the answer to each problem in another way. (See Max's papers, Figure 7.)

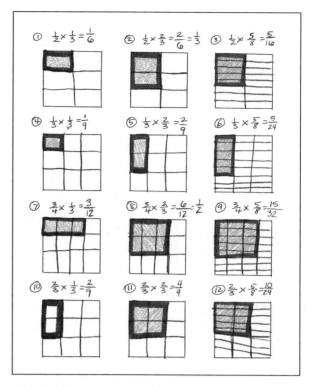

▲▲▲▲▲▲**Figure 5** *Althea divided the squares and represented each of the products correctly.*

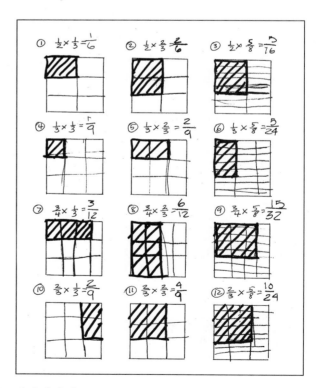

▲▲▲▲▲▲**Figure 6** *Sandra's drawing for Problem 8 gave the correct answer but represented the problem $\frac{3}{3} \times \frac{2}{4}$, not $\frac{3}{4} \times \frac{2}{3}$.*

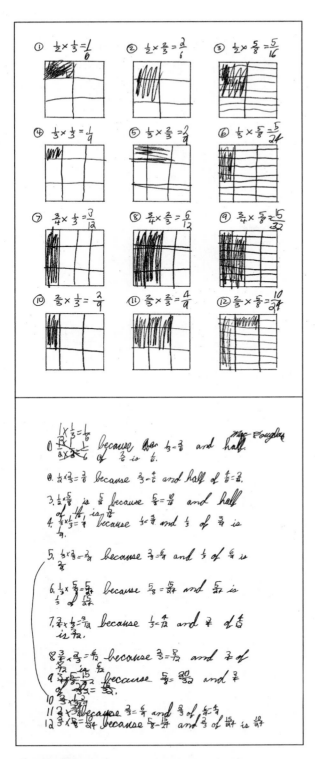

1. $\frac{1}{2} \times \frac{1}{3} = \frac{1}{6}$
2. $\frac{1}{2} \times \frac{2}{3} = \frac{2}{6}$
3. $\frac{1}{2} \times \frac{5}{8} = \frac{5}{16}$
4. $\frac{1}{3} \times \frac{1}{3} = \frac{1}{9}$
5. $\frac{1}{3} \times \frac{2}{3} = \frac{2}{9}$
6. $\frac{1}{3} \times \frac{5}{8} = \frac{5}{24}$
7. $\frac{3}{4} \times \frac{1}{3} = \frac{3}{12}$
8. $\frac{3}{4} \times \frac{2}{3} = \frac{6}{12}$
9. $\frac{3}{4} \times \frac{5}{8} = \frac{15}{32}$
10. $\frac{2}{3} \times \frac{1}{3} = \frac{2}{9}$
11. $\frac{2}{3} \times \frac{2}{3} = \frac{4}{9}$
12. $\frac{2}{3} \times \frac{5}{8} = \frac{10}{24}$

1. $\frac{1}{2} \times \frac{1}{3} = \frac{1}{6}$ because $\frac{1}{3} = \frac{2}{6}$ and half of $\frac{2}{6}$ is $\frac{1}{6}$.

2. $\frac{1}{2} \times \frac{2}{3} = \frac{2}{6}$ because $\frac{2}{3} = \frac{4}{6}$ and half of $\frac{4}{6} = \frac{2}{6}$.

3. $\frac{1}{2} \times \frac{5}{8}$ is $\frac{5}{16}$ because $\frac{5}{8} = \frac{10}{16}$ and half of $\frac{10}{16}$ is $\frac{5}{16}$.

4. $\frac{1}{3} \times \frac{1}{3} = \frac{1}{9}$ because $\frac{1}{3} = \frac{3}{9}$ and $\frac{1}{3}$ of $\frac{3}{9}$ is $\frac{1}{9}$.

5. $\frac{1}{3} \times \frac{2}{3} = \frac{2}{9}$ because $\frac{2}{3} = \frac{6}{9}$ and $\frac{1}{3}$ of $\frac{6}{9}$ is $\frac{2}{9}$.

6. $\frac{1}{3} \times \frac{5}{8} = \frac{5}{24}$ because $\frac{5}{8} = \frac{15}{24}$ and $\frac{5}{24}$ is $\frac{1}{3}$ of $\frac{15}{24}$.

7. $\frac{3}{4} \times \frac{1}{3} = \frac{3}{12}$ because $\frac{1}{3} = \frac{4}{12}$ and $\frac{3}{4}$ of $\frac{4}{12}$ is $\frac{3}{12}$.

8. $\frac{3}{4} \times \frac{2}{3} = \frac{6}{12}$ because $\frac{2}{3} = \frac{8}{12}$ and $\frac{3}{4}$ of $\frac{8}{12}$ is $\frac{6}{12}$.

9. $\frac{3}{4} \times \frac{5}{8} = \frac{15}{32}$ because $\frac{5}{8} = \frac{20}{32}$ and $\frac{3}{4}$ of $\frac{20}{32} = \frac{15}{32}$.

10. $\frac{2}{3} \times \frac{1}{3} = \frac{2}{9}$

11. $\frac{2}{3} \times \frac{2}{3} = \frac{4}{9}$ because $\frac{2}{3} = \frac{6}{9}$ and $\frac{2}{3}$ of $\frac{6}{9} = \frac{4}{9}$

12. $\frac{2}{3} \times \frac{5}{8} = \frac{10}{24}$ because $\frac{5}{8} = \frac{15}{24}$ and $\frac{2}{3}$ of $\frac{15}{24}$ is $\frac{10}{24}$

▲▲▲▲▲▲**Figure 7** *Max's papers showed his ability to solve the problems with squares and also by reasoning numerically.*

Multiplying with and without Rectangles, Version 1

PROMPT

Solve each problem in two ways, numerically and by drawing a rectangle.

1. $2\frac{1}{2} \times 5$
2. $\frac{1}{3} \times 4$
3. $1\frac{1}{2} \times 1\frac{1}{2}$
4. $4 \times 1\frac{1}{3}$
5. $1\frac{1}{4} \times 2\frac{1}{2}$

Provide each student with a sheet of squared paper. (See Blackline Masters.) This assessment is similar to the previous one, *Multiplying with Rectangles,* and is also appropriate after the students have experienced the lesson in Chapter 4, "Drawing Rectangles." In this assessment, the problems involve a combination of whole numbers, fractions, and mixed numbers. As well as providing important insights into individual students' understanding and skills, the assessment also provides valuable information for planning further instruction.

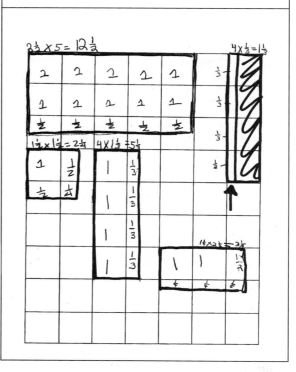

▲▲▲▲▲▲Figure 8 *June's numerical solutions for all of the problems involved the distributive property, breaking apart one of the factors, doing two multiplications, and combining the results for a final product. She correctly drew a rectangle for each problem.*

$1. \ 2\frac{1}{2} \times 5 = 12\frac{1}{2}$

$2\frac{1}{2} + 2\frac{1}{2} + 2\frac{1}{2} + 2\frac{1}{2} + 2\frac{1}{2} = 12\frac{1}{2}$

$2. \ \frac{1}{3} \times 4 = 1\frac{1}{3}$

$\frac{1}{3} + \frac{1}{3} + \frac{1}{3} + \frac{1}{3} = \frac{4}{3} \text{ or } 1\frac{1}{3}$

$3. \ 1\frac{1}{2} \times 1\frac{1}{2} =$

$1 \times 1\frac{1}{2} = 1\frac{1}{2} \qquad 2\frac{1}{4}$

$\frac{1}{2} \times 1\frac{1}{2} = \frac{3}{4}$

$4. \ 4 \times 1\frac{1}{3} = 5\frac{1}{3}$

$1\frac{1}{3} + 1\frac{1}{3} + 1\frac{1}{3} + 1\frac{1}{3} = 5\frac{1}{3}$

$5. \ 1\frac{1}{4} \times 2\frac{1}{2} =$

$1\frac{1}{4} \times 2 = 2\frac{1}{2} \text{ or } 2\frac{4}{8} \qquad 2\frac{4}{8} + \frac{5}{8} = 2\frac{9}{8} \text{ or } 3\frac{1}{8}$

$\frac{1}{2} \times 1\frac{1}{4} = \frac{5}{8}$

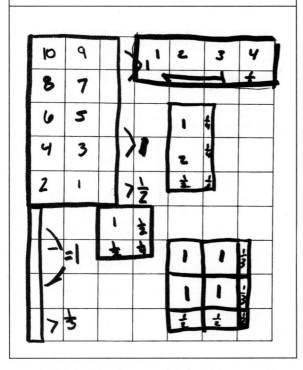

▲▲▲▲▲▲Figure 9 *Indira relied on repeated addition for problems that involved a whole number factor. She correctly drew a rectangle for each problem.*

Multiplying with and without Rectangles, Version 2

PROMPT

Solve each problem in two ways, numerically and by drawing a rectangle.

1. $3 \times 3\frac{1}{3}$
2. $3 \times 2\frac{1}{4}$
3. $1\frac{1}{2} \times 1\frac{3}{4}$

For this assessment, students are not given squared paper but instead sketch their own rectangles for each problem. This version is another way to assess whether students understand how multiplication connects to the area of rectangles and if drawing rectangles is an accessible strategy for the students. While some students find this version more difficult, others appreciate the opportunity to sketch the rectangles for themselves.

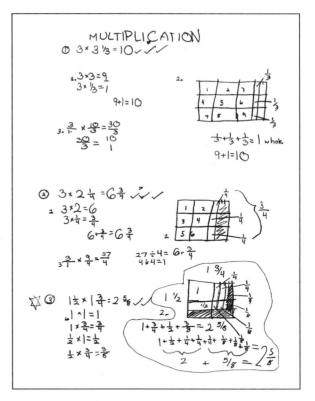

▲▲▲▲▲▲**Figure 11** *Celia solved the first two problems each in three ways, using the standard algorithm as one of the ways.*

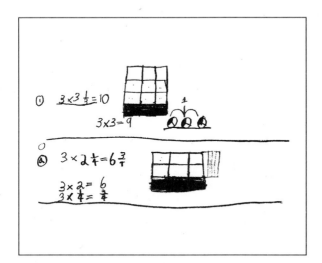

▲▲▲▲▲▲**Figure 10** *Paul was able to complete only two of the problems, and his paper indicated that he was not comfortable drawing rectangles to solve these problems. For the first, he resorted to drawing circles, and for the second, he relied on reasoning numerically.*

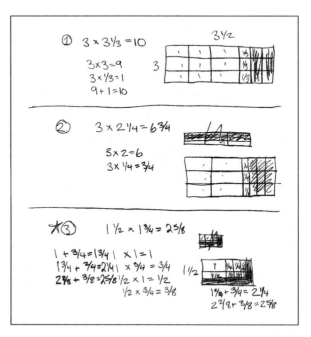

▲▲▲▲▲**Figure 12** *Anita made false starts drawing rectangles for two of the problems but was finally able to do so correctly.*

Assessments   147

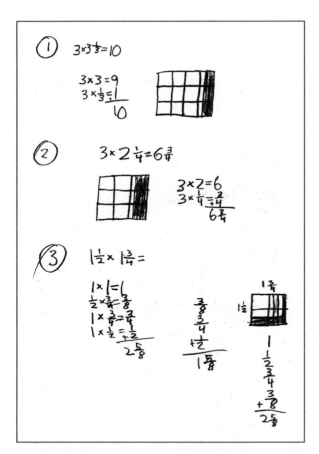

① $3 \times 3\frac{1}{3} = 10$

$3 \times 3 = 9$
$3 \times \frac{1}{3} = 1$
$\overline{10}$

② $3 \times 2\frac{1}{4} = 6\frac{3}{4}$

$3 \times 2 = 6$
$3 \times \frac{1}{4} = \frac{3}{4}$
$\overline{6\frac{3}{4}}$

③ $1\frac{1}{2} \times 1\frac{3}{4} =$

$1 \times 1 = 1$
$\frac{1}{2} \times \frac{3}{4} = \frac{3}{8}$
$1 \times \frac{3}{4} = \frac{3}{4}$
$1 \times \frac{1}{2} = \frac{1}{2}$
$\overline{2\frac{5}{8}}$

$\frac{3}{8}$
$\frac{3}{4}$
$+\frac{1}{2}$
$\overline{1\frac{5}{8}}$

1
$1\frac{1}{2}$
$\frac{3}{4}$
$+\frac{3}{8}$
$\overline{2\frac{5}{8}}$

▲▲▲▲▲▲Figure 13 *Pierre solved all three problems correctly. For the third problem, he found four partial products and then combined them.*

Explain Your Reasoning

PROMPT

Solve the following problems. Show how you solved them and explain your reasoning.

1. $4\frac{1}{3} \times 7$
2. $5\frac{5}{6} \times \frac{1}{2}$

Provide each student with a copy of *Explain Your Reasoning*. (See Blackline Masters.) This assessment provides a format for assessing students' ability to compute and explain their reasoning. It's important for students to know how to compute accurately and efficiently, but it's also important for them to understand and make sense of the methods they use. The prompt is one that the students are familiar with from most of the work they do. While the particular papers shown here involved the students in multiplying mixed numbers, whole numbers, and fractions, you can use this assessment with any problems. Once students are familiar with the format and the kinds of explanations that are acceptable to you, this assessment is particularly effective for checking their understanding and skills.

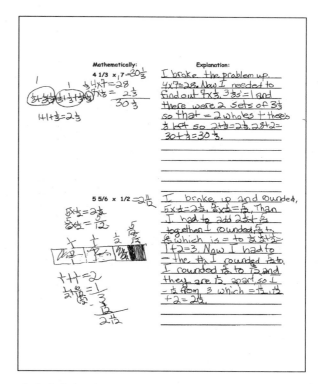

▲▲▲▲▲▲**Figure 14** *Annie's paper showed that she used a variety of strategies for solving the problems.*

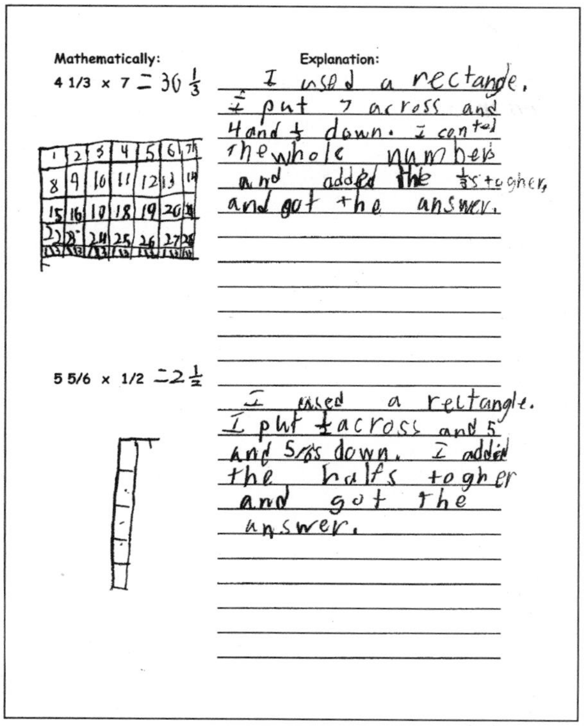

▲▲▲▲▲▲**Figure 15** *Eddie used a rectangle to solve each problem, a method he had recently mastered.*

Mathematically:
4 1/3 x 7
4x7=28
7x1/3 = 7/3 = 2 1/3
28 + 2 1/3 = 30 1/3
Explanation:
① If you brake apart number one you start by multipling 4x7 which is 28 and then you multiply 7x1/3 becaus you can't multiply 4x1/3 because they are part of the same number. So 7x1/3 is 7/3 which = 2 1/3. Then you add 28+2 1/3 which = 30 1/3.
5 5/6 x 1/2
5x1/2=2 1/2
5/6 x 1/2 = 5/12
2 6/12 + 5/12 = 2 11/12
What I did here is the same thing as number one. I broke apart the equation into 5x1/2 and 5/6x1/2. 5x1/2=2 1/2 and 5/6x1/2=5/12. You add the together and you get 2 11/12.

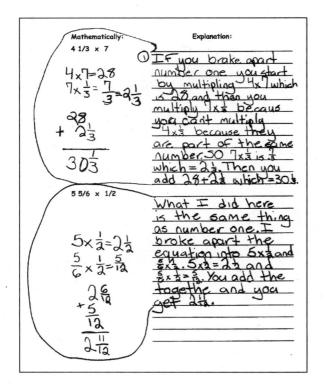

Figure 16 *Sachi used the same method for both problems, one that she relied on regularly when multiplying mixed numbers.*

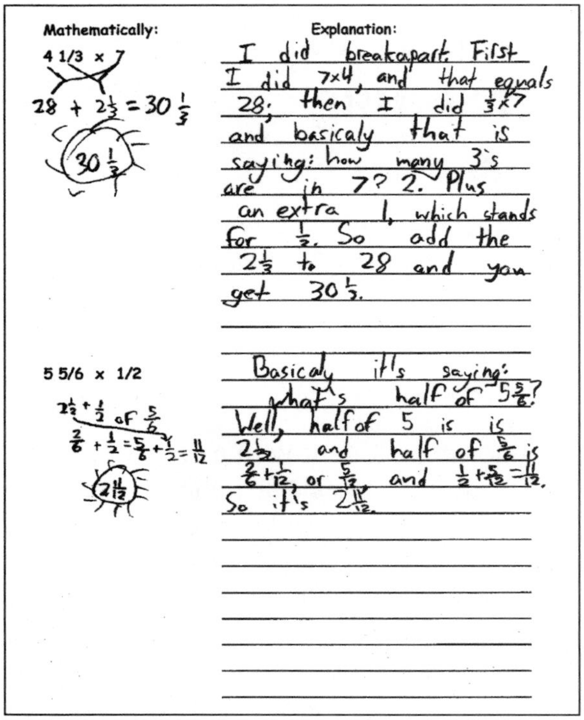

Mathematically:
4 1/3 x 7
28 + 2 1/3 = 30 1/3
30 1/3
Explanation:
I did breakapart. First I did 7x4, and that equals 28; then I did 1/3x7 and basicaly that is saying: how many 3's are in 7? 2. Plus an extra 1, which stands for 1/3. So add the 2 1/3 to 28 and you get 30 1/3.
5 5/6 x 1/2
2 1/2 + 1/2 of 5/6
2/6 + 1/2 = 5/6 + 1/2 = 11/12
2 11/12
Basically it's saying: what's half of 5 5/6? Well, half of 5 is is 2 1/2, and half of 5/6 is 2/6 + 1/12, or 5/12, and 1/2 + 5/12 = 11/12. So it's 2 11/12.

Figure 17 *Pierre was confident about his math ability and solved the problems correctly.*

Problems with $\frac{3}{4}$ and $\frac{1}{4}$

PROMPT

Solve the problems and explain why each answer makes sense.

$\frac{3}{4} + \frac{1}{4}$

$\frac{3}{4} - \frac{1}{4}$

$\frac{3}{4} \times \frac{1}{4}$

$\frac{3}{4} \div \frac{1}{4}$

$\frac{1}{4} \div \frac{3}{4}$

Provide each student with a copy of *Problems with $\frac{3}{4}$ and $\frac{1}{4}$*. (See Blackline Masters.) This assessment presents students with two fractions—one-fourth and three-fourths—and asks them to add, subtract, multiply, and divide them. They divide the fractions twice, reversing the dividend and divisor in the second division problem. The assessment gives a snapshot view of students' understanding of the four operations, reviewing what students have learned previously about adding and subtracting fractions as well as what they're currently studying about multiplication and division.

I've used this assessment in several different ways. Sometimes I've given it to students before they begin to learn about multiplying and dividing to give the students a hint of what they'll be learning. I tell the students that I don't expect them to be able to do what I haven't taught yet and they should do their best and write *I don't know* next to a problem that they can't solve. In this way, I can assess students' previous experience with all four operations. Sometimes I've given the assessment after I've taught about multiplication but before the students have thought very much, if at all, about dividing fractions. Again, I'm careful to tell the students that I don't necessarily expect them to know how to do the last two problems but that their papers will help me know what I need to teach. I also use the assessment after the students have been introduced to division of fractions. And sometimes I've given this same assessment twice, before I've done very much teaching about multiplication and division and then again afterward, with other fractions, giving the students a chance to see their own progress.

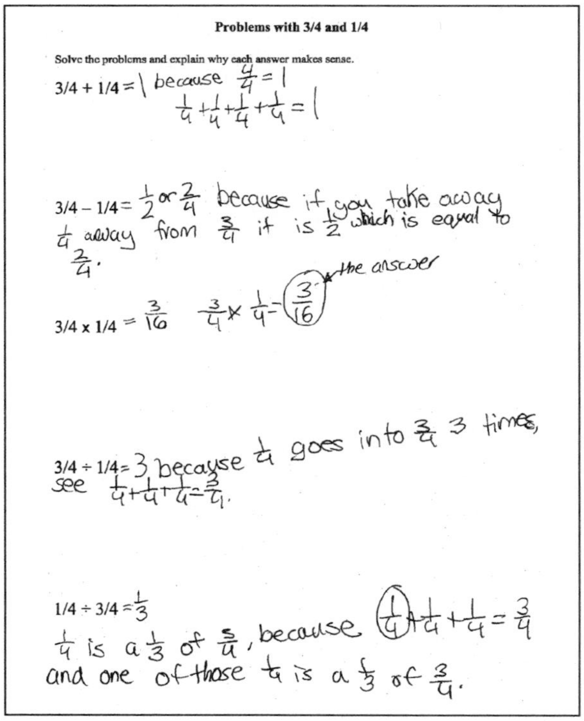

Problems with 3/4 and 1/4

Solve the problems and explain why each answer makes sense.

3/4 + 1/4 = 1 because $\frac{4}{4} = 1$

$\frac{1}{4} + \frac{1}{4} + \frac{1}{4} + \frac{1}{4} = 1$

3/4 − 1/4 = $\frac{1}{2}$ or $\frac{2}{4}$ because if you take away $\frac{1}{4}$ away from $\frac{3}{4}$ it is $\frac{1}{2}$ which is equal to $\frac{2}{4}$.

3/4 x 1/4 = $\frac{3}{16}$ $\frac{3}{4} \times \frac{1}{4} = \frac{3}{16}$ ← the answer

3/4 ÷ 1/4 = 3 because $\frac{1}{4}$ goes into $\frac{3}{4}$ 3 times, see $\frac{1}{4} + \frac{1}{4} + \frac{1}{4} = \frac{3}{4}$.

1/4 ÷ 3/4 = $\frac{1}{3}$

$\frac{1}{4}$ is a $\frac{1}{3}$ of $\frac{3}{4}$, because $\frac{1}{4} + \frac{1}{4} + \frac{1}{4} = \frac{3}{4}$ and one of those $\frac{1}{4}$ is a $\frac{1}{3}$ of $\frac{3}{4}$.

Figure 18 *Maggie solved all five problems correctly.*

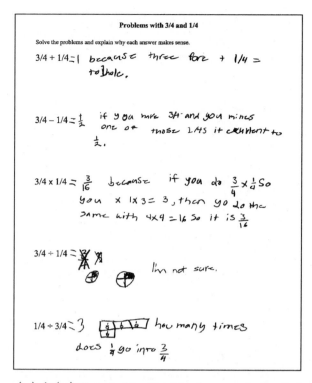

Figure 19 *Damien's paper revealed his confusion about dividing fractions, including interpreting the last problem incorrectly.*

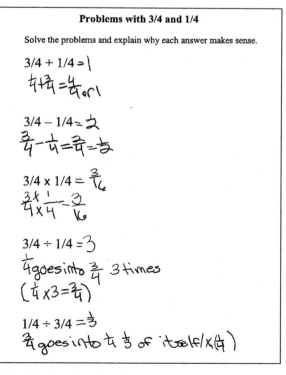

Figure 21 *Carla's answer to the multiplication problem was incorrect. She interpreted the problem correctly as $\frac{1}{4}$ of $\frac{3}{4}$, but then her numerical reasoning was incorrect.*

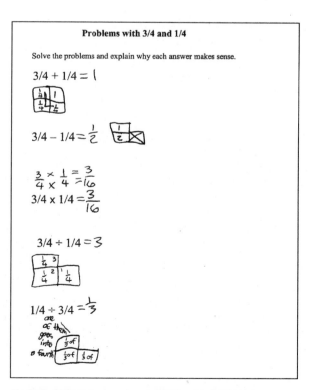

Figure 20 *Sabrina used drawings to explain four of the five problems.*

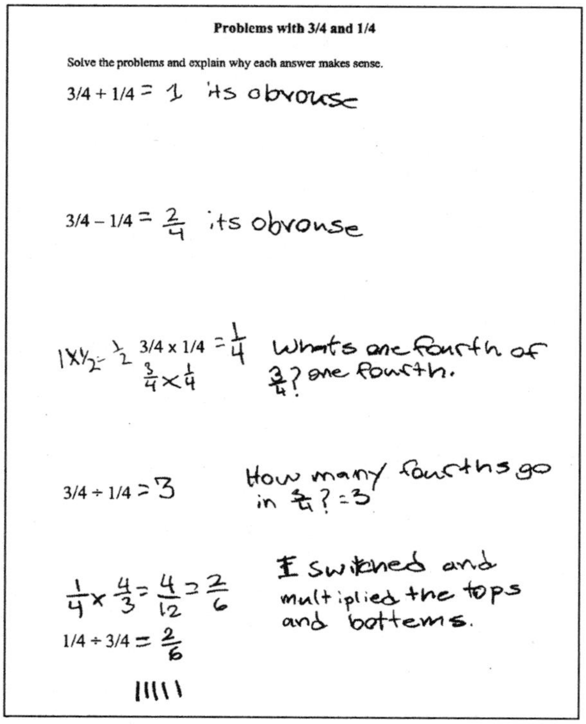

Figure 22 *Annie gave numerical explanations for her solutions.*

Five Problems
PROMPT

Choose any two numbers and use them for five problems—addition, subtraction, multiplication, and two division problems. At least one number must be a fraction or mixed number. Explain your answers.

This assessment is similar to the previous assessment, *Problems with $\frac{3}{4}$ and $\frac{1}{4}$,* but it allows each student to choose the fractions or mixed numbers to use for the problems. This assessment is appropriate after students have had experience using all four operations with fractions. This assessment not only gives you a snapshot of students' abilities to add, subtract, multiply, and divide fractions but also gives you insights into students' level of comfort. Some students chose fractions that they thought would be easy for them while others chose fractions to give themselves more of a challenge. Some students thought that they were choosing easy fractions but found that the challenge was more than they had anticipated. After I looked over the papers, I had students share them in pairs, each explaining to the other how he or she reasoned. I found it useful for students not only to explain their reasoning again but also to hear how their classmates reasoned, and I had partners switch several times. Sachi and Celia were surprised that they had the same answers but then realized that their fractions were equivalent; Sachi had chosen one-half and one-third while Celia had chosen two-fourths and one-third. You can repeat the assessment and ask students to choose other fractions or specify that they must choose two mixed numbers or some other combination.

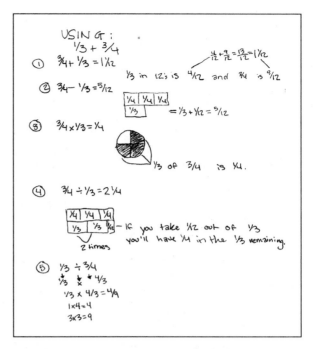

▲▲▲▲▲**Figure 23** *Gloria chose the fractions $\frac{3}{4}$ and $\frac{1}{3}$. She solved all five problems correctly and explained her solution strategies.*

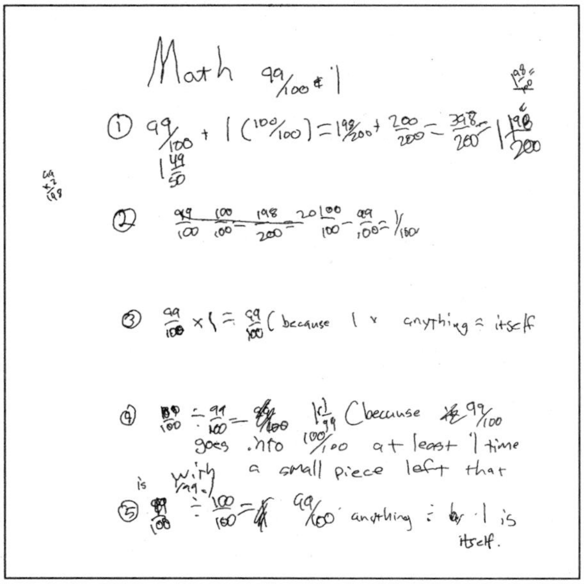

▲▲▲▲▲**Figure 24** *Craig wanted a challenge and chose $\frac{99}{100}$ and 1. He found it easy to subtract them and to multiply and divide by 1, but the others posed problems for him.*

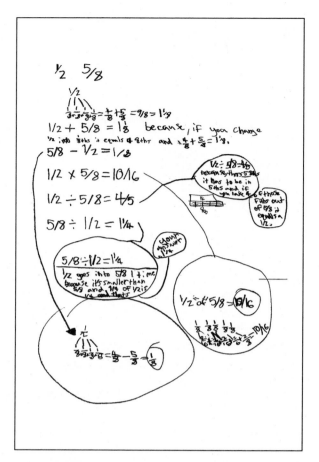

▲▲▲▲▲**Figure 25** *Brendan chose $\frac{1}{2}$ and $\frac{5}{8}$ and solved all but the multiplication problem correctly.*

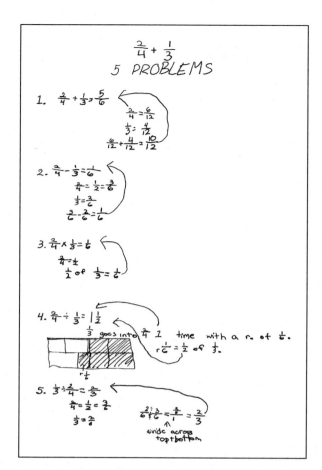

▲▲▲▲▲**Figure 26** *Celia correctly solved all five problems with $\frac{2}{4}$ and $\frac{1}{3}$; her explanations were easy to follow.*

An Experiment with Mice

PROMPT

For an experiment with 20 mice, $\frac{3}{5}$ got vitamins with their food. How many mice got vitamins? Explain.

Provide each student with a copy of *An Experiment with Mice.* (See Blackline

Masters.) This assessment asks students to apply their knowledge of fractions to a problem-solving situation. While the problem can be solved by representing the problem numerically as $\frac{3}{5} \times 20$, none of the students did this. However, most were able to make sense of the situation and solve the problem correctly. Students' solutions showed whether they understood the concept of three-fifths and could relate it to the context of twenty mice.

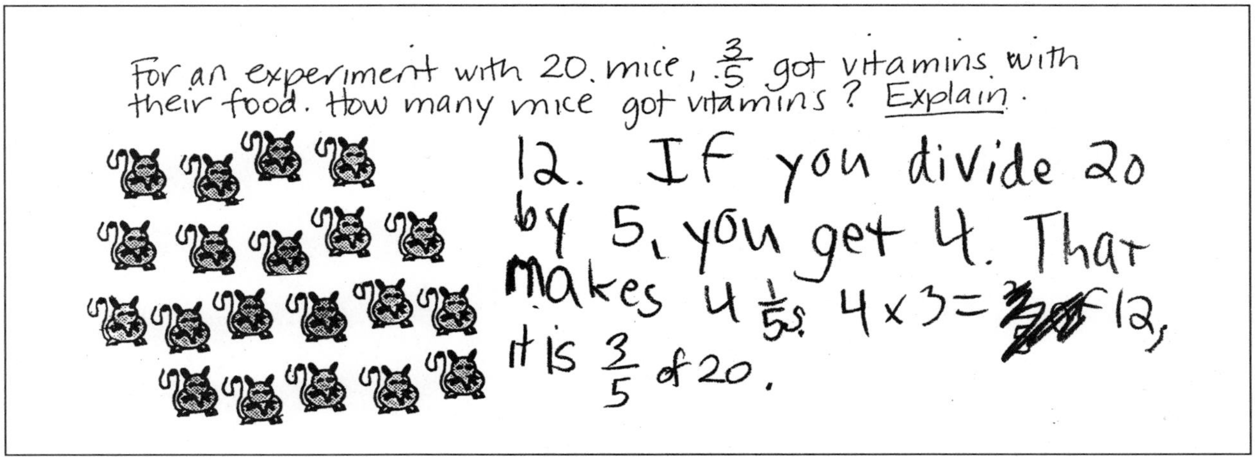

For an experiment with 20. mice, $\frac{3}{5}$ got vitamins with their food. How many mice got vitamins? Explain.

12. If you divide 20 by 5, you get 4. That makes 4 $\frac{1}{5}$s. 4 x 3 = 12. It is $\frac{3}{5}$ of 20.

▲▲▲▲▲▲Figure 27   *Elizabeth knew that there were four $\frac{1}{5}$s in 20 and used that information to solve the problem.*

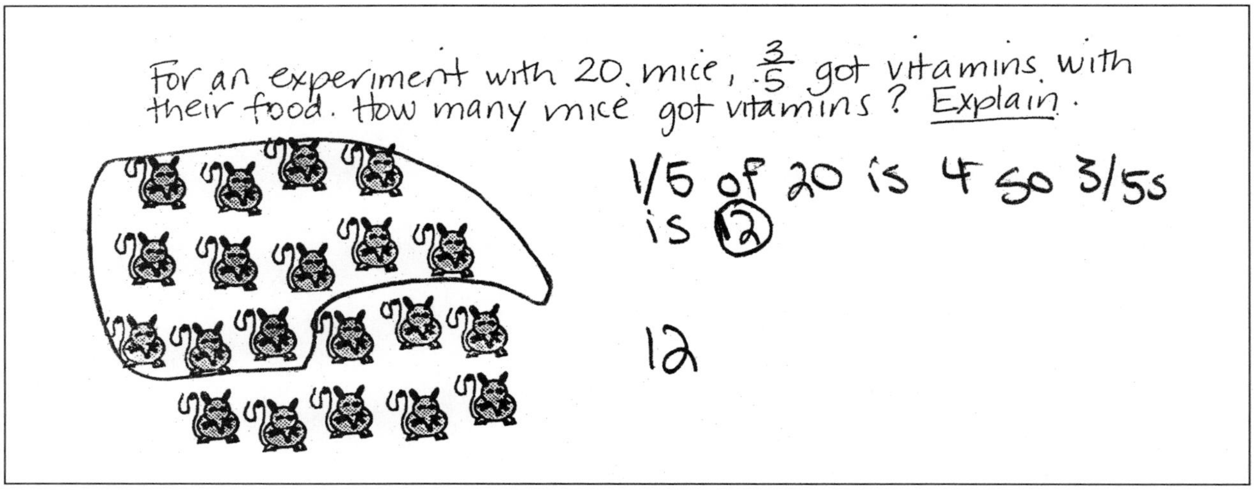

For an experiment with 20. mice, $\frac{3}{5}$ got vitamins with their food. How many mice got vitamins? Explain.

1/5 of 20 is 4 so 3/5s is ⑫

12

▲▲▲▲▲▲Figure 28   *David correctly reasoned that because $\frac{1}{5}$ of 20 was 4, then $\frac{3}{5}$ of 20 was 12.*

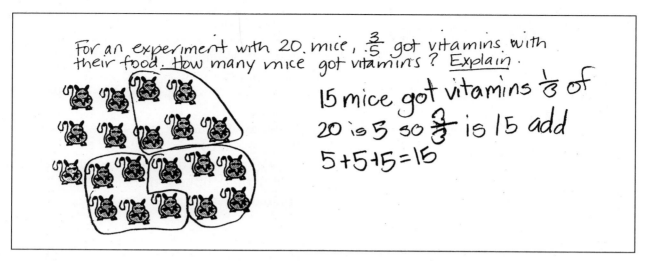

For an experiment with 20 mice, $\frac{3}{5}$ got vitamins with their food. How many mice got vitamins? <u>Explain</u>.

15 mice got vitamins $\frac{1}{3}$ of 20 is 5 so $\frac{3}{3}$ is 15 add 5+5+5=15

▲▲▲▲▲▲Figure 29   *George was not able to solve the problem correctly.*

Two Ways

PROMPT

Solve the problem in two ways. Show all your work. Explain how you solved it on the lines below.

Provide each student with a copy of *Two Ways*. (See Blackline Masters.) This assignment provides another format for assessing students' ability to compute and explain their reasoning. It's essentially a quiz with just one division problem, and you can repeat this assessment as often as needed for different problems. There are three goals for this assessment. One is to find out if students can compute successfully, an important goal of instruction. A second is to learn how they reason, which is valuable for guiding further instruction. A third goal is to see if students can use two different methods, an indication of their flexibility in reasoning numerically, an important indicator of number sense. For the papers shown, students were asked to identify the strategies they used from the tool kit for dividing fractions. (See Chapter 12.)

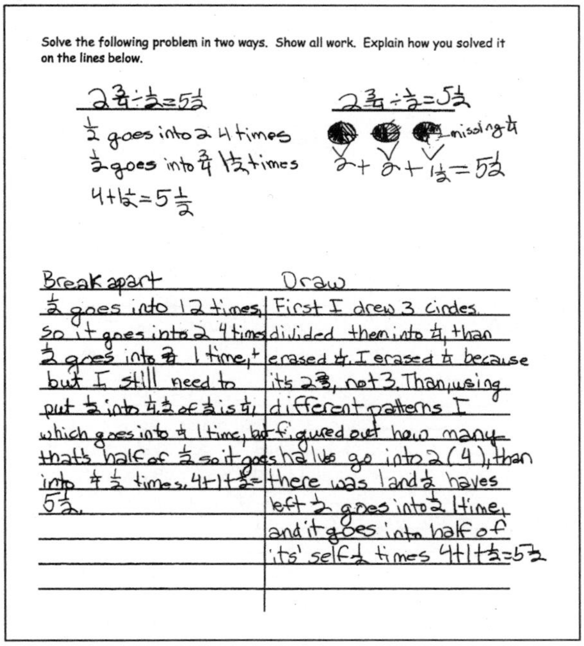

▲▲▲▲▲▲Figure 30 *Annie's answers were correct and her explanations were clear.*

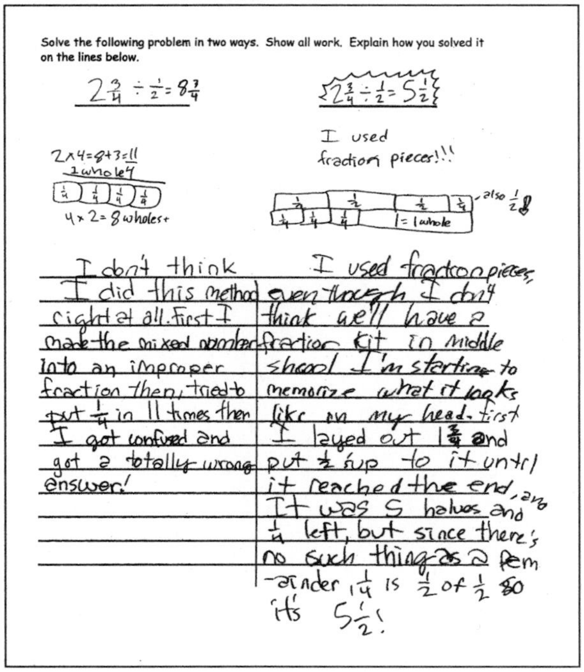

▲▲▲▲▲▲Figure 31 *While Helene's paper revealed her confusion, it also showed the success that she could have when working with a concrete model for the fractions. Her paper gave information that could help guide further instruction.*

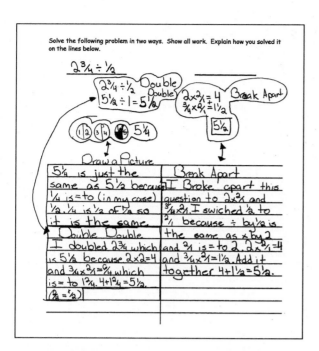

Solve the following problem in two ways. Show all work. Explain how you solved it on the lines below.

$2^3/_4 \div 1/_2$

$2^3/_4 \div 1/_2$ Double Double
$5^1/_2 \div 1 = 5^1/_2$

$2 \times 2 = 4$ Break Apart
$3/_4 \times 2/_1 = 1^1/_2$

$5^1/_2$

(1/2)(1)(1 1/2)(2 1/4) $5^1/_4$

Draw a Picture

Draw a Picture	Break Apart
$5^1/_4$ is just the same as $5^1/_2$ because $1/_4$ is = to (in my case) $1/_2$. $1/_4$ is $1/_2$ of $1/_2$ so it is the same. Double Double I doubled $2^3/_4$ which is $5^1/_2$ because $2\times2=4$ and $3/_4 \times 2/_1 = 6/_4$ which is = to $1^2/_4$. $4+1^2/_4 = 5^1/_2$. ($2/_4 = 1/_2$)	Break Apart I Broke apart this question to $2\times2/_1$ and $3/_4\times2/_1$. I swiched $1/_2$ to $2/_1$ because ÷ by $1/_2$ is the same as × by 2 and $2/_1$ is = to 2. $2\times2/_1 = 4$ and $3/_4\times2/_1 = 1^1/_2$. Add it together $4+1^1/_2 = 5^1/_2$.

▲▲▲▲▲▲**Figure 32** *Sachi explained three solution strategies for the problem—draw a picture, double double, and break apart.*

BLACKLINE MASTERS

The Multiplying Game Record Sheet
The Multiplying Game
The Quotient Stays the Same
Multiplying with Rectangles
1-Inch Squares
Explain Your Reasoning
Problems with $\frac{3}{4}$ and $\frac{1}{4}$
An Experiment with Mice
Two Ways

The Multiplying Game
Record Sheet

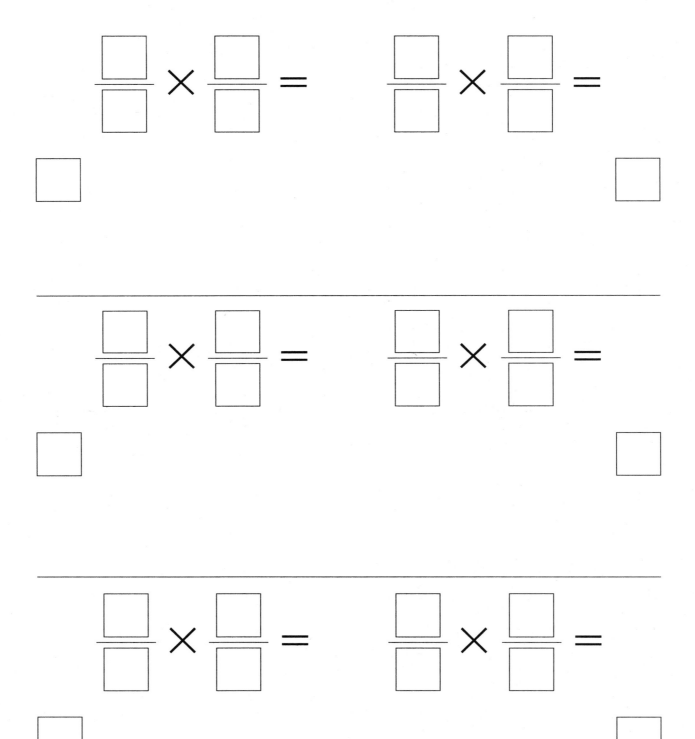

The Multiplying Game

You need:
  a partner
  a die

Rules
1. You need a game board with three rounds like this.

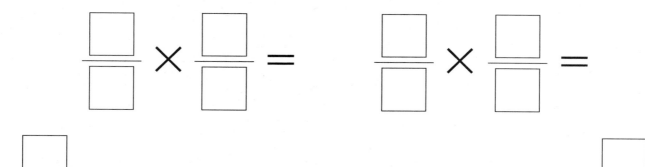

2. Players take turns rolling the die and writing the number in one of their spaces for that round. Once a number is written, it cannot be changed. The boxes to the side are reject boxes that give one chance to write a number that you don't want to use in the problem.

3. After writing a number, pass the die to the other player.

4. Play until both players have recorded two fractions. (Your reject box may be empty if you used your first four numbers for the fractions.)

5. Multiply your two fractions. Check each other's answers.

6. The winner of the round is the player with the smaller product. Explain how you know which answer is smaller.

7. Play three rounds.

   From *Lessons for Multiplying and Dividing Fractions, Grades 5–6* by Marilyn Burns. © 2003 Math Solutions Publications

The Quotient Stays the Same

÷ Problem	Check	× Problem
$2 \div \frac{1}{6} =$		$2 \times$
$2 \div \frac{1}{4} =$		$2 \times$
$2 \div \frac{1}{3} =$		$2 \times$
$2 \div \frac{1}{2} =$		$2 \times$
$2 \div 1 =$		$2 \times$
$2 \div 2 =$		$2 \times$
$2 \div 4 =$		$2 \times$

$2 \div \frac{2}{3} =$

$3 \div \frac{3}{4} =$

$3 \div \frac{3}{8} =$

$3 \div 1\frac{1}{2} =$

Multiplying with Rectangles

① $\frac{1}{2} \times \frac{1}{3} =$

② $\frac{1}{2} \times \frac{2}{3} =$

③ $\frac{1}{2} \times \frac{5}{8} =$

④ $\frac{1}{3} \times \frac{1}{3} =$

⑤ $\frac{1}{3} \times \frac{2}{3} =$

⑥ $\frac{1}{3} \times \frac{5}{8} =$

⑦ $\frac{3}{4} \times \frac{1}{3} =$

⑧ $\frac{3}{4} \times \frac{2}{3} =$

⑨ $\frac{3}{4} \times \frac{5}{8} =$

⑩ $\frac{2}{3} \times \frac{1}{3} =$

⑪ $\frac{2}{3} \times \frac{2}{3} =$

⑫ $\frac{2}{3} \times \frac{5}{8} =$

Explain Your Reasoning

Solve the following problems. Show and explain your reasoning.

Mathematically: **Explanation:**

_____

_____

_____

_____

_____

_____

_____

_____

_____

_____

_____

_____

_____

_____

_____

_____

_____

_____

_____

_____

_____

Problems with $\frac{3}{4}$ and $\frac{1}{4}$

Solve the problems and explain why each answer
makes sense.

$\frac{3}{4} + \frac{1}{4} =$

$\frac{3}{4} - \frac{1}{4} =$

$\frac{3}{4} \times \frac{1}{4} =$

$\frac{3}{4} \div \frac{1}{4} =$

$\frac{1}{4} \div \frac{3}{4} =$

An Experiment with Mice

For an experiment with 20 mice, $\frac{3}{5}$ got vitamins with their food. How many mice got vitamins? Explain.

From *Lessons for Multiplying and Dividing Fractions, Grades 5–6* by Marilyn Burns. © 2003 Math Solutions Publications

Two Ways

Solve the following problem in two ways. Show all
work. Explain how you solved it on the lines below.

_____   _____

INDEX

addition
    of rectangles, to multiply mixed numbers,
        52–53
    repeated, multiplying as, xi, 2, 3, 4–5, 11,
        12, 15
algorithms
    standard, for dividing fractions, ix–x, 109–10
    standard, for multiplying fractions, ix–x, 22,
        33, 56
assessments, 139–58
    An Experiment with Mice, 139, 155–56
    Explain Your Reasoning, 139, 149–50
    Five Problems, 139, 153–54
    Halfway Between, 139, 141–42
    Multiplying with and without Rectangles,
        Version 1, 139, 145–46
    Multiplying with and without Rectangles,
        Version 2, 139, 147–48
    Multiplying with Rectangles, 139, 143–44
    overview, 139
    Problems with 3/4 and 1/4, 139, 151–52
    teaching notes, 139–40
    Two Ways, 139, 157–58

Blackline Masters, 159–69
    An Experiment with Mice, 168
    Explaining Your Reasoning worksheet, 166
    Multiplying Game record sheet, 161
    Multiplying Game rules, 162
    Multiplying with Rectangles worksheet,
        164–65
    Problems with 3/4 and 1/4 worksheet, 167
    Quotient Stays the Same worksheet, 163
    Two Ways worksheet, 169
board
    recording student ideas on, 10, 44–45
    student self-confidence at, 39
break-apart method of division
    student use of, 129, 133
    terminology, 125–26
break-apart method of multiplication
    assessment, 145

statements on, 2, 3, 6–9, 12, 17–18
    teaching, 10

challenge problems, 120–22
chart paper, for *Tool Kit for Dividing Fractions*
    lesson, 123, 124
circles
    estimating with, 27
    representing division with, 78–81, 87, 92,
        100–109, 128, 131, 132, 134
    representing multiplication with, 21
complex fractions, 93
computation errors, 56
concrete examples. *See also* ribbon strategy
    connecting division with fractions to, 113–14

denominators
    changing fractions to same denominators,
        130
    fraction comparisons and, 62, 141–42
    multiplying, 14, 21–22, 33
    in *Multiplying Game,* 60–61
dice
    for *Multiplying Game,* 57, 59–61, 66
    random behavior of, 59
distributive property, break-apart method and,
    10, 125–26, 145. *See also* break-apart
    method of multiplication
dividends
    breaking apart, 71–72
    divisors larger than, 111
    doubling, x, xiv–xvi, 79–80, 114, 119,
        130–31, 133
    introducing terminology, 89, 96
    reversing order with divisor, 71
division. *See also* division of fractions
    checking by multiplying, 69, 71
    grouping model of, 73–74
    as groups of a number contained in another
        number, 70–71
    by one, 71
    with remainders, 71, 111–12

division (*continued*)
　　as repeated subtraction, 68, 70, 79, 115
　　reversing order of dividend and divisor, 71
　　by same number, 71
　　sharing/partitioning model of, 73–74
　　by two, and multiplication by one-half, 85,
　　　　87–90, 95
　　whole number, 67–74
division of fractions. *See also* division
　　break-apart method of, 125–26, 129, 133
　　challenge problems, 120–22
　　changing division problems to multiplication
　　　　problems, xiv–xv, 84–96, 114–15, 125,
　　　　126, 129
　　checking by multiplying, 80, 91, 97, 98,
　　　　100–101, 116, 119, 131
　　concrete examples of, 113–14
　　converting fractions to improper fractions,
　　　　130, 133–34
　　developing student understanding of, 75
　　dividing by one-half, xv, 75–76, 77–79, 87–90,
　　　　113–16
　　doubling the dividend and the divisor, x,
　　　　xv–xvi, 79–80, 114, 119, 133
　　by fractions, 79–81
　　as multiplying by "flipping" fractions, 97–109,
　　　　115, 119–21, 133
　　patterns in, 84–96, 102–5
　　preparing for, 67
　　quotient patterns, 77, 81
　　relating to multiplication, 87–96, 151–52
　　with remainders, 111–12
　　representing with circles, 78–81, 87, 92,
　　　　100–109, 131, 132, 134
　　representing with long division, 78, 118
　　representing with rectangles, 92
　　sharing/partioning model of, xiii
　　standard algorithm for, ix–x, 109–10
　　statements about, xii–xiv
　　strategies for, x, xiv–xvi, 79–80, 114, 119,
　　　　123–27
　　student reasoning about, x, 77–81
　　using subtraction, 79
Division Patterns lesson, 84–96
　　extensions, 95–96
　　overview, 84
　　questions and discussion, 96
　　teaching directions, 84–86
　　teaching notes, 86–87
　　time required for, 84
division sign (÷), as "into groups of," 71
division statements
　　multiplication statements and, 67–69
　　sharing/partitioning model of division and, 68
　　student examples of, 69
　　understanding division of fractions with,
　　　　76–77
　　for whole numbers, 67–74
　　zero and, 69
Division with Remainders lesson, 111–22

lesson, 116–22
　　materials, 111
　　overview, 111
　　questions and discussion, 122
　　teaching directions, 111–12
　　teaching notes, 112–16
　　time required for, 111
divisors
　　doubling, x, xiv–xvi, 79–80, 114, 133, 199
　　introducing terminology, 89, 96
　　larger than dividend, 111
　　reversing order with dividend, 71
doubling strategies
　　dividends and divisors, to divide, x, xiv–xvi,
　　　　79–80, 114, 119, 130–31, 133
　　mixed numbers, to multiply, 41, 45
　　multiple doubling, 130–31, 133
Drawing Rectangles lesson, 33–45
　　extensions, 43–44
　　lesson, 36–44
　　overview, 33
　　questions and discussion, 44–45
　　teaching directions, 33–35
　　teaching notes, 35–36
　　time required for, 33

equivalent fractions, 63
errors. *See also* misconceptions
　　computation, 56
　　as opportunities for learning, x, 48
estimates, 23–32
　　with circles, 27
　　indicating with wavy lines, 25, 32
　　about multiplying mixed numbers, 25–30,
　　　　36–37, 39, 41, 48, 49–51
　　with rectangles, 29
　　student understanding of, 23–25
Experiment with Mice, An, assessment, 139,
　　155–56
　　worksheet, 168
Explain Your Reasoning assessment, 139, 149–50
　　worksheet, 166
explanations. *See also* reasoning
　　value of, 96
　　written, 122, 157–58
Extensions, xvii

factors
　　doubling, 41, 45
　　reversing order of, 2, 3, 6, 11, 12, 17
fingers, dividing fractions with, 78
Five Problems assessment, 139, 153–54
"flipping" fractions. *See also* reciprocals
　　calculation errors, 107
　　division as multiplication using, 97–109, 115,
　　　　119–21, 125, 126–28, 130, 133
　　terminology, 99–100, 125
fourths, 77–81, 91
　　assessment, 151–52
　　patterns in, 91, 104–5

fraction comparisons
    comparing to one-half and one-third, 62–63
    denominators and, 62
    difficulty writing about, 66
    equivalent fractions and, 63
    fractions with different denominators, 141–42
    product size, 61–62
    reasoning about, 61–64
fraction instruction
    contents of book, xi–xvi
    goals for, xvii
    lesson structure, xvii–xviii
    using this book, xviii
Fraction Kit Guide, The, 114
fraction kits, 13, 114
    checking division with, 116–17
    for *Division with Remainders* lesson, 111
    student use of, 130
    understanding remainders with, 116–17
    Web site information on, xvi
fractions
    complex, 93
    dividing by, 75–76
    equivalent, 63
    improper, 31, 56, 130, 133–34, 137
    remainders represented as, 71
fraction sentences
    clarity of, 62
    practice with, 65

games, *Multiplying Game,* 57–66
goals for fraction instruction, xvii
grouping model of division, 73–74
groups, division statements about, 71
groupwork, 83

half
    comparing other fractions to, 62–63
    dividing by, xv, 75–76, 77–79, 87–90
    dividing other fractions by, 113–16
    doubling mixed numbers containing, to
        multiply, 41, 45
    multiplying by, and dividing by two, 85,
        87–90, 95
Halfway Between assessment, 139, 141–42
"how many fit?" method, 129

improper fractions
    alternative ways of expressing, 31
    converting fractions to, as division strategy,
        130, 133–34, 137
    converting mixed numbers to, 56
Introducing Division of Fractions lesson, 75–83
    lesson, 77–93
    overview, 75
    questions and discussion, 83
    teaching directions, 75–76
    teaching notes, 76–77
    time required for, 75
    written assignment, 81–83

Introducing Multiplication of Fractions lesson,
    11–22
    lesson, 14–21
    materials, 11
    overview, 11
    questions and discussion, 22
    teaching directions, 11–13
    teaching notes, 13–14
    time required for, 11
invert-and-multiply strategy, xiv–xvi
    changing division problems to multiplication
        problems and, 125
    including in strategy tool kit, 123
    parental teaching of, 109
    preparing students for, 97–109
    presenting to students, 112, 119–22
    student understanding of, 107–8, 113, 116,
        117, 137
    verifying answers with, 117

lessons
    contents, xi–xvi
    structure of, xvii–xviii
Lessons for Extending Fractions, Grade 5,
    x, xvi, 10
Lessons for Introducing Fractions, Grades 4-5, x,
    xvi, 13, 114
long division, representing division of fractions
    with, 78, 118

Making Estimates lesson, 23–32
    extensions, 30
    lesson, 25–31
    overview, 23
    questions and discussion, 31–32
    teaching directions, 23–24
    teaching notes, 24–25
    time required for, 23
    writing assignment, 30
Materials, xvii
misconceptions. *See also* errors
    about multiplying two mixed numbers, 46–50
    as partial understanding, 24
mixed numbers
    converting to improper fractions for dividing,
        130, 133–34, 137
    converting to improper fractions for
        multiplying, 56
    dividing by fractions, 80–81
    doubling, to multiply, 41, 45
    estimates about multiplying, 25–30, 36–37,
        39, 41, 48, 49–51
    exploring methods of multiplying, 49–56
    multiplying by mixed numbers, 46–56
    multiplying using rectangles, 33–42, 51–55
    multiplying whole numbers by, 36–42
    partial products in multiplying, 52–56
    sharing methods for multiplying, 41–42
    student misconceptions about multiplying,
        46–50

multiplication. *See also* multiplying fractions

    break-apart method of, 2, 3, 6–9, 10, 17–18

    checking division of fractions with, 80, 97, 98, 100–101, 116, 119, 131

    checking division with, 69, 71

    division as, by "flipping" fractions, 97–109, 115, 119–21

    patterns in, 102–5

    product size, 2, 3, 9–10

    relating division of fractions to, 87–96, 151–52

    as repeated addition, xi, 2, 3, 4–5, 11, 15

    reversing order of factors, 2, 3, 6, 11, 12, 17

    showing with circles, 21, 27

    showing with rectangles, 2, 3, 5–6, 11, 12, 15–17, 19–21, 22, 27, 33–44, 51–55

    of whole numbers, xi, 1–10

    by zero, 99

multiplication statements

    about fractions, 11–22

    whole number division and, 67

    for whole numbers, 2–10

multiplicative inverses. *See also* "flipping" fractions

    introducing, 99–100

    terminology, 125

multiplying fractions. *See also* multiplication

    changing division problems to multiplication, xiv–xv, 84–96, 114–15, 125, 126, 129

    converting mixed numbers to improper fractions, 56

    doubling strategies for, 41, 45

    estimating answers, 23–32

    introducing, 11–22

    methods for multiplying mixed numbers, 49–56

    multiplying numerators and denominators, 14, 21, 22, 33

    partial products in, 52–56

    product size, xi–xii

    as repeated addition, xi

    standard algorithm for, 22, 33, 56

    statements about, 11–22

    student reasoning about, ix–x, xi, xii

    student understanding of, xi–xi, 24

    student understanding of algorithms for, ix–x, 56

    using rectangles, 42–43, 143–48

    by whole numbers, 13–14

Multiplying Game

    game board, 57–59

    record sheet, 57, 161

    rules, 57, 59–60, 62, 65–66, 162

    scoring alternatives, 65–66

    strategic thinking in, 59

    student reaction to, 63

    time allowed for, 66

    winning, 61

Multiplying Game lesson, 57–66

    extensions, 65–66

    lesson, 59–65

    materials, 57

    overview, 57

    questions and discussion, 66

    teaching directions, 57–58

    teaching notes, 59

    time required for, 57

Multiplying Mixed Numbers lesson, 46–56

    extensions, 55

    lesson, 49–55

    overview, 46

    questions and discussion, 56

    teaching directions, 46–47

    teaching notes, 47–49

    time required for, 46

Multiplying with and without Rectangles, Version 1 assessment, 139, 145–46

Multiplying with and without Rectangles, Version 2 assessment, 139, 147–48

Multiplying with Rectangles assessment, 139, 143–44

    worksheet, 143–44, 164–65

negative numbers, 2

numerators

    multiplying, 14, 21–22, 33

    in *Multiplying Game*, 59–61

    terminology, 59–61

of, using for *times,* xii, 12, 14

one

    division by, 71

    as factor, 9–10

Overview, xvii

paraphrasing, to model correct use of terminology, 89, 100

parents, strategies taught by, 109

partial products

    computation errors in obtaining, 56

    in multiplying mixed numbers, 52–56

patterns, in division and multiplication of fractions, 84–96, 102–5

Problems with 3/4 and 1/4 assessment, 139, 151–52

    worksheet, 167

products

    comparing, 61–62

    reversing order of factors and, 2, 3, 6, 11

    size of, xi–xii, 2, 3, 12, 13, 18–19, 61

quotients

    introducing terminology, 89, 96

    patterns in, 77, 81

Quotient Stays the Same lesson, 97–110

    extensions, 108–9

    lesson, 100–109

    materials, 97

    overview, 97

    questions and discussion, 109–10

teaching directions, 97–99
teaching notes, 99–100
time required for, 97
worksheet, 99, 163

randomness, of dice rolls, 59
reasoning. *See also* assessments
    assessment of, 149–50
    comparing fraction size, 62–63
    comparing fractions with different
        denominators, 141–42
    developing student flexibility in, xvi
    about dividing fractions, x, xi–xiv, 77–81,
        81–82
    about fraction comparisons, 61–64
    helping students with, 10
    about invert-and-multiply strategy,
        107–8, 113
    about multiplying fractions, ix–x, xi, xii, 59
    about multiplying mixed numbers, 25–31
    about patterns, 86
    recording student ideas on board, 44–45
    about relationship between division and
        multiplication, 85–86
    about remainders, 111
    repeating student ideas, 89
    student explanations of, 96, 122, 149–50,
        157–58
reciprocals. *See also* "flipping" fractions
    introducing, 99–100
    student understanding of, 94
    terminology, 125
rectangles
    adding partial squares in, 40–41, 52–53
    dividing fractions with, 92
    dividing into squares, 34, 37–38, 52
    drawing, 33–45
    estimating with, 29
    marking units, 34, 37
    multiplying fractions with, 42–44, 143–48
    multiplying mixed numbers with, 33–42,
        51–55
    partial squares, 35–36, 38, 55
    representing division with remainders
        with, 113
    showing multiplication as, 2, 3, 5–6, 11, 12,
        15–17, 19–21, 22, 33–44, 51–55
    size of, 35, 37–38
    value of method, 33, 35
remainders
    challenge problems, 120–22
    deciding how to handle, 111
    division with, 111–22
    in long division problems, 118
    representing as fractions, 71
    representing as whole numbers, 71
    student understanding of, 115
    understanding with fraction kits, 116–17
    visualizing with circles, 132
ribbon strategy

for division with fractions, 113–14, 123–24
    student use of, 126–29, 134
risk taking, x, 24

self-confidence, of students, 39
sharing/partioning model of division, xiii,
    73–74
    division statements and, 68
sixths, 91–92
spinners, for *Multiplying Game,* 57
squared paper, for multiplying rectangles,
    145–46
strategic thinking, in *Multiplying Game,* 59
strategies. *See also* invert-and-multiply strategy
    break-apart method, for division, 125–26,
        129, 133
    break-apart method, for multiplication, 2, 3,
        6–9, 10, 12, 17–18
    changing division to multiplication
        problems, 126, 129
    changing fractions to same denominators,
        130
    checking by multiplying, 131
    circles, for division, 78–81, 87, 92, 100–109,
        128, 131, 132, 134
    circles, for estimates, 27
    circles, for multiplication, 21
    converting mixed numbers to improper
        fractions for division, 130, 133–34, 137
    converting mixed numbers to improper
        fractions for multiplication, 56
    doubling, for dividing fractions, x, xiv–xvi,
        79–80, 114, 119, 130–31, 133
    doubling, for multiplying fractions, 41, 45
    "flipping" fractions, 97–109, 115, 119–21,
        125, 126–28, 130, 133
    fraction kits, 13, 111, 114, 116–17, 130
    "how many fit?" method, 129
    multiple, value of, 109, 123, 132
    ribbon strategy, 113–14, 123–24, 126–29, 134
    student exploration of, xiv–xvi
    student flexibility with, xvi, 123–37
    student preferences for, 126
    student reasoning about, 149–50
    tool kit for dividing fractions, 123–27
    types of, 125–26
struggling students
    providing assistance to, 122
    strategies and, 137
subtraction
    of fractions, 65–66
    solving division problems with, 68, 70,
        79, 115

Teaching Directions, xvii
Teaching Notes, xvii
thirds
    comparing other fractions to, 62–63
    patterns in division and multiplication of
        fractions, 96, 103–5

Time, xvii
times
    as "groups of," 2, 3, 5, 11, 12, 14, 15
    student understanding of, x, xi, xii
    using *of* for, xii, 12, 14
Tool Kit for Dividing Fractions lesson,
       123–37
    extending, 135
    lesson, 126–36
    materials, 123
    overview, 123
    questions and discussion, 137
    student development of toolkit, 129–31
    student use of toolkit, 132–36
    teaching directions, 123–25
    teaching notes, 125–26
    time required for, 123
    worksheet, 129–31
Two Ways assessment, 139, 157–58
    worksheet, 169

vocabulary
    break-apart method, 125–26
    denominators, 60–61
    distributive property, 125–26
    dividend, 89, 96
    divisor, 89, 96
    multiplicative inverses, 99–100, 125
    numerators, 59–61
    paraphrasing, to model, 89
    quotient, 89, 96

reciprocals, 94, 99–100, 125
requesting student use of, 89, 96

wavy lines, indicating estimates with, 25, 32
Whole Number Division lesson, 67–74
    lesson, 69–73
    materials, 67
    overview, 67
    questions and discussion, 73–74
    teaching directions, 67–68
    teaching notes, 68–69
    time required for, 67
Whole Number Multiplication lesson, 1–10
    lesson, 4–10
    overview, 1
    questions and discussion, 10
    teaching directions, 1–2
    teaching notes, 2–4
    time required for, 1
whole numbers
    dividing, 67–74
    dividing by fractions, 81–83
    dividing by one-half, xv, 75–76, 77–79, 87–90
    multiplying, xi, 1–10
    remainders represented as, 71

zero
    division by, 69
    division statements and, 69
    as factor, 2, 3, 9–10, 12, 18–19
    multiplication by, 99